BACKTRACKING

SPEEDWAY NOSTALGIA FOR FANS OF THE 70s, 80s AND 90s

VOLUME 2

Edited by TONY McDONALD

First published in November 2016 by
Retro Speedway
Tel: 01708 734 502
www.retro-speedway.com

Copyright Retro Speedway

Designed by Jan Watts
Cover design: William Clayton

Printed by Premier Print Group (London)
Distributed by Retro Speedway
103 Douglas Road, Hornchurch, Essex, RM11 1AW, England
Distribution email: subs@retro-speedway.com

ISBN 978-0-9927427-3-7

BACKTRACKING

SPEEDWAY NOSTALGIA FOR FANS OF THE 70s, 80s AND 90s

VOLUME 2

Edited by TONY McDONALD

Acknowledgements

RETRO SPEEDWAY would like to thank the following writers for their editorial contributions: Martin Neal, Rob Peasley, Richard Bott, Andrew Skeels, Doug Nicolson and Rob McCaffery.

Most of the photographs in this book are reproduced with the kind permission of John Somerville, who proudly owns by far the largest collection of speedway images in the world. We would encourage you to view it online by visiting the John Somerville Collection website at www.skidmarks1928. com

Sadly, a couple of notable doyen photographers who have contributed to this book, and whose many years' dedication to the sport forms part of John's vast collection, are no longer with us. However, we would wish to posthumously thank the late Alf Weedon and Wright Wood, while also crediting their fellow 'snappers' Ken Carpenter, John Hipkiss, Don Ringrow, Julie & Steve Magro, Dave Kindred, Mike Patrick and Trevor Meeks.

Our thanks also to designers Jan Watts and William Clayton, as well as our good friends at *Speedway Star,* Richard Clark, Andrew Skeels and Dave Fairbrother.

Cover photographs
Front (clockwise): Terry Betts (King's Lynn) leading Gordon Kennett (White City); Ole Olsen (Coventry); Kelly Moran (USA); and Tony Davey (Ipswich).
Back: Martin Dugard (Oxford).

Contents

Introduction

HOT on the heels of *Backtracking Volume 1* we welcome you back for a second huge helping of nostalgia in this new series of books featuring highlights from the past 12 years of our bi-monthly *Backtrack* retro magazine.

One of the major interviews in this edition is with Ole Olsen, who overcame his initial reticence and agreed in 2008 to reflect on his past achievements. The triple World Champion was still the Speedway Grand Prix race director at the time, totally absorbed by the here and now, and couldn't understand why anyone would now want to read about his feats for Denmark, Wolverhampton and Coventry. But, as it turned out, he warmed to the nostalgia vibe and in the end had so much to say that we had to spread the interview over two issues. The tape recorder might still have been whirring in Ole's office now if I hadn't had a return flight to catch.

Whether you agree with his outspoken views or not, Olsen always has plenty to say and most of it makes sense. He is one of the sport's most intelligent operators, a deep thinker who has never stopped trying to improve the sport.

We met up again last year at the London offices of BSI, the Speedway Grand Prix and Speedway World Cup rights holders, where his youngest son Torben is employed as the company's speedway managing director. Torben showed his father and I into a meeting room, where Ole was happy to be interviewed on camera for our forthcoming *Memories of Coventry Speedway* and *History of the World Pairs* DVDs.

The Great Dane also happily helped to promote our *Ole Olsen Racing* DVD by posing for pictures holding the sleeve (as PC did with *Peter Collins Racing*). Ole was genuinely pleased that we produced a double-disc set showcasing more than 100 of his most important races. He appeared equally happy to receive from us a pristine copy of the programme for the 1966 British-Nordic Final at Sheffield, his first meeting in the UK.

And I was humbled when, completely unprompted, he made a point of saying: "I want to thank you for what you are doing at Retro Speedway. As you know, I'm not usually one to look back but it's a good thing that you are doing."

Even a forward-thinker like Ole appreciates that the past can inform the future.

1 Terry Betts spoke to us in issue 26 and you can read what the King's Lynn legend said in this edition of Backtracking.
2 Gordon Kennett was our cover man for issue 16.
3 All five Collins brothers, Peter, Les, Phil, Neil and Stephen, were interviewed in issue 27.
4 American superstar and double World Champion Bruce Penhall joined our writing team for a few years.

Interviewing Olsen is easy. You place the microphone in front of him, or point the camera at him, and he's away . . . just like dropping the clutch in his Coventry heyday 40 years ago, there is no stopping him. Others need more gentle coaxing to travel back in time, especially if their journey invokes memories of personal pain and hardship. Because we're not just talking speedway here, we are dealing with humans and, often, that means some suffering.

Ole Olsen in 2015, promoting our DVD showcasing many of his greatest races.

You hear about your old heroes moving to the other side of the world to begin a new chapter in their life and tend to assume it's all hunky dory. But when you eventually track down Allan Emmett, one of my favourites from supporting Rayleigh as a kid in the early 70s, in Australia, you find out he has been through the mill.

You talk to Tony Davey – and if there is a more humble, down to earth ex- star rider, then I have yet to meet him – and discover that he has had to cope with family tragedy.

'Shrimp' has subscribed to the magazine from Day One, never misses a copy and was over the moon this year when he finally got his hands on the elusive issue 11 (published in 2005) to complete his collection.

The great thing our team of writers and interviewees have is the benefit of hindsight, the luxury of being able to see things for how they really were, not how they may have seemed all those years ago. In his interview, Martin Dugard agrees that he was too much of a 'home boy' at Eastbourne, where he had two spells under the management of his father Bob, and admits he should have spread his wings much further to advance his career. He admits, too, that when he flew the Eagles' nest, he should have landed at Cradley Heath instead of Oxford. As you will see, his reasons for saying so are illuminating.

That's the beauty of *Backtrack*. Martin is now wise enough and mature enough to reveal his innermost thoughts on his career some 30 years after the event, whereas he could not have spoken with such candour, in *Speedway Star* or *Speedway Mail*, at the time it was unfolding.

Invariably people take years to bare their soul. Some four decades had elapsed before former West Ham and Wembley rider Tony Clarke confessed to us that he had been involved in the theft of bikes and other equipment from the Russian party at the 1972 World Final. The leading question couldn't be avoided and, fair play to him, he made no attempt to dodge the issue. On the contrary, he attempted to justify the crime with which he will forever be associated!

We will continue to prompt, probe, coax and ask searching questions which produce compelling interviews that can't be found anywhere else.

We will keep striving to preserve the sport's history in words, pictures and on film.

And if volumes one and two of *Backtracking* are well received, look out for the series continuing in 2017 . . .

Tony Mac
November, 2016

By Tony McDonald ● Issue 59 (2013)

IDENTITY CRISIS

Modern teams may look unified in matching race suits but is it, as Tony Mac suggests, a case of professionalism at the expense of the individualism that made our leather-clad heroes of the 70s and 80s so popular and much more easily identifiable? . . .

WHEN Elite League teams voted in favour of wearing colour co-ordinated team kevlars in the mid-90s it was hailed as one of the best decisions ever taken by British speedway bosses.

Simon Wigg, one of the sport's deepest thinkers, regularly called for the unification of colours to ensure that all seven team members looked virtually identical.

Wiggy was always campaigning for the sport to adopt a more professional approach and he reckoned matching team uniforms was one positive way to improve the sport's image. He reasoned that if football, rugby and cricket teams take to the field wearing identical kits, with only numbers on their backs to distinguish them as individuals, then speedway should follow suit.

Ivan Mauger with the famous leathers, designed in his old school colours, that he wore to three World Final victories in the 70s.

Now I loved Wiggy's passion for our sport and most, if not all, of his theories on how speedway could be improved were spot on. Sadly, most of them fell on deaf ears in SCB and BSPA corridors of power but the team kevlars idea was eventually adopted and became firmly established to this day.

But as with most things 'new', it was not exactly original. As far back as the 50s and throughout the 60s a number of teams wore appropriate coloured football or rugby jerseys over the top of their black leathers. OK, so they were not as stylish as multi-coloured kevlars, which are skin-tight by comparison, but the question of team identity had obviously crossed the minds of promoters long before Simon pushed for it.

Coventry and Newport donned gold and black tops; Wolves the Old Gold made famous by the Wanderers from up the road at Molineux; Exeter wore green and white halves; Poole preferred blue and white striped shirts; Newcastle were in familiar black and white hoops; and West Ham donned a replica of the claret and sky blue shirt worn by their local football club (even though the speedway Hammers' always wore red and royal blue, never claret and sky blue).

The football or rugby shirt was a cheap and simple way of bringing a dash of colour to the

8

sport in a largely black era in which only a handful stood out above the drabness – the 'White Ghost' Ken Le Breton, 'Little Boy Blue' Nigel Boocock and 'The Red Devil' Mike Broadbank all caught the eye in coloured leathers.

The billowing rugby and football shirts may look a bit naff now when you study action pictures taken in that era but they were of their time and few questioned it.

Even after team shirts went out of fashion, several individual riders continued to stand out in their chosen coloured fabrics. In our last issue of *Backtrack,* former Bradford star Sid Sheldrick explained that he wore a white football shirt over his leathers so that his mum would recognise him more easily from her seat in the stand as he roared around Odsal in the early 70s.

Although one of the smallest riders, Reading's Richard May was unmistakable in his light blue Reading FC shirt with white collar and cuffs.

Ivor Brown's white shirt became his trademark at Cradley Heath in the 60s and before him George White dazzled in (what else?) all-white leathers for Swindon. But in 1971 – my first full season watching speedway – it was the white shirt and boots of Romford's accident-prone Aussie Bruce Edgar that made him impossible to ignore. It was hardly a statement of sartorial elegance, though –

Getting shirty: Nothing like the trusty old football or rugby jersey to add a dash of colour to otherwise drab attire. Covering up here are Poole trio from 1966, Pete Smith, Ronnie Genz and Colin McKee.

9

his attire soon turned brown the next time he bit the Brooklands dirt for the umpteenth time.

But that's the point. I remember Bruce not for his paltry points return or the fact that he struggled to complete a race. His plain and simple white shirt made him stand out from the rest.

The management must have seen something in him – or at least his clothing – because midway through the '71 season they decided to discard the conventional body colour and experiment with white tops, which the home riders were asked to wear over their leathers. There was an action rider motif transfer stuck on the front, with the RAF roundel printed at the top of the sleeves and three stars down the arm. At least that's what Charlie Benham's shirt looked like when Romford faced Hull Vikings.

But Charlie's team-mate Brian Foote, never a conformist, decided to cut his sleeves in half, or maybe he just rolled them up, which made the top layer of cotton look ridiculous. The white shirts experiment was swiftly abandoned as a bad exercise and the Bombers – including the orange-leathered Bob Coles – were allowed to do their own thing again the following week.

Howard Cole of King's Lynn was another who became intrinsically linked with a white top.

Wearing white boots was an obvious way to catch the eye. Olle Nygren got such a kick out of seeing Ken Le Breton's 'ghostly' look at Ashfield in the 50s that he decided to paint his black boots white when turning out for Wimbledon and West Ham.

White boots and a tartan scarf were also what gave Scotland's Bert Harkins his individuality at Wembley and Sheffield in the early 70s, although Bertola would probably have ridden dressed in a kilt if they'd let him.

There was something about white leathers that oozed class. Remember how resplendent our columnist Malcolm Simmons looked when he first strode out at the start of the 1976 season in his new all-white set with red and blue trim. In that glorious week in which he won the Internationale at Plough Lane and the British Final at Brandon, he looked every inch the supreme stylish that he was. His slick gating and ability to stay upright longer than just about anyone else meant he didn't have Bruce Edgar's cleaning bill either.

That same year, which he crowned by reaching his one and only World Final, Sheffield's Doug Wyer unveiled a flashy set of white leathers that pushed fashion boundaries even further with the addition of tassels to both sleeves.

Also in '76, Hackney's Keith 'Chalky' White ditched his Leicester team leathers for a set designed in the colour of his name.

It was really after Barry Briggs and Ivan Mauger started appearing with stars and stripes on the sleeves, legs and chest of their multi-coloured leathers in the late 60s and early 70s that things started to change more dramatically. Some riders became instantly recognisable *because* of their leathers, especially after *Speedway Star* brought full colour to their covers from the start of the 1970 season. Before then, as a kid, you'd stare for hours at the black and white images on every page of the sport's must-have weekly and try and guess what colours all the different shades of grey represented.

Perhaps the most standout example from this period was John 'Tiger' Louis who, in his first full season of racing in 1970, could be instantly spotted a mile away in his yellow and black striped leathers to underpin his nickname. The cleverly conceived 'Tiger' tag stuck with him throughout his career and even today us dinosaurs still refer to the Ipswich co-promoter as 'Tiger John'. His son is simply known as Chris Louis but his 'old man' will always be 'Tiger John'.

When I saw JL appear centre stage at a tribute evening in his honour near Foxhall a few years back, I was pleased to see that not only does he still have his last set of stripey leathers, he can still fit into them, too.

Dave 'Tiger' Beech, one of my boyhood favourites at Rayleigh, never wore striped leathers but

Tiger earned his stripes: John Louis in 1970, at the start of his first full season with Ipswich.

Swindon (1970), Wolverhampton (1970), Leicester (1972) and Rye House (1979).

Sweden, represented here at the 1977 World Pairs Final by Anders Michanek and Bernt Persson, were one of the first national teams to adopt matching coloured leathers.

Talking of checks, when Joe Owen donned his black and white set in the mid-70s, no-one was left in any doubt that he was representing Newcastle Diamonds.

Ole Olsen, one of the greatest team-riders ever seen, combined the best of both worlds – team identity and individuality – when he unveiled a unique set of yellow and black leathers in 1972. He went to the trouble of having the same design of his team Wolverhampton's racejacket woven into the fabric and the No.1 on his back, which negated the need to wear a conventional Wolves body colour. Sam Ermolenko did the same thing in 1988. Unfortunately for Ole, the authorities took a dim view of his enterprise and he soon had to revert to wearing a jacket.

Ray Wilson was part of the trend-setting Leicester side of 1969, when they became the first British League team to wear identical leathers – red and yellow with two black stripes above and below a red lion on the right arm. On the left arm was just a single union jack. No-one was more stylish than Ray, who took to wearing red boots. Leicester really was a team in every sense that year, using the same seven riders in all of their 38 league and cup matches – an incredible feat that will almost certainly never be repeated.

My team Hackney also adopted a more colourful look in 1969, with Len Silver's Hawks turning out in blue, white and yellow leathers. A year on, when colour television was making its mark, three other BL sides, Swindon, Poole and Wolves, followed suit by having their own team leathers made. They were very simple designs – in the Pirates' case, the name 'POOLE' appeared horizontally in blue on a white sleeve. It was crying out for the skull and crossbones to be added but these were much simpler times. At least Swindon went to the trouble of including a robin on their white sleeves.

The 1971 Glasgow Tigers appeared in matching red leathers with white sleeves but resisted the temptation (and cost) of adding some stripes to further distinguish them from the rest. The same applied to those Tigers at second division Teesside, who settled for plain red and white halves.

My other favourite team, Rayleigh, looked more colourful from the start of '71 in blue and yellow

Romford's Brian Foote leads Reg Wilson of Hull in 1971, during Bombers' brief experiment with white tops.

Green piece: Some say green is unlucky but several riders were happy to be associated with the colour. None more so than Simon Wigg, pictured here outside Richard Knight, in the tasselled stripes of Mildenhall Fen Tigers.

leathers, although, strangely, they were not identical sets. Geoff Maloney had two white stripes down his pale yellow sleeves, Dingle Brown and Alan Jackson had none. Between the two white stripes on Allan Emmett's sleeves there was a blue strip. Terry Stone was the only one who had blue sleeves. Tiger Beech favoured all-yellow, while Bob Young wore a suit in turquoise blue.

Maybe a cock-up somewhere in the manufacturing process was the simple explanation for these subtle differences but no-one questioned it. Despite all riders wearing Rockets' basic colours, they were still able to retain a little individuality.

At Halifax, Eric Boocock and Greg Kentwell had been wearing red for some time but in 1972, the entire Dukes team were kitted out in the club's colours of red, white and blue. With echoes of Poole's simplistic design, the riders' Christian names were added to the forearm of the sleeve. To see common British names such as 'Eric', 'Bill', 'Mike' and 'John' stitched on to leather was very much a sign of the times.

The '72 season also heralded a uniform-looking Cradley Heath team. Bizarrely, though, instead of leathers produced in their traditional green and white, they were a hideous shade of burgundy. I could never work that one out. Maybe the designer was colour blind. This was not long before the rudderless Cradley management took the even stranger decision to drop the traditional 'Heathens' nickname and re-name the team 'United'. The least said about this particular identity crisis at Dudley Wood the better.

An increasing number of BL2 clubs cottoned on to the team leathers theme. Boston and Bradford both had them by '72 and the following year Berwick came to the party in yellow and black.

King's Lynn were seen in a few different sets of team leathers during the 70s and there was a spell in 1979 when the good, old fashioned football jersey (yellow with two green stripes) made a brief comeback. When Stars' general manager Martin Rogers moved to Leicester the following year he had his Lions riders in a get-up of red shirts with two yellow stripes, although before long an order went in for proper team leathers.

This uniformity was not confined to Britain, though. The Polish national team wore matching red and white suits in the 1973 home Test series against Great Britain. The Stal Gorzow team that toured English tracks in 1977 all wore the same red, yellow and black suits.

That year we also saw the first duo turn out in identical kit for the World Pairs Final, when Swedes Anders Michanek and Bernt Persson lined up at Belle Vue in blue and yellow leathers made by Halvarsson. Two years earlier, at Norden in Germany, Sweden had been the first World Team Cup finalists to wear matching coloured leathers.

As the 70s progressed, team leathers went out of favour as 'rider power' took hold at the top level and all the superstars, eager to maximise exposure for their sponsors, had several sets of custom-made leathers to choose from. The leather manufacturers themselves were among the first companies to sponsor riders. Rivetts, Lewis, Suzuki, Highwayman, TT, Sportac, Interstate, GTS, BN, BD . . . everyone seemed to be getting in on the act as the big names tried to outdo each other in the fashion stakes.

Three of a kind: Davey Watt, Darcy Ward and Chris Holder on World Cup duty for Australia in matching kevlars.

Wiggy pushed hardest for matching race suits.

A couple of colourful and imaginative team designs appeared at Rye House and Mildenhall. Although the red, white and blue of the Rye House team sponsor, heating company Infradex, had no connection whatsoever to their club colours of yellow and blue, Rockets certainly looked the part from 1977.

Their big National League rivals, the Fen Tigers, looked equally impressive in yellow and black leathers with stripe sleeves and tassels that were a throwback to the original tasselled twosome, John Louis and Dougie Wyer.

But there was a more conservative look about the 1979 Crayford team in their black leathers with red and yellow side panels bearing the name of their stadium owners, Ladbrokes. When Terry Russell switched the Kestrels from Crayford to Hackney in 1984, he had his team decked out in the new combined colours of yellow, blue and red. The following season their colours were changed to blue and white. It was no surprise that Terry clearly liked his boys to look a team in every sense. He was BSPA chairman when colour co-ordinated team kevlars were introduced in British speedway in the mid-90s.

Many believe a return to team suits that first appeared here in 1969 has been one of the best things to happen to the sport over the past few decades. After all, speedway prides itself on being the only motorsport with proper team racing and a team ethos. So it make senses for all seven men (or four in the World Cup) to look like a team rather than a collection of individuals.

But I'm not convinced. And it's not just the fact that the old iconic team emblems – the ace of clubs, the skull and crossbones, etc – have, sadly, been almost obliterated by suits awash with sponsors' names and logos that troubles me.

On my rare visits to Arena-Essex (OK, Lakeside), I struggle to distinguish one rider from another, particularly on dark nights and where the air fence obscures the view of them from all but the shoulders upwards as they roar round the bends. From that distance, they are faceless men in full-face helmets, indistinguishable from each other.

I prefer the 'olden days' when riders wore distinctive, personalised leathers which made many of them instantly recognisable. Even the ones who felt more comfortable in less flashy designs – Stan Stevens refused to part with his all-black leathers right up to his retirement in the mid-70s – could be easily identified by what they wore. In many cases, their choice of leathers characterised them as people.

There was a sense of anticipation at the start of each season as you peered over the pit fence on opening night and wondered what design your favourite rider had come up with over the winter months? A change of track usually called for a new set of leathers, especially if he'd been transferred from a team in which the riders wore identical suits.

Leathers were a big part of a rider's individual identity and character. Like a second layer of skin. I know I'm an old fogey, but wouldn't young newcomers to the spectating ranks today find it easier to relate to certain riders if their on-track heroes were allowed to wear exactly what they liked on race nights?

How ironic that it was Simon Wigg, the man who did most to influence the BSPA into adopting matching team suits, who spent virtually the whole of his illustrious racing career sporting bright green racewear and livery that very few others would dare to wear for superstitious reasons.

It's what helped Wiggy to stand out from all the rest.

On 2 Minutes With...
ROY TRIGG

How did you first get into speedway?

I've been a speedway supporter from the first time my parents took me to Wimbledon, when I was about eight or nine-years-old. My Idol back then was Ronnie Moore and he still is to this day.

Who was your favourite promoter, and why?

Jack and Charlie Knott from my season at Poole. They were real gentlemen and loved their speedway.

What was your favourite track?

Cradley, which was a great shape with lots of racing lines, and Leicester's Blackbird Road, which always seemed to be immaculately prepared each time I raced there.

Was there a track you didn't enjoy visiting?

My least favoured track was Coventry. I have no complaints about the track itself but for some reason or other I could just not get going around the place.

Who did you most enjoy partnering on track?

My favourite race partner was Les McGillivray. We had a three-year partnership at Hackney and our styles – Les on the inside and me taking the outside gate – seemed to work a treat. Les was a great guy.

What was your worst crash or injuries?

My career was free of any serious injuries. A dislocated shoulder and broken collarbone were my worst injuries, something for which I'm always grateful.

What have you done since you stopped riding speedway?

I retired and emigrated to New Zealand with my wife Tracy and our three sons, Tony, Lee and Scott, in 1974, having thoroughly enjoyed my speedway career with no regrets and only good memories of my years in the game. I'm now 70 and still work full-time for Auckland City Council maintaining children's playgrounds. My spare time is taken up with Kayaking and campervaning and following the grandkids' rugby and netball careers.

TERRY
BETTS

THE nameplate just to the right of the entrance to this impressive rural retreat would be reassuring to speedway traditionalists who are resistant to change. It reads 'Saddlebow House', home to Terry Betts, or Mister King's Lynn as he is universally known.

The same blue-eyed boy who put the small market town on the speedway map well before the name of the Saddlebow Road track, where 'Bettsy' shone brilliantly for the Stars for 14 years, was changed to the Norfolk Arena.

Buster and Jonathan Chapman, the two men grafting to sustain speedway at Lynn these days, could do with discovering another Bettsy – and recapturing the many thousands who made the Saturday night pilgrimage to see him lead his team from the front.

Sue Betts welcomes me inside and we head through to the sprawling back garden, at least as long as the straights at Lynn, to begin the search for her husband, who is always busying himself doing one job or another. We stroll along the manicured lawn, beyond the snooker room where Terry keeps a restored two-valve Jawa and a vintage JAP that once belonged to post-war Aussie legend Vic Duggan. And then he appears from almost nowhere, looking as fit and very much as he did when he retired from racing in 1980.

We're in sunny Shepreth, a delightful village just a few miles from the Cambridge end of the

Home from home: Terry in 2008.

M11 motorway, where Sue and Terry, who were married in 1965, have lived since 1988. "I built the place myself and it took me four years," explains Terry, now 64. He points towards the adjacent plot of land, where their previous house had stood, tucked behind the filling station and Leyland dealership that Terry ran. "Briggo used to live there until we knocked it down and built the house we're in now. He came to stay one weekend and ended up being here for 14 years!"

Cars belonging to Barry and his son Tony are parked on the driveway at the front of Saddlebow House. "He leaves them with us because it's easier for him to get to and from Stansted airport," Terry explained, leading me back inside to the room where he keeps most of his speedway memorabilia spanning a fine career spanning three full decades.

There are FIM gold medals for the two World Team Cups he won as a valued member of the Great Britain sides of 1972 (eight points at

Terry with two of his biggest friends in speedway, mentor Colin Pratt and Barry Briggs in 1972.

Olching, Germany) and 1973 (nine at Wembley), plus the World Pairs title he and Ray Wilson shared in '72, but he points instead to probably the most symbolic memento of all – the Lynn Trophy he received for winning the first-ever meeting staged at King's Lynn in May 1965.

In the kitchen, Bettsy settles down to reflect on his early struggles to make the grade . . . the trouble he had partnering the great, though selfish, Ove Fundin at Norwich; the clashes with officialdom that hacked him off so much that he walked away from the sport for a year at the age of 21 and almost took up car racing; why he wasn't welcome back at Wolverhampton for some time after he "ran off with the promoter's girlfriend!"; the time a hooligan Aussie fan almost cost him an eye on a Lions tour; and how the persuasive tongue of fellow Essex man Maurice Littlechild literally got him back on track at Lynn.

But those revealing stories are for inclusion in issue 2 of our new sister magazine, *Classic Speedway*. For the specific purpose of the era covered by *Backtrack*, we'll fast-forward now to 1970 and the major turning point in the career of Terry Betts that changed his life and set him on the path to legendary status at his beloved King's Lynn and international stardom.

"It all changed for me when my old mate Pratty broke his neck in the Lokeren road crash and had to retire from racing," says Terry, explaining the dramatic effect Colin Pratt had on him. "Until then I'd never been professional enough as a rider. I just wanted to race, I loved it, but I didn't want to do all the other stuff. I hated cleaning my bike.

"I'd known Colin since I was 16, when I was still too young to drive. We lived near each other, so when we both had broken bones at the same time, he would collect me and we'd go to Epping Hospital together for treatment.

"When we raced against each other, we were very competitive but we were also work-mates, because he used to work at my dad's garage at White Roding during the day.

"Pratty's equipment was always immaculate, he'd spend hours in the workshop getting everything just right. I was the complete opposite and he was forever telling me how shabby my bike looked and how I never paid attention to my engines. I'd fit a new engine, leave it in for 30 meetings, then buy a new one! That's why I never did any good in the BLRC at Belle Vue, a big track where you needed a fast motor. My engine was always absolutely knackered by the end of the season."

"But after recovering from the broken neck he suffered in the Lokeren road crash (1970), when he had more time on his hands, he put a lot of effort into making me a better all-round rider. He told me I'd never win anything, or reach a World Final, if I didn't learn to gate. And that meant paying a lot more attention to my clutch, which he'd meticulously take apart and maintain for me."

The 1972 season was Terry's best. He and 'Willie' were crowned World Pairs champions at Boras in Sweden and he gave solid support to Ivan Mauger as GB retained the World Cup at Olching, Germany. On the domestic front, he progressed from being a happy-go-lucky No.1 to world class status, achieving his highest-ever final British League match average of 10.46. He was the top Brit, with only Mauger, Ole Olsen and Anders Michanek above him in the rankings.

"You can put all of that down to Pratty," he says with typical modesty. "Without him behind me, I wouldn't have raised my game the way I did."

One of the individual highlights of '72 saw Terry win a title he wishes he had never had to compete for. His Littlechild Trophy success at King's Lynn, held in honour of the man who had talked him back into speedway and took a paternal interest in him, is one that meant a lot, albeit tinged with sadness at Maury's death due to cancer earlier that year.

"Maurice was so straight, such a nice guy, and it was because of him that I stayed loyal to King's Lynn," explained Terry. "Ipswich wanted me at one stage but the only tracks I would have considered joining were Wimbledon and Hackney because, apart from Lynn, they were my two favourites.

"Funnily enough, Ronnie Greene, the Wimbledon promoter, once had a right go at me when I turned up for the Internationale meeting in dirty leathers. He threatened me by saying: 'You won't ever get another booking at this track. You make sure you clean them before you step out on my centre green'. But he was good to me and would often invite me to Plough Lane just to ride in an extended second-half. I thought he and Charles Ochiltree were a couple of genuine top promoters.

"Whether I would have done so well under Len Silver at Hackney, I don't know. Maybe he would have been too laid-back, too much like me. Len really used to wind Pratty right up with his stunts.

"Perhaps I should have ridden for Greene earlier in my career, in the late 60s, because he never stood for any nonsense and that would probably have done me a lot of good, instead of freelancing like I was at King's Lynn. I probably needed a bit more discipline.

"But I could never leave Maurice and after he passed away, I stayed there for his widow Violet, his son Alan and Cyril Crane. I can honestly say that I never had a problem with Cyril."

Betts confirmed what his former team-mate Malcolm Simmons first revealed in his 2006 book – that early on in his King's Lynn days, he struck a unique, private deal with the Lynn management that rewarded him handsomely down the years. As well as his customary guaranteed points money, he also received a cut of turnstile takings. "It worked out well for me but it could have gone the other way – none of us knew when King's Lynn opened how successful it would prove to be," he said.

"I used to be paid a guaranteed maximum," he revealed. "The way I saw it, I could then ride with total freedom and give my best without worrying about dropping a point here and there and worrying about how that might damage my average. I never looked at averages anyway, although I know Simmo did."

Bettsy didn't abandon his trademark laid-back demeanour to attain the brilliant results achieved in 1972 and the seasons that followed. As he explained, his last-minute dashes to meetings, often arriving seconds before the parade, were simply part of his routine rather than a lack of professionalism.

"I'd always leave home at Bishops Stortford at 5.30pm and I'd pull into the car park at King's Lynn at around 7.15. I'd go in the back way, through narrow, winding lanes that few people knew about, to save time. The journey always involved high speed driving and plenty of overtaking but that's how I liked it. I wasn't one for getting to meetings early – as Pratty always did – and then sitting around for an hour or so. I liked to arrive while the adrenalin was still pumping, so that I could more or less jump straight on the bike and go.

"We did have one or two scrapes, though. I remember Maurice driving us to Newport and me having to get changed into my leathers in the back of his car. I took the bike straight off the trailer, rode it through the pits and onto the track for Heat 1!"

Friendly rivalry with Simmo

IT'S fair to say that King's Lynn were often a one-man team until Terry had Malcolm Simmons for company at the top of the scorechart from 1968. Simmo even managed to pip Terry for the No.1 spot at the end of 1973 but Bettsy regained pride of place the following year, when Malcolm reached the conclusion he would be better off moving on to become a No.1 in his own right at Poole.

Betts and Simmons remained good friends and Terry agrees that their friendly rivalry, although intense on the track, brought the best out of them both. "Definitely. Simmo and me were chalk and cheese – he always had immaculate bikes, just like Pratty did, but we also both wanted to beat each other in the second-half. When Howard Cole was Lynn's third heat leader, the three of us had some great scratch race finals. We always split the points money equally between us anyway, so all you had to lose was the damage caused by hitting the fence – and that's just what I did one night. I reckon I've had more crashes in second-half finals than at any other time!" he laughed.

Second-half finals at King's Lynn were always lively affairs with Howard Cole, Terry and Malcolm Simmons all wanting to end the night on a winning note.

Proud first winner of the Littlechild Trophy in 1972, with Violet Littlechild and Cyril Crane.

"Once, I chased Simmo so hard that I drifted wide and broke my arm on one of the lamp standards that used to hang over the fence at King's Lynn. I didn't crash, I just slowed down and pulled on to the centre green. Al Littlechild thought I'd only pulled up because Simmo was beating me but I knew I'd broken my right forearm. Look, I've still got the lump there now," he says, rolling up his sleeve to reveal arms that Popeye would have killed for. And yes, the lump is still visible.

"It's fair to say that we both wanted to be King's Lynn's No.1, it was a matter of personal pride. Simmo joining us from West Ham gave me the kick I probably needed. It's easy to become stagnant when you stay at one club for such a long time. It's easy to slip into the comfort zone and, perhaps looking back, I wonder if I'd become a better rider had I moved around. The trouble with King's Lynn was that the track was

Simmo serves the injured Bettsy a drink from the World Team Cup trophy.

Pushing his motor to the limit at Saddlebow Road.

too good – everybody who came there loved it. I never had hang-ups about any tracks, although big ones were my biggest bugbear because, as I said, I never had quick enough motors.

"Simmo had more talent on a bike than me but he never quite believed in himself enough. I also thought it was possible to psyche him out at times. We'd pit next to each other at King's Lynn and I could see what he was thinking sometimes, which part of the track he'd want to ride."

Mike the Bike and a trophy at last
THE same year Simmons left to fulfil his potential at Poole, King's Lynn honoured Terry with a richly deserved testimonial meeting, on Sunday, May 4, 1975. It was just a month or so after the club unleashed its new 16-year-old sensation Michael Lee, the hottest property in speedway and a World Champion in the making.

"I never had the same rivalry with Michael that I'd had with Simmo," says Bettsy. "You could see right from the start that he was a special, young talent and I wanted to encourage him all I could. Well, no bugger helped me when I first started riding. Michael was the future of King's Lynn and that suited me.

"Did he listen to advice? Yes, he did. The trouble was, he listened to too many people!" laughed Terry.

Before 1977, the nearest Terry had come to winning team honours with the Stars were third place finishes in the 1972 and '73 British League, while East Anglian rivals Ipswich beat them emphatically in the 1976 KO Cup Final. A year later, though, Betts and new British Champion Lee led Lynn to a thrilling 79-77 aggregate cup final victory against Reading – the club's only major trophy success of the BL era.

Betts was happy to see the rapidly emerging Lee assume the mantle of King's Lynn No.1 but, at 35, he wasn't quite ready to drift into retirement, despite what one or two others may have suspected. At the end of the 1978 season he could still point to an average a tad over eight points a match as evidence of his enduring qualities but King's Lynn were looking to shake off their Cinderella tag and compete on level terms more regularly with the glamorous teams from the big cities.

Terry wanted to help young Michael Lee.

In the winter of 1978-79, with Betts apparently non-committal about his racing future, they set their sights on Reading's England star Dave Jessup and splashed out a then record £18,000 to lure him away from Smallmead early in '79.

Sad way to say 'goodbye'

KING'S Lynn's former general manager Martin Rogers has always maintained that, with no firm indication from Betts that he would be pitching up for another season in the gold-and-green, it was reasonable to assume that Lynn would need serious reinforcements come the start of the '79 racing campaign.

In his book, *King's Lynn Speedway – Forty Years On,* published in 2005, Rogers wrote: "Bettsy had not obviously reached his use-by date but with Michael Lee now the people's choice, Terry was not the indispensable figurehead of previous years. The cat and mouse negotiations in which club and rider engaged on an annual basis were beginning to lose something of their old urgency.

"Crucially, Peter and Judy Thurlow, whose Abbeygate Group had backed Terry for half-a-dozen years, wanted Dave Jessup at Saddlebow Road. Their input was just one of the factors that drove the pursuit and eventual signing."

With Lee and Jessup, arguably England's top two by then, spearheading Stars' attack, there was no scope to include Bettsy either in terms of the constraints of the team structure or financial budget.

"I don't know how they got the idea that I was completely packing up or what they read into it," says Terry. "I'd enjoyed the '78 season, it had been a reasonable one, and at the end of it I probably said that I didn't know what I'd be doing the following year. Usually, they would come round and see me – Martin lived quite near us – but they didn't this time. In the meantime, I kept reading all the stories in the press that King's Lynn were after Jessup."

As one of the most likeable and universally popular guys the sport has ever known, you would be hard pushed to hear a bad word said about Terry Betts and, conversely, he is not given to criticising others. His body language cannot disguise, though, how disappointed and saddened he was at the manner in which his time at the club came to an end.

"There was a lot of fuss at the time," he continues. "and Violet Littlechild was most unhappy when she heard I wouldn't be in the team for '79." She no doubt recalled her late husband's declaration, in 1967: "You can take it that as long as I'm promoting at Saddlebow Road, Terry Betts will be riding for the Stars."

Betts claims that Cyril Crane was equally keen for him to remain part of the furniture at Lynn but, by then, Martin Rogers had been promoted from his previous roles as PRO and announcer to general manager – the man paid to make the big decisions on behalf of the promoting company, Norfolk Speedways.

Martin offered Terry the chance to remain an influential figure within the club in a part-time rider/ coach capacity, for which he would be paid a retainer.

"Martin came to me in, I think, about February time and asked if I fancied the idea of becoming rider/coach. I said to him sarcastically: 'What, one week I can ride and the next I'll drive the others around in a coach!'

"He explained that it wasn't possible to fit in Michael, Jessup and me because of the points limit. He said I'd be in the team whenever one or both of them was away on international duty but his plan wasn't for me. I couldn't continue in speedway on a part-time basis – it was all or nothing," says Terry. "I told him: 'Bugger it, you know what you can do with your speedway. I'll pack up then'.

"I don't think Violet and Cyril knew too much about all of this, although of course they were there in front of the press on the day Jessup signed. But Violet went ballistic when she heard I wouldn't be in the team. She said that I had to stay, so we all agreed to meet up in Newmarket, where Martin had to try and explain why I couldn't be fitted in after they had signed Jessup. Violet said: 'I don't care what you do, Terry has got to stay here'.

"In the end, I said: 'It ain't a problem, I'm retiring'.

"I think Cyril was away at the time and he later rang me and said: 'You've got to stay'. But I told him I didn't want to ride for him (Martin) any more.

"It wasn't the way I wanted to pack up but that's how it happened.

"I was disappointed with Martin – and I said to him: 'I thought you was my mate'. It was more or less through me that he got into speedway, because he was reporting for the Chelmsford paper and started covering King's Lynn every week.

"He used to drive me to meetings and travel everywhere with me, even abroad. He'd handle all my continental bookings, negotiate fees for open meetings, arrange my flights and do virtually everything for me. We had a really good working relationship – he was 100 per cent behind me.

"Sue and I even went to his wedding (to Lin) – and there were only two other people there!"

So Betts signed off for the Stars after scoring 6,799.5 points from 658 matches in all competitions between 1966 – the club's first league season – and the end of 1978. His league tally of 4,522 is almost twice as many as the 2,492 of Michael Lee, who is next in the all-time list. Terry recorded

Leading Ipswich's Tony Davey and Stars team-mate David Gagen.

Farewell but not goodbye, Terry signing off at the end of 1978. Little did he know he had ridden his last race for King's Lynn.

105 maximums (85 full, 20 paid).

"After I knew I'd be leaving King's Lynn, we decided to go ahead with our plans to buy Bridge Garage, the Leyland dealership business, at Shepreth. I took it over on April 1st, 1979 and there were seven blokes working there at the time."

Reluctant Reading Racer

BUT the last chapter of the Terry Betts' speedway story hadn't quite been written. He explained: "Reading came on the phone and asked me to ride for them in '79. I said 'no' at first but then John Davis came here to try and tempt me to ride, promoter Bill Dore was very persuasive and they kept offering me good money.

"I kept saying that I'd retired but it was still up in the air whether we would go through with the business. In the end Reading made me such a good offer that I agreed to carry on riding for another year. "

As Racers' third heat leader with respectable figures of a little less than eight points a match, he gave Davis and Jan Andersson solid support in an improving Reading side that was on the up.

"I've got no gripes whatsoever with anybody at Reading, the people there treated me brilliantly. But after being at King's Lynn for 14 years, I felt like a guest rider every week. It just didn't feel right. The local derbies were down in Exeter, Poole and Swindon, whereas I'd been used to Ipswich and Leicester.

"I got on with everybody fine, although I didn't have the most successful season. I did my job and got paid for it but I wasn't particularly enjoying it.

"And then I realised that I was doing it for all the wrong reasons. I was doing it for the money. I knew I'd have to re-assess things before the start of the following season."

With a teenage Tony Briggs, the son of one of his biggest mates in speedway, about to begin his shale career in Reading colours for 1980 and the club continuing its high profile pursuit of success now that Dave Lanning had joined the promoting team, Bettsy was all set for a second season at Smallmead. His hopes of bowing out gracefully, though, literally suffered a serious blow when his Jawa engine seized during Racers' pre-season practice/press day.

He said: "After my motor blew, I came away from the track that day and thought to myself, 'I don't know if I want to be doing this'. I didn't have another engine and I told the Reading management that I'd had it and couldn't face another season of hassle. We'd be running the business for almost a year and my mind was on that a lot of the time. Although my long-term mechanic, John Coote from King's Lynn, continued to help me, along with a London-based guy called Alan who did my southern meetings, it was a strain combining the business with speedway.

"I told Reading that the only way I could continue was if they provided me with a new engine. Anyway, I never heard a word from them. There was only a week between the practice and our first scheduled meeting but it wasn't until the Monday evening – race day – that Lanning phoned me here at about six o'clock to ask where I was.

"I reminded him that I didn't have a bike to ride and that no-one from Reading had bothered to get in touch with me in the previous week, so I'd decided to knock it on the end. He said: 'You won't be able to retire, you'll miss it too much'. Understandably, he wasn't happy but I reckoned that, by then, I wasn't too high on Reading's priority list. Looking back, if they'd phoned me during that week, I would have been there the following Monday – I'd have borrowed a bike, I wouldn't have wanted to let them down – but no-one called."

Betts' abrupt retirement didn't damage Reading's quest for the championship – they won the 1980 title amid a blaze of publicity – but Terry doesn't look back on his handling of the situation with

Reading never felt like home to the Lynn legend.

any pride.

"I felt a bit for Reading, because they had been good to me in the year I'd spent with them," he admits. "Afterwards, I felt I'd let them down, it wasn't how I wanted to finish my career. I regret it now. I wished I'd done another full season for them and been able to plan my retirement. I'd like to have visited all the tracks knowing it was the last time. But as it turned out, it wasn't a nice way to finish it. If Lanning hadn't said that I was bound to miss speedway, I probably wouldn't have been so determined to prove him wrong!

"I suppose, I'd gone to Reading to prove a point to Martin Rogers, to make the point that I wasn't ready to pack up. Who knows, under different circumstances, I might have continued at King's Lynn for another four years.

"I rode in a few testimonial meetings in 1980, and went back to Lynn for the Pride of the East at the end of that year, and I still felt OK. I weigh more or less same now as I did when I was riding and I found the riding part relatively easy.

Back at Lynn as team manager with advice for Henka Gustafsson.

That's my girl: Terry celebrates with wife Sue after winning the 1971 Southern Riders' Championship at Wimbledon, one of his favourite tracks. **Right:** Together at home in 2008.

When Briggo asked me to do a few of his Golden Greats meetings, the fact that I hadn't been on a bike for a number of years didn't bother me. When I rode in the first one he ran in 1988, I hadn't been on a bike for eight years.

"When I was riding at my peak, I never practiced before my first meeting of the season and I never had any kind of fitness regime. One winter, in the early 70s, I decided it would be a good idea to get myself a bit fitter, so I went out for a jog one morning, tripped up the kerb and cut all my knee. I thought, 'bugger this!'. I remained fit by working in the garage and the building work I'd done through the years."

As a footnote to his unhappy departure from Lynn, amid all the regrets, he admits he did very well financially from the move to Reading, who paid an expensive £10,000 fee for him.

"Because I'd been at King's Lynn for so long and hadn't asked for a transfer, I was due a big lump sum of whatever any club paid for me," explained Bettsy. "So most of what Reading paid to King's Lynn came to me."

Much as he still loved racing, Terry vowed to himself that he would go out at the top and not drop into the second grade National League, where he would have secured star status for a few more years and, of course, scored lots more points.

"I did have offers from National League tracks but they didn't interest me. But if Martin had left King's Lynn, it might have been different. I would have been tempted . . .

"It's a pity Simmo didn't take it over (with Bill Barker) a bit earlier. I would have gone back there and ridden for Simmo. But by the time they took over from Martin there in 1988, it was too late for me.

"In an ideal world, I would have had three or four more years at King's Lynn and then retired. King's Lynn was a big part of my life and I enjoyed every minute of it," added Terry.

Golden boy returns

Helping to promote Retro Speedway's King's Lynn Superstars DVD, on which he features prominently.

THE break from speedway didn't come easily. "Suddenly, my whole life had changed. One minute I was a full-time rider, the next I was working at the garage. I didn't go to speedway again for a long time afterwards, I got rid of my bikes and everything else. Most of my engines had blown up anyway!"

But King's Lynn hadn't quite seen the last of its former golden boy. Promoter Bill Barker and the club's former main sponsor Peter Thurlow talked Terry into returning as team manager in 1990.

"I'd never done team managing but Alan Littlechild said he'd share the duties with me. I gave it a go, and we had two top riders in Henka Gustafsson and Mark Loram but I found that I really had little to do. The formula had changed from when I rode, so you couldn't make any tactical changes anyway. Apart from trying to gee up the boys, your hands were tied. They needed a team-motivator rather than a manager and I found it frustrating.

"It was a totally different era from when I rode and some of them were a bit temperamental. I found myself having to bite my tongue, otherwise I might have upset a few people. I don't think I was cut out to be a team manager anyway.

"Mark didn't give a monkey's which races you put him out in and Henka was a diamond. He had so much natural ability – he couldn't start but, by Christ, could he come from the back. What a gifted racer – I thought it was only a matter of time before he won a World Final.

"Like Michael Lee, he was a massive waste of talent. He really needed someone to get hold of him and keep him on the right track."

Success can be measured in different ways. In terms of winning major titles, Terry is the first to acknowledge that he didn't do himself full justice individually. He was certainly good enough to have qualified for more than the one World Final he reached in 1974.

But Terry and Sue, as down-to-earth as each other, have done very well for themselves. Alongside their house – built on a corn field and which, even allowing for the downturn in the housing market, is worth the best part of £1million – the six-acre site includes several units that he has converted into flats, offices and retail outlets that net them rental fees. "We were offered around £2m for the units last year but turned it down," says Terry, who remains busy attending commercial truck and van auctions, carrying out building work and tending to anything that needs doing around their various properties.

"Whatever money I made from speedway I always sunk into my businesses and property. We didn't take holidays and I always worked through the winters. I prefer to be on the go and wouldn't want to retire and take it easy. I'd be bored stiff.

"Our son and youngest, Terry junior (33), works with me. We've got a really good working relationship but I steered him away from taking up speedway. In fact, we've been so busy that last year was the first since I was nine-years-old that I didn't go to a speedway meeting.

"But Buster (Chapman) has always made me welcome back at King's Lynn. He's put in a lot of money and hard work there and I wish him well. If ever he needed me, I'd always do anything I can to help him."

Terry and Sue also have two daughters – Trudi (38), who lives nearby and has a son James (7), who is showing glimpses of his grandad's two-wheeled skill in national BMX circles, and Toni (41), who lives in San Francisco with her American doctor husband and their three children, Thomas (11), Will (5) and Emily (2).

"Speedway has been good to me and I enjoyed more or less every minute of it," Terry concluded.

BRIEF ENCOUNTERS WITH… Kurt Hansen

How did your move to the UK come about?

My first trip to England was in 1982, to an Olle Nygren training school at King's Lynn. Then at the end of the 1983 season Mike Lohmann arranged three second-half meetings – at Hackney, which was postponed, then at Reading and finally at The Shay, Halifax. Me

and my team-mate from Slangerup, Peter Olsen, were two youngsters from Denmark who travelled to England for 14 days and had a great time racing and learning.

Which clubs did you ride for over here?

The only club I rode for in England was the Dukes of Halifax (1984 and 1985). I was thinking, 'wow, I'm gonna be a pro, living off my beloved sport, riding in great stadiums (compared to Danish standards at the time)' and all the people in and around the club were very welcoming.

How different were the tracks and the racing in the UK?

I found the tracks VERY grippy when I first came over, and the banking of The Shay was very difficult to adapt to. But I think I came to terms with them OK. Wolverhampton and The Shay were tracks I liked.

What was the highlight of your British speedway career?

It must have been the Northern Riders' Championship in

1985, when I came third behind Neil Evitts and Eric Monaghan.

And the low point?

The low point was definitely my first race with Halifax. We went to Newcastle and on the first bend of the first race of the second lap, I was taken off by a bike with no rider on it and ended up in hospital with a seriously damaged left leg.

Did you receive any special treatment because you were Danish?

I think I might have been treated a little differently. Eric and Bonnie Boothroyd brought my lunch to all away matches and tried to take me in, like one of their own.

When did you realise it was time to go back home?

Halfway through the 1985 season I realised that it was time to go home. I felt really isolated living up north, all my Danish mates were living in the middle or south of England, so I had a discussion with Mr. Boothroyd.

Any regrets?

The only regret I can think of is that I never fulfilled the ambitions I had when I first went over. It all came to an end with that discussion (with Eric) around what a great opportunity I had waiting for me at home, working at my father's garage and maybe taking it over in a couple of years, although it never worked out that way.

By Richard Bott ● Issue 41 (2010)

WORLD CLASS ODSAL DESERVES FULL RESPECT

If, as most suspect, Bradford's Odsal Stadium is now 'dead' as a speedway venue, isn't it time we gave the old place a decent funeral? Richard Bott relives the highs and lows of the famous West Yorkshire venue . . .

IT may well have been the ugly duckling of World Final venues but it was arguably the best race track in the country when it closed 13 years ago after being revamped to FIM specifications to stage the 1985 and 1990 finals.

But the BSPA knew the FIM axe was ready to fall on Odsal as a World Final venue after 1990.

The official reason was that the stadium's reduced capacity of 25,000 no longer met the minimum requirement. Unofficially, it was no secret that Bradford, both the environment and the stadium, was considered 'unfashionable' in FIM circles.

Grandiose plans to turn Odsal into 'the Wembley of the north' had only partially materialised and, ironically, the multi-billion pounds construction of the 'new' Wembley ended the pipe dream of Bradford, or anywhere else, housing a new national stadium.

Sadly, of course, Wembley has been lost to speedway for three decades and Bradford, even for league racing, since 1997.

There was plenty of drum beating at the time about the closure being only temporary while Odsal was transformed into a 21st century 'Superdome' but nothing happened and the building of a corporate hospitality complex on what was the pits bend, for the Bradford Bulls rugby league club, effectively read the 'last rites' to speedway at Odsal Top.

If the roar of speedway bikes is to be heard again in Bradford it is going to have to be at a new venue – and what are the chances of that in these austere times?

Now, in the Grand Prix age, all roads lead to Cardiff's Millennium Stadium and here, there and everywhere around Europe.

Wembley was, and always will be, regarded as the spiritual home of speedway's blue riband events and Bradford never stood a chance of being compared in the same light, with or without a revamped Odsal.

For a start, it's 'up north', where the perception is that the motorways are cobbled and the pigeons fly backwards to keep the muck out of their eyes. And Odsal, often maligned as 'just a big hole in the ground', is more like the mouth of an extinct volcano.

But if there is nowhere like Wembley, old or new, there is nowhere like Odsal, either.

It is, and always has been, unique. The sheer magnitude of the place (it once attracted a crowd of 102,578 to a rugby league Challenge Cup Final replay) can take your breath away when you come

A packed Odsal in the immediate post-war boom period. Note the extra spectators standing above the first bend terracing. Below: refurbished stadium and a new, wider track for the 1985 comeback season.

through the turnstiles at the top of the 'volcano' and look down into this man-made amphitheatre.

Open to the elements because the planned covered seating was never finished, it can be a cold, wet, inhospitable place on a bad night and I can vouch for that having reported on rugby league there for the past 12 years.

But on a good night (and there have been plenty of those over the last 60 years) Odsal comes alive whether it be for speedway, rugby league or even when it became Bradford City's temporary home after the horror of the Valley Parade fire in 1985.

And let's be fair. If Wembley is warmly remembered for 'signing off' with an epic World Final, in 1981, when Bruce Penhall triumphed so spectacularly, what about Odsal's two individual World Finals, in 1985 and 1990?

The '85 final, the first to be staged in England after Wembley and the Football Association gave speedway the boot, took a while to get going, until the rain stopped and the track dried out, but it

Bradford star Kenny Carter chasing Paul Thorp of Stoke and Belle Vue's Chris Morton off the banking in the British semi-final of the World Championship at Odsal in May 1986. It was Carter's last meeting before his tragic death.

Per Jonsson, the eventual champion, leading his closest challenger Shawn Moran during the thrilling 1990 World Final.

built to a dramatic, nerve-shredding climax.

Denmark's Erik Gundersen outwitted his fellow countryman Hans Nielsen and America's Sam Ermolenko in the first three-man run-off since 1960, to retain his title.

It was a huge gamble staging the '85 final at Odsal but where else in England could it go at the time?

Even then, it took the foresight and determination of Bradford Metropolitan Council to seize the nettle of opportunity because although speedway had prospered at Odsal in the post-war boom years and again, briefly, in the early 70s, it had withered and died again.

Peter Royston, of the *Bradford Telegraph and Argus* evening newspaper and with a genuine love for the sport, wrote an emotional article for *Speedway Star's* World Final preview issue in August 1985: "This was to be the year Bradford finally found a place on the sporting map.

"Bradford City were in the second division for the first time for 48 years and after decades of neglect Odsal was being given an expensive facelift in preparation for its biggest occasion for years – the World Speedway Final.

"Then came that dreadful day in May when 56 people perished when fire swept through the Valley Parade main stand as Bradford City celebrated their Third Division championship success.

"So Bradford, which for years had yearned for sporting success, found itself the centre of world attention in a way it never wanted.

"We sports-minded Bradfordians haven't had a lot to shout about over the years. The occasional champion, like heavyweight boxer Richard Dunn, show-jumper Harvey Smith and Olympic swimmer Adrian Moorhouse. But not a lot else.

"But there was always Odsal, the enormous hole in the ground which was turned into a sports

37

Unsung hero Eric Boothroyd prepared a superb track for the '90 World Final.

stadium by corporation rubbish tipping during the 30s.

"I have always been proud of Odsal. I saw my first speedway meeting there when that master showman Johnnie Hoskins opened the track in June 1945. We watched from primitive wooden-sleepered terracing in those days, cheering on the likes of Alec Statham, Ron Clarke and Oliver Hart. It is hard to believe that some league matches in those early post-war years pulled in as many fans as there will be at Saturday's World Final.

"Some of us have long dreamed of Odsal becoming the Wembley of the North. The potential was always there but not the money. Now, ironically, because Wembley can no longer accommodate speedway, the cash has somehow been found to transform Odsal into one of the north's major sporting venues.

"It may not be the biggest stadium in the country and it certainly isn't the smartest, even after one-and-a-half million pounds has been spent on refurbishing it. But the place simply exudes atmosphere. We are proud to be presenting speedway's showpiece and we are going to make a success of it. After all that has gone before, we deserve our moment of glory in Bradford."

The week after the World Final, I had my say in *Speedway Star* and wrote: "The myth-breakers did their best. Bradford Metropolitan Council, who sing that slogan to prove they are no Yorkshire puddings when it comes to moving with the times, tried so hard to transform the ugly duckling of Odsal into a beautiful white swan for England's first individual World Final outside Wembley.

"There is NO substitute for the old place with the twin towers but Bradford did us proud. And if this horrendous summer had relented sufficiently to give us a dry track from the start, I am sure we would be drooling about an epic among world finals.

"Instead, half-finished Odsal gave us half a classic. An early string of processional heats on a track saturated by the morning's rain, which made the man off No.1 gate an odds-on favourite every time, was followed by a completely different ball game when the sun came out, stayed out and they scraped off the sodden muck.

"Suddenly, it was REAL speedway, competitive, colourful, controversial and in true story-book style, a cliff-hanger until the very last page.

"Half-finished Odsal? If the council go ahead with the remainder of their ultra-ambitious £10million refurbishment, the transformation will be complete and the place will hold 65,000 instead of 40,000. But for those of us who remember the state of the old stadium just a year ago, we can have nothing but praise for the council's efforts. Without Bradford's single-minded determination to provide a stadium to fulfil FIM requirements, England would not have had a World Final at all this year."

Belle Vue promoter Stuart Bamforth, who sold the famous Manchester circuit a year or two later, faced with the crippling cost of rebuilding it under the new safety measures demanded by the government, was largely responsible for giving us a track worthy of a World Final, just as Eric Boothroyd did five years later after the Halifax Dukes had moved lock, stock and barrel from The

Shay to the revamped Odsal in 1986.

The 1990 final also went to a run-off, Sweden's Per Jonsson seeing off the challenge of America's Shawn Moran, after the pair had tied on 13 points.

And that World Final was hailed as a classic, giving Odsal the ultimate seal of approval.

Philip Rising wrote in *Speedway Star:* "Take a bow, Odsal. The 1990 World Final will live in the memory for a long time. There was universal and justified praise for the racing strip provided and the presentation of the meeting from start to finish. The considerable efforts of those involved are worthy of the highest praise.

"The BSPA undertook the handling of the meeting and came out of the whole affair with credit. Although the stadium was by no means full, the atmosphere on a warm, pleasant evening was tremendous. Odsal did us proud."

Kelvin Tatum, one of England's three finalists that night after being the only one in 1985, said: "It was a brilliant World Final, like it should be. The FIM people must take note. The track was brilliant, a real speedway track."

And *Speedway Star's* Richard Clark, in his report of the final, wrote: "This was real racing. It was what made you a speedway fan in the first place. When Munich memories conjure up merely a wonderful setting and nothing else, Vojens a feeling of being gatecrashers at a Danish party, Amsterdam an ill-conceived FIM political football that should have been booted into touch, Odsal will be remembered for giving most punters what they want – racing and a final that should rightly

Bradford Dukes after their 1990 Gold Cup Final victory over Oxford, the first national trophy in the West Yorkshire club's long history. Standing, left to right: Paul Thorp, Stuart Parnaby, Andy Smith, Neil Evitts. Kneeling: Gary Havelock, Glenn Doyle, Marvyn Cox.

Odsal Stadium viewed from the pits bend before the 1992 World Semi-Final.

Bouncing back, the Bradford Northern team of 1970. Left to right: Alan Knapkin, Gary Peterson, Alan Bridgett, Alf Wells, Peter Thompson, Sid Sheldrick, Robin Adlington. On bike: Dave Schofield.

be remembered as a classic."

As one of *Speedway Star's* columnists at Odsal for both finals, I sought out the unsung hero of the 1990 final, BSPA vice-chairman and Bradford co-promoter Eric Boothroyd – a man with years of experience as a track specialist.

He told me: "If people have gone away tonight saying it has been a great World Final, then I am delighted. I am delighted I was able to call on all the expertise in track preparation I have accumulated over the years and been able to put it together on the night that really matters.

"I worked very hard on the track because I wanted to put one down that showed we in England still have the expertise to prepare the perfect racing circuit.

"We always put plenty of dirt down at Bradford because it makes for good racing. That has been proved here tonight. At the halfway stage, six or seven riders could still have won the meeting. I haven't missed a World Final for a long time and I believe this one has been the best since Wembley in '81.

"Wembley wasn't always the best World Final venue because it was a one-line track – a bit like Munich and Gothenburg. I don't want to knock Gothenburg but it has always been said: 'Stick on the line there and no-one gets by you'. There are always problems when you have a track in a stadium that wasn't built for speedway. Odsal was. I wasn't involved with the track preparation here for the 1985 final but it was a good final once it came to the boil.

"What helped me this time was that I had two weeks to prepare the track and the weather was kind. You live by the weather. You have to keep watching the weather and get the right balance between what to put on and what to take off.

"I hope this World Final will show Bradford up in a better light. The president of the CCP, Gunter Sorber, is over the moon about tonight's final. Surely that has to mean something? Maybe he will go back to the FIM and say: 'We must stop knocking Bradford the way we have in the past'.

"I would like to think we have a chance of staging another World Final here. But who knows what will happen in four or five years' time."

What did happen was that the one-off World Final was soon replaced by the Grand Prix format and Bradford was in effect dumped.

Also, the Bradford Dukes found it easier to win trophies than attract fans and with cruel irony speedway ended at Odsal the very year, 1997, the Dukes were crowned Elite League champions.

Halifax Dukes had moved out of The Shay, crippled by rent demands, and then been hit by the tragic death of their No.1 box office star Kenny Carter in 1986, their first season at Odsal.

But with two of Bradford's famous sporting sons, Bobby and Allan Ham, at the helm in the early 90s, the Dukes went on a roll, winning seven team trophies and producing the 1992 World Champion, Gary Havelock, who triumphed at Wroclaw in Poland.

Kelvin Tatum, Mark Loram, Simon Wigg and Joe Screen were other top English riders who wore Dukes' colours and revelled on the best track in the country.

But speedway was losing its appeal at the turnstiles and the crowds melted away at Odsal, just as they had done in the mid-70s after the likes of Alan Knapkin, Dave Baugh, Robin Adlington and the late Gary Peterson had lured five-figure crowds to the old stadium for the first time since the early post-war years.

It was second division speedway, introduced to Odsal midway through the 1970 season when Mike Parker transferred his Nelson Admirals team to Bradford, but it clicked with the public after a barren 10 years.

I was Parker's press officer at Nelson and got involved in the Odsal operation with my old pal Bob Radford.

The team was called Bradford Northern, adopting the name of the rugby league club, and they were virtually unbeatable at home on a difficult track restricted in shape by the rugby pitch.

"Other teams didn't like coming to Odsal because it was an awkward shape but it suited me," recalls Knapkin, a bespectacled former grass-tracker and scrambler who rattled up more than 1,000 points in his five years with Bradford.

"Gary Peterson was the real star – a great rider but an absolute loony. Sadly, of course, he got killed in a track crash at Wolverhampton in 1975."

Knapkin, who ran a motorcycle shop in Manchester, has one regret about his time at Odsal. He bought out Mike Parker, Les Whaley and Bill Bridgett halfway through the 1973 season when the attendances were starting to fall.

"I thought I could get the crowds up again and changed the team name from Northern to Barons, because I knew a lot of the supporters didn't like the connection with rugby league."

Knapkin only ran the promotion for a year before, in turn, selling out to Jim Streets. "I lost a few thousand pounds but I'm sure Jim lost a lot more. The experience of being a promoter didn't sour me and I enjoyed my time in speedway. I was 27 when I started riding speedway and if I had my time again, would have started a lot earlier."

The Bradford boom had bust and the track closed in 1975, just as it had done in 1960.

When it reopened in 1985 it had a new track with big, wide sweeping bends and was 'made' for speedway.

A year earlier, in September 1984, three Belle Vue riders, Chris Morton, Peter Collins and Larry Ross, staged a series of demonstration races under the watchful gaze of FIM officials.

This was followed, in 1985, by three World Championship qualifying meetings to further establish

The wide open spaces of Odsal were suited to the six-man race format for the 1988 World Pairs semi-final.

that the track was up to standard.

Ironically, the first of the three, a World Team Cup qualifying round, was held on Sunday, May 12 – the day after the Bradford City fire disaster. What an omen!

But speedway was back at Odsal and, apart from the 1985 and 1990 individual World Finals, staged World Pairs and World Team Cup Finals and qualifying rounds.

England last won the World Cup at Odsal in 1989, although the event was marred by the horrific first-race crash which saw all four riders taken to hospital and Erik Gundersen left fighting for his life.

Thankfully, the little Danish dynamo survived, even if he has never ridden since. The question remains: will we ever see anybody ride speedway at Odsal again?

If not, at least give the old place some respect.

On 2 Minutes With...
PHIL WHITE

How did you get started in speedway?

My dad took me to watch at Sheffield and I thought it was fantastic. I knew that's what I wanted to do.

As a fan, Arnie Haley was a big favourite of mine and he was the first recognised rider I ever beat. It must have been embarrassing for him being beaten by a junior in the second-half but he came over and congratulated me. That was a really nice thing to do and it meant so much to me.

Which team-mate did you most enjoy partnering on the track?

Shawn Moran at Sheffield. He was such a fantastic guy and I probably had the best view you could have of him ... from behind! He was so generous and he would leave you room and look after you. He was a gentleman – he was so good, he could afford to be. I partnered Dave Morton for a season too, which I enjoyed. The team spirit was fantastic and we were all mates.

Ivan Mauger was involved at Sheffield at the time and if you did something and came in and saw him smiling and giving you praise, it was a really good feeling.

Career highlight/proudest moment?

I was just a jobbing middle order rider. I was never really one for individual meetings and I never got very far in the World Championship – I just liked the team doing well and taking points off a rider.

What have you done since you stopped riding speedway?

Geoff Hall Motorcycles used to sponsor me and I'd worked for them in the winter, so I got a full-time job there for a while. Purely by coincidence, my wife at the time's uncle had been for a trial flight in a Cessna, so I had a go and I liked it. I started having a few lessons and got my private licence.

I worked for Kwik Fit, then did a job for Midland Bank as a gofer but all the time I kept up my flight training and gained my commercial pilot's licence. I didn't miss speedway because I had something to focus on.

After getting my licence I got a job with British Regional Airways flying a British Aerospace Jet Stream 41. These days I'm working for Flybe on an Embraer, which is a state of the art Brazilian-made jet.

TONY
CLARKE

SUPPORTERS of West Ham in the swinging 60s will have no trouble recalling Tony Clarke, a popular and key member of Hammers' treble-winning team in his first season of racing and one of the sport's biggest personalities.

These days, you would probably struggle to recognise the once blond tough guy of the track as the slim 70-year-old man in glasses and longish hair who now drives a minicab for a hard-earning living near his home at Nunhead in south London.

The last few years have been tough for the former England international and British Lions hero. He suffered a stroke last summer and showed *Backtrack* the scar that runs the length of the left side of his neck where surgeons operated to repair arteries that had become blocked through years of heavy smoking.

Despite his brush with death, he defiantly continues to smoke like a trooper, although he says he has cut down to 30 or 40 cigarettes a day. "There's no point in stopping now," he says, reaching out

Tony leading Swindon's Bob Kilby at West Ham in 1969, his best season.

Home comforts: on parade for the Lions with Gote Nordin at Wembley in 1971.

Newport Wasps' No.1 in 1972.

for his packet of Golden Virginia that is perched on his favourite armchair. It's the only pleasure I've got left in life!"

'Tearaway Tony's' racing career peaked in 1969, the year before the start of the *Backtrack* era, when he topped injury-hit West Ham's averages. The following winter he starred for the Lions on their tour of Australia and New Zealand but was never able to recapture that brilliant form once the 70s dawned.

He left Custom House for London rivals Wembley at the start of 1971, a move that suited him well and felt like coming home. Born at nearby Kensal Rise on July 6, 1940, Tony was taken to his first speedway meeting by his father at Wembley in the late 40s and was a regular there on the pits bend terraces on Thursday nights.

Offering solid support to heat leaders Bert Harkins, his old West Ham team-mate Sverre Harrfeldt and the fast emerging young Dave Jessup, 'Clarkey' averaged more than seven points a match for the Lions, who were in their second season back at the Empire Stadium.

Tony had been a victim of the Rider Control system when he was directed from West Ham to Oxford, a track he says he hated, in 1966 and he was given no choice in the matter again after Wembley pulled out of the British League at the end of '71.

This time he was re-allocated to Newport, an often bumpy and square-shaped track few riders relished visiting, but in a struggling team destined for the wooden spoon he topped their averages with a CMA of 7.15 from 35 matches.

From the start of his career in 1960, as a raw rookie falling off regularly in practice rides at Rye House, when his father George told him he would never make a rider, until his retirement in 1975, he claims he only ever owned JAP machinery. It remains a regret that he resisted the switch to Jawa . . . although he did briefly get his hands on a few of the Czech-made bikes through ill-gotten means.

It's part of speedway folklore that Tony was imprisoned for dishonestly handling stolen goods, namely three complete Jawa machines, plus wheels, tyres and various other items of racing equipment belonging to the six Russian riders who were in England in September 1972 to contest the World Final at Wembley.

"Yeah, I nicked 'em," Tony admits without hesitation when asked if the rumours were true.

"In those days the Russians used to bring over lots of bikes, engines and equipment – not to use as spares, but to sell while they were here to get their hands on some western currency. I didn't have the money to buy it from them, so I thought, 'f*** it, I'll help meself'. Simple as that. They had everything stored in a lock-up near Wembley Stadium car park – anyone could have nicked it.

"There were three of us involved – me, my brother Terry and his mate (Ben Griffiths), who supplied the van we used."

Tony and his brother were arrested, and subsequently released on bailed. four days after the World Final. He is convinced he knows how and why the police were on his tail so quickly.

"I know who grassed us up, although he would never admit it," says Tony.

"I'd told another rider what I intended to do but he didn't turn up to collect the bikes as arranged. The next thing, the Old Bill swooped on Terry's place, where we'd hidden all the gear. We had a nice, little garage business going at Hounslow at the time of our arrest.

"I woke up one morning and when I looked out of my window I could see police waiting for me. I tried to get hold of my brother to tell him what I thought was going on but I couldn't reach him by phone and that was it – the Old Bill came down and collared us both.

"I got 15 months and eventually served about a year in prison."

While on bail release, Tony rode for two British League clubs in 1973.

Wimbledon Dons early in the 1973 season. Standing, left to right: Cyril Maidment (team manager), Graeme Stapleton, Pete Wigley, Tony Clarke, Neil Cameron, Bert Harkins. Kneeling: Reg Luckhurst and Tommy Jansson, with Trevor Hedge on machine.

He had been reluctant to join Newport Wasps from defunct Wembley in 1972 and described the weekly journey from his north London home to South Wales as "murder". The much shorter trip to home meetings at Wimbledon the following season came as a welcome relief.

His average had dipped to around 5.00 by then, though, and he admits: "I wasn't riding that well and then I had a ruck with Cyril Maidment (Dons' manager). We were riding at Poole and after scoring two points in my first heat, Maido pulled me out and put in our reserve, Graeme Stapleton. I couldn't see how he could do that, so I told him: 'I'm not going all the way down to Exeter (which was our next meeting) if you've going to do this to me, so go f*** yourself'. That was the end for me at Wimbledon."

After 12 official matches for Dons, Tony was released in July and, after a period of two months spent running his garage

Tony at the WSRA dinner in 2007.

business, agreed to join Wolverhampton for the last eight weeks of the season. He rode only seven matches for Wolves (CMA 4.55) but helped them to beat Leicester in the Midland Cup Final and gave best support to Ole Olsen with a match-winning nine points on his return to Wimbledon.

But the past caught up with him.

In November 1973 Tony was sentenced to 15 months imprisonment at Middlesex Guildhall Crown Court, where, along with his younger brother, he was convicted of dishonestly receiving three Jawa bikes, eight wheels and tyres and two boxes of spares.

After sentencing, Tony was taken to Wormwood Scrubs prison in west London but after a few uncomfortable weeks there he was transferred to "a nice easy jail" at Spring Hill open prison in Aylesbury, Bucks.

"Three weeks after I was sent down, my brother was jailed for three years for ringing cars – and, in fact, we ended up doing time together at Spring Hill. We arranged for a load of whisky, vodka and fags to be brought in for us to sell but that ended when other inmates grassed us up."

After spending the 1974 speedway season at her majesty's pleasure, Clarke made a comeback with Wolves in '75. But the year out had taken its toll – 26 matches yielded a 3.16 average. At 33, he decided it was time to quit.

"I'd had enough of racing by then," he recalls. "When you're maintaining your own bike and doing everything yourself, you get fed up with it. My heart wasn't in it anymore, I'd lost interest."

Despite spending all nine seasons of his career in the top flight, Clarke admits he never took speedway seriously enough.

"I enjoyed it, it was good fun, but speedway was never life and death for me, like it was for Briggo and Ivan Mauger. I remember being with the British Lions in Australia and the other boys in the team were up early in the morning after every meeting to clean their bikes. They'd be cleaning their

Tony at home in 2010 with a Wembley plaque, one of few career mementoes he kept.

wheel spokes and I'd think, 'that won't make the bike go any faster'. I'd just kick the s*** off my bike, make sure the chains were clean and check that nothing was breaking, and that was it – my cleaning was done.

"I had all the ability in the world. I just didn't have good enough equipment."

Not that he found it easy to live without speedway. "I missed it for 10 years and it was hard to do other things," he says. "I tried to get my boy, Ian, into speedway and I used to take him to the Hackney training school in the early 80s. But he didn't really like it much."

Following his divorce from his first wife, Tony had sadly become estranged from his three children, Ian, Julie and Angela, for a long time. Sadly, Ian, died aged 37 following a brain aneurysm in 1999. Happily, Tony is now back in touch with his daughters, who both get on well with his Sri Lankan-born wife, Easterine.

Tony and Easterine, who is a qualified doctor and accountant, met in a nightclub at Greenford in north London in 1980 and were married nine years later. He jokes: "I only went out for the night . . . and I ain't been able to get rid of her since!"

Joking aside, Tony went on to say: "I'd have been f***** years ago if it wasn't for her. No ifs and buts about it, I'd have knocked it on the head years ago. I would have been dead. I used to ask myself, 'what's the point of it all?'. Once you stop doing the things you like, what is the point in getting up in pain and walking around in pain all day long? I see it with the people we take to hospital for treatment."

The couple have run their small mini cab business, a two-car enterprise called At Your Service Cars, from their home for the past seven years.

"It's absolutely dead at the moment and we're relying on corporate clients to see us through the recession," sighs Tony.

"I was out on a cabbing job last year when I became ill. I made a misjudgement and slightly bumped the car. Half-an-hour later I did it again. And then half-an-hour after that it happened a third time.

"I came home, made myself a coffee and the cup slipped straight through my hand. I saw my doctor and two days later he sent me to Kings College Hospital, where they did lots of tests on me. I was allowed to go home but then they phoned me and said, 'you'd better get up here a bit quick'. They whizzed me straight in and did the operation. I'd suffered a stroke."

A diabetic, Tony revealed that he still suffers from bouts of depression but the days of him consuming three bottles of whisky in a weekend are happily gone. "One (alcoholic) drink is enough for me now. My body can't handle it anymore," he says.

"I took Easterine to the 1981 World Final at Wembley and we went to Wimbledon during their Conference League era when Ronnie Moore came over from New Zealand. But I only watch speedway on telly these days. I find it boring."

* Some three years after the above interview, Tony Clarke died at his south London home early in 2014, aged 73, following a long battle with a series of major health problems.

Tony had suffered a stroke in 2010 and a second one in April of 2013, shortly before being diagnosed with lung cancer. He underwent 32 sessions of radiation treatment, only to be told by doctors that the cancer had spread to his brain. More radiotherapy treatment followed before, in December 2013, he was given three-and-a-half months to live.

He hung in there for a little longer than that but his brave fight ended when he died peacefully at home while being cared for by Easterine, his wife of 34 years, and Marie Curie nurses.

BRIEF ENCOUNTERS WITH… Leif Berlin Rasmussen

Which UK teams did you ride for?

Wolverhampton from 1975 to 1977.

What were your first impressions of the UK?

It was something new. I was young and it felt strange to come over and drive on the left side of the road. I could not speak English, so it was very hard for the first half-year.

Did you have an 'English dad' or did you have to fend for yourself?

I was alone but there were many sweet supporters who were very helpful.

What did you miss most about home?

My family and friends.

What was your favourite 'hang out' in Britain?

I had no favourite but I enjoyed going up in the bar after the racing.

Was there anything about the UK that you could never understand or get to grips with?

I think it went very well – you have the same humour as Danes!

How different were the tracks and the racing in the UK?

It was professional. You rode almost every day, whereas at home I had been working and rode mostly at weekends and sometimes on Wednesdays. So you could say it was a completely different life.

Did you receive any special treatment because you were Danish?

No, I do not think so. Maybe the supporters were more

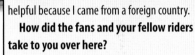

helpful because I came from a foreign country.

How did the fans and your fellow riders take to you over here?

Everybody were very helpful.

What was the highlight of your British speedway career?

It was always a highlight when we won at our home track, when the audience was also happy and we had done our job.

Were you treated any differently when you returned home after riding over here?

I rode only for a few years after I went home. I could not get myself organised in Denmark and I also had children who pulled at me, so I stopped riding.

When did you realise it was time to go back to Denmark?

I had my second child with my wife and could not earn enough money for everything, so it was somewhat involuntarily that I stopped.

Any regrets?

Yes, I regret that I went home and did not give it a chance

What are you up to now?

I've been a course manager on a golf course for the last 20 years, although I am retired now. I have a daughter who lives in Birmingham and has lived there for almost 15 years, so it is doubtful if she will come to Denmark and live, but for us it's not so far away. We enjoy England and still have friends from back then we can stay with, so it's nice.

By John Berry ● Issue 47 (2011)

HOW TO REDUCE GUESTS BY POOLING RESOURCES

JOHN BERRY recalls the cost-cutting days of the miner's strike, the three-day week, the banning of Swedes and offers a possible solution to the guest rider problem that still plagues the sport today . . .

MOANING about the way speedway has been and is run in the UK is easy and I know many within the sport resent me expressing my opinions. They consider me to be snide and sniping but in my defence, just about every problem I have soap-boxed about has been my long-held view. More importantly, these are views I had expressed to the right people at the right time and I would like to think that each time I have made a negative comment I have also offered a positive alternative.

Sometimes in the old days these alternatives were accepted; more often than not they were dropped into the 'too hard' basket or did not suit vested interests. However, I would like to believe my carping is acceptable if it offers constructive suggestions.

And so here is my two pennyworth on the question of how to manage without guest riders.

The question of how to cover for absent riders in team speedway has always been difficult. Surely then, the first thing to do is to look at reducing the number of times guests are needed. In the 'good old days' it was rare, indeed, for a star man to be injured and therefore require cover, while rider replacement was more than adequate for numbers two and three. Second strings and reserves could be replaced by one of the many junior riders attached to every team.

So the lion's share of guest use, then and now, is to cover for non-injury unavailability.

During the 1973-74 winter the BSPA had the collective balls to declare that any rider who could not make themselves available for all official British fixtures (other than for international duty) could not ride in the British League. Well, actually, they didn't say that.

What they said was that the arrangement whereby star Swedish riders could miss British fixtures in order to go back and race in Sweden (at the BL's expense) would cease. But as all the other riders racing in Britain had no such liability, then effectively the one thing embraced the other. I should point out this was at the time when Arthur Scargill was the de facto Prime Minister, Edward Heath was wringing his hands, electricity was in short supply and the three-day week was upon us. The speedway public therefore accepted the decision as a cost-saving measure and, indeed, the effect of the miners' strike might well have influenced some of the promoters' decision-making.

When the promoters made that call for the 1974 season, many top class Swedes were excluded from the (then) British League. Reading took a season out that year while waiting for their new stadium to be finished, so Anders Michanek wasn't badly missed, although he took the opportunity to concentrate on the World Championship that year and won it at a canter.

Other Swedes who missed out that year were: Bernt Persson (Cradley Heath), Soren Karlsson (Coventry), Christer Sjosten (Coatbridge), Bengt Jansson (Hackney),Tommy Nilsson (Hackney), Richard Hellsen (King's Lynn), Hasse Holmqvist (Oxford), Christer Lofqvist (Poole), Bengt Larsson (Sheffield) and Tommy Jansson (Wimbledon).

Two veteran Swedes, Soren Sjosten (Belle Vue) and Olle Nygren (Ipswich), were given the go-ahead to continue racing in the BL throughout '74 because they were both long-term UK residents and married to English women.

That was an impressive list of names to manage without but the sky did not fall in. In fact the BL coped quite well given the difficult political circumstances. By 1975, with the three-day week a distant memory, enough individual clubs bitched about having lost their top man that, having bitten the bullet and endured the potential pain of coping for the first difficult season without the Swedes, the British promoters, under pressure from Charles Foot who wanted to maintain good relations with SVEMO and Reading who wanted Mich to spearhead the Racers in their newly-built stadium, backed down and the Swedes were allowed back in.

Swedish stars Bernie Persson, Anders Michanek, Bengt Jansson and Christer Lofqvist, pictured before the 1972 BLRC, were all banned from competing in the 1974 British League.

Ipswich youngsters Mike Lanham (left) and Dave Gooderham taking their chance in this battle with Neil Cameron at Poole in 1975.

There was, however, a minor change to the previous arrangement. Up until the banning of the Swedes, the cost of their air fares was shared between all tracks. From 1975 onwards, those promoters who employed a 'commuting Swede' became responsible for paying his rider's fares, which were not inconsiderable in those days of airline regulation.

At the time, the decision to allow the Swedes back seemed insignificant. In hindsight it was a disaster. From then until now, on just about every question involving foreign riders, UK promoters have steadfastly refused to draw any lines in the sand and the door was opened to allow Czechs, Poles and all manner of foreign wannabes an opportunity to try their luck.

One should also point out that had the BSPA stuck to its guns, then there would have been a whole heap of top class riders ready, willing and available to replace any short-term injured BL top men.

So with no BL riders having to miss meetings in order to race elsewhere and with medium-to-long-term injury cover available in the shape of uncontracted foreign stars, then surely rider replacement would have been more than adequate to cover for the odd one-off absences. It wouldn't have been difficult to work around the various World Championship events in the fixture list if only a few British domiciled riders were affected.

As previously stated, covering for injury to riders two or three in a team, rider replacement was always the best option. Second strings and reserves? That is what a team's junior riders were there for, and if the overall standard of teams had been reduced by having no commuting riders, then the difference in standard between a number four and a number eight would not be that great.

I know that, at Ipswich, supporters loved to see the reserve riders, such as Mike Lanham, Ted Howgego, Trevor Jones and Dave Gooderham, being given a chance to flex their muscles against the big boys, and it gave those riders opportunities for experience and advancement.

Of course, all of the above presumes the promoters in both leagues could work together for the common good, that a sensible method of equalisation of rider strengths could be maintained and that riders were all under central contracts. Yes, I know, some presumption, given the mood of the time, but I'm just showing here *how* it could have been done.

Part-time stars should join central pool

OK, let's move on to modern times and accept the situation as it is today. And once again we have to presume promoters are prepared to put British speedway in front of their own narrow interests on the understanding that everyone would benefit in the long-term.

It has always seemed a nonsense to me that a promoter can trawl through lists of riders from all over the world and simply add any of them to his 'asset list'. Surely, if a rider wishes to race in the UK it should be arranged through the central administration?

In my plan a rider would submit his details to the BSPA, along with his financial demands and availabilities. If those demands are considered reasonable he then joins a 'provisional pool' of riders for the first year after his application has been accepted and makes himself available to fill in for any team in the event of a short-term gap becoming available through absence or injury. The buzzword these days is for a rider 'pool'. Well, this would be it.

EC riders would need to specify which league they were aiming for. Non-EC riders would obviously only be available to the top league and would be subject to rigorous ability checks.

Now it might well suit some riders not to want to commit to a full season with one club. Indeed, that seems to be more and more the case with SGP riders anyway. So it may be that these riders might actually wish to remain as a 'pool' rider on a full-time basis. This certainly makes more sense than the current situation where a promotion can juggle its team around from month to month and stick in an SGP rider for a few weeks, or whenever he can fit in the odd meeting.

In my Utopian world, all rider assets are contracted to the BSPA and not to individual promotions. It is the central office that does all the contract negotiating and placing of riders, permanent or temporary. During each close season, riders and promoters can each submit (secret) wishes for change. A rider might wish to move from a team and a promoter might wish to move a rider on – perhaps even to change leagues. They would make a confidential application to the central administration at the end of the season and be added to the list of provisional riders looking for a permanent home.

This enlarged pool of riders would now be allocated to teams by the central administration, which would look at all the various requests and move riders around to balance up team strengths, taking into account where possible the wishes of all parties but reserving the right to final decision-making.

Those riders who either do not wish to commit to a full season and those for whom a permanent team place cannot be found become the nucleus of the next season's 'pool', to be joined by new applications from riders wishing to join UK speedway.

Old fashioned Rider Control? Not really, because firstly the parties would nominate for change anyway and also the decisions would not be made by a committee made up of promoters with vested interests.

The National League (today's third tier) simply would have no guest facility available to it.

Obviously my system does away with transfer fees, which must be to the benefit of the sport. The current system is plain silly. Everyone holds football up as well run but how can it be well run if those teams with the greatest income (or having the richest sugar daddies) can just buy their way to the top?

Spectacular Russian No.1 Emil Sayfutdinov is one current day star who could be made available to British teams again via a central pool system advocated by John Berry.

In speedway, the retain and transfer system is simply unhealthy and pointless. It pushes up costs, not only in direct transfer fees but also because promoters are forced into Dutch auctions when it comes to negotiating with riders. I mean, how daft do you look when, after paying out £40K on a rider, you find he decides to opt out of British racing the year after you signed him and is now worth zilch?

Now remember, this is a 'discussion paper'. It makes no claim to being the finished article, not least because I (in common, it seems, with many of today's promoters) do not know all the current twists and turns of today's team building small print.

I also make a couple of quite large assumptions. The biggest is that the promoters are prepared to accede power to a central administration. That done, the logic of abandoning the retain and transfer system and putting the sport's interests in front of promotional point-scoring would be a doddle.

Of course, there could be far more radical action involving a whole new competition format with entirely different 'playing conditions' but that really would require a giant leap of faith.

How did you first get into speedway?

It was 1970-something and we lived about 300 yards from the dog track at Romford. Every week one of the away riders would come down our road looking for the speedway track (the Bombers, of course raced at Brooklands, home of Romford FC, and not at the greyhound stadium). It became a regular thing, so we used to go out and wait and direct them. I was only about 10 or 11 at the time and we started going to watch the speedway.

The first year we were doing junior grass-track seriously, my younger brother Colin and I had to share a bike because we couldn't afford two, but I was older than him so I was riding a 100cc bike in a 150cc class. I still finished second in the championship, though!

My brother was better than me at junior grass-track but when we got into speedway his heart wasn't in it and he didn't really want to do it.

Who was the best promoter you rode for?

It had to be Len Silver, he was the best. He was a real showman and very good to me.

What was your favourite track?

I preferred the smaller ones. Aside from Eastbourne and Rye House, I liked Hackney, Newcastle, Middlesbrough and, strangely, Berwick. At Shielfield Park it wasn't just the track, it was the people – they made the meeting. When I joined Middlesbrough, the other track I would have gone to was Oxford – I loved it.

And ones you never looked forward to visiting?

Workington and Exeter. Exeter scared me, it was daunting. That banking – I've never seen anything like it.

Which team-mate did you most enjoy partnering on the track?

Rye House team-mates Ashley Pullen and Karl Fiala. I knew exactly where they would be. Kelvin Mullarkey was the same.

What was the proudest moment of your career?

Winning the KO Cup with Rye House in 1979. For the away leg the whole team travelled up by train and all the bikes were loaded into one van, which three mechanics drove up there. After the meeting we all went back on the sleeper train because we were riding at home the next day, while the mechanics travelled back overnight. That's what we used to do if we had a one-off match in the far north or Scotland. It was a great way to travel back. The journey up seemed to take forever but after the meeting we'd have a couple of drinks, head straight to our berths on the train and wake up at King's Cross.

In the winter of 1980-81 I spent two-and-a-half months riding in South Africa, where we competed in an unofficial Test series. A fantastic experience.

What have you done since you stopped riding speedway?

I got a job straight away driving a van for an office equipment company. I did that for two or three years when they asked me to open a furniture warehouse, which I did. I was there for nine years when I was poached by one of their suppliers to work in their sales office.

From there I decided to go self-employed. I now do courier work, mainly delivering for printers, with a good long-term friend of mine and the company is called Pimpernel Trading, based in Enfield. I've done lorry driving and the European bit, so it suits me.

JAMIE
LUCKHURST

IF you were to compile a list of 'oddest first speedway injuries' I suppose falling off a banister in a trotting track on a Spanish island could be top of the list – but that was the fate of a young Jamie Luckhurst.

His father, former England international and World Finalist Reg Luckhurst, had become involved in Ian Hoskins' speedway venture in Majorca at the Son Pardo trotting track in the early 70s, and young Jamie and his brother Jeremy had taken to the lifestyle like any youngsters living life in the sun – very actively.

"I loved Majorca," recalls Jamie. "After school we went down to the beach every day. I was too young to ride speedway but I used to ride round on the back of the water carrier, doing things and mucking-in, but one day I had a bad accident. Jeremy and I used to slide down the banister of a big staircase that went down to where the bikes were warming-up at the bottom of the stadium. I went over it one day and it was about a 20-foot drop.

"I can't remember hitting the ground or ending-up in hospital but my right wrist was poking to the right, almost hanging-off, and both bones were broken."

Canterbury Crusaders of 1984. Standing, left to right: Neville Tatum, Rob Tilbury, Reg Luckhurst (team manager), Alan Mogridge, Dave Mullett, Jamie Luckhurst. Kneeling: Barney Kennett, Kevin Brice.

So began a list of niggling injuries that, with one notable exception, were not too serious on their own but would eventually sap the energy and enthusiasm of the charismatic youngster.

Back home in Kent, the racing bug had clearly been inherited from Reg, a former star at West Ham and Wimbledon, as both brothers took to junior grass-track, supplemented by trips down to the local Kentish beaches to mark a track out and race.

"My father was a true professional. He had a large workshop and one at home, too, where both Jeremy and I kept two to three speedway bikes and trials bikes. He dedicated his life to us."

At the same time mum Gloria was secretary of the junior grass-track club, so the brothers had full backing from both parents.

At 16 Jamie progressed into speedway, taking second-half rides at Canterbury and his dad's former track Wimbledon in 1981. Thirteen meetings for the Crusaders with an average of just under four was a satisfactory start, capped by being nominated for the Junior Championship of the British Isles, then an annual fixture at his home Kingsmead track.

"I suppose they'd noticed me because I'd won the British Junior Grass-track Championships, along with the Welsh and English titles and club events on numerous occasions, so they thought I was going to be reasonably good at speedway.

"A lot of us came through at the same time . . . Marvyn Cox the year before me, then Andy Galvin, Andrew Silver, Simon Cross and Nigel De'Ath."

A useful four points in the under-21 meeting suggested a bright start but the next year was to be frustrating. Apart from a handful of appearances as a stop-gap for Wimbledon, he found himself back in second-halves.

"It wasn't a bad start but when you're that young expectations are high. I was frustrated in '82 but I was still doing second-halves and grass-track, so I was still pretty occupied."

Former international and World Finalist Reg Luckhurst passing on his vast experience to eldest son Jamie.

Jamie hits the front at Hackney in the 1984 NL Fours, with team-mate Dave Mullett and Edinburgh duo Sean Courtney and Bobby Beaton chasing.

Persistence paid off, though, and 1983 saw Jamie establish himself in a Canterbury team that starred the likes of Denzil Kent, Kelvin Mullarkey and local legend Barney Kennett. Missing only four matches, Jamie earned himself an impressive six-plus average. What was the reaction from the senior riders to this young upstart?

"I don't think they liked it too much because I was able to beat them. Not always but we generally got on all right and travelled together most of the time."

The next season saw Jamie hit the heights as Crusaders' No.1 in only his second full season, running a creditable eight point CMA. Individual honours came in open meetings at Arena-Essex and Canterbury.

Jamie puts his rapid rise at Canterbury down to dedication. He says: "I'd trained very hard during the winter because I wanted to be No.1 by the end of the season and I also wanted to win my first open meeting at Canterbury, which I did as well.

"What I wanted was achieved in that off-season (1983-84). I used Sports Techniques, which involved 'visualising'. I would practice starts in my head. I used to see me standing on rostrums. I could smell the dope and oil."

Psychology was clearly the key, along with a huge commitment to fitness: "I'd walk and jog and with every step I thought, 'that's going to make me better'. I wanted to be fit, faster, more positive and achieve what I wanted. I'd had a broken wrist the previous year and I wanted to get things right.

"I'd realised psychology was the key when I was about 13 or 14. At a couple of meetings there were people who, on their day, were faster than me but to beat them you had to be stronger mentally. You had to make the perfect start and put your bike where they were or wanted to be."

The mind could be a hindrance too, though. As Jamie explains, he saw a character trait in himself that was to affect his racing.

"I've got a very flippant personality. If everything's going great, I actually lose interest. I could

Lucky boys: Jamie and Jeremy followed their father to Wimbledon. Below: Jamie, on the inside, and Jeremy leading for Dons at Milton Keynes in 1985.

be 100 per cent one week, then nothing the next. That wasn't psychology, just a natural trait of my personality."

It was that trait that compromised his career on the shale as much as the injuries that gradually sapped his enthusiasm, as events were to prove.

The 1985 season saw the seismic shift in the balance of power in speedway that saw multiple defections from the British League to the National League, then enjoying weekly coverage on cable and satellite television. Among the tracks making the jump was one of the brightest stars in speedway's firmament, Wimbledon. A place for Jamie beckoned at a venue he readily calls 'home', a track he'd been visiting regularly since childhood.

"Dad had raced there in the 60s and early 70s, so it was a place where I felt I belonged. The stadium was brilliant, the supporters were always proactive and supporting you. It was one of the better tracks and stadiums to race in at the time. The promotion was that professional you hardly ever saw them. You knew you were there but they kept themselves to themselves. Every time you turned up everything was done."

Jamie and Wimbledon were the perfect fit. He earned another eight-point average in 1985 while supporting fellow Dons' stars Mike Ferreira and Roger Johns. Further individual successes came at Arena-Essex, Eastbourne and home at Plough Lane in the Marlboro Southern.

The youngster's flair for publicity made him a popular interviewee in front of the Screen Sport cameras.

"I wanted to self-promote because all the time you're in front of the cameras or riding or winning, the more likely you were to attract and keep sponsors. My view was, 'it's not going to do any good if I'm just sat in the pits doing nothing or reading a book'. You've got to be out there actually doing something about it."

Jamie was idolised by young female Wimbledon fans.

1987 brought a nasty experience at Ipswich.

The effort paid-off, resulting in works sponsorship from Godden. "In fact I think I was sponsored for everything: carburettors, chains, leathers, even tyres from the Wimbledon supporters. I didn't really pay for anything!"

Riders who cultivate a glamorous image can often feel a backlash from supporters and even riders. Did this apply to Jamie?

"If other fellow riders did resent me they never showed it to my face. When I was riding really well I turned my intentions into my head instead of letting them out. I'd just sit and watch people and think, 'I'm going to beat you'. My whole feeling was directed towards beating the fastest fella that night."

In 1985 he earned British League bookings for Ipswich, a season in which Jamie estimates he rode in as many as 110 meetings.

"I just wanted to win races and keep winning. I had no other distractions in my life. I just wanted to get on a bike and get in front."

Success continued in 1986, when Jamie's average for Dons rose to just below 10. "I think I had an 11.5 average at home. I remember Steve Schofield beat me once and I had a breakdown and a fall but apart from that I just dropped points in a couple of other rides at home all year.

"I was good round Wimbledon and reasonable away. I wasn't ever the best rider in the world but I've beaten a couple of world champions. I rode so much and I was very fit at that stage – not just for speedway but in general. I was doing five or six meetings a week.

"When I wasn't racing I was training, or riding a unicycle, BMX or trials and using weights and practicing yoga. I was very proactive.

"When I started to get better I never sat in the pits nor touched the bike. I sat in the grandstand and watched everything that went on out on the track. At that point I still believed that I could be World Champion. I was training my body and mind to be the world's best," he says.

Just as things were going so well for him in south London, 1987 proved to be a disaster. Failure to agree terms with Wimbledon led to a step up into the senior division with Ipswich and a chance to progress at the higher level.

"I didn't want to leave Wimbledon but they weren't going to pay me as much as I thought I was worth. I didn't particularly want to go to Ipswich and, in fact, through that winter I decided that I really didn't want to ride. This is where I went into my 'flippant' state."

In his first couple of meetings for Witches Jamie had a couple of accidents, one of which was to play a significant part in his life as much as his speedway career.

"I got knocked out at Ipswich, broke my wrist and compressed two vertebrae in my neck. What I didn't realise at the time was that I had delayed concussion for six months. I was slurring my speech and was very slow, mentally. That accident hindered the rest of my career.

"But I didn't fully assess that until after I'd finished racing, when I realised just how slow my reactions had become since the crash."

For Jamie, the split-second 'edge', so vital in gaining a head start at the tapes and spotting chances to pass, had gone.

"I'd lost that instinctive keenness without realising it. I don't know if it was physical or mental but something slowed my brain down. They say a really bad head injury can take 10 years to repair itself, because of the scar tissue, which obviously you can't see. The confidence was there, that never left me, but there was a case when I was driving and Jeremy reminded me about turning on my lights, and I'd say: 'What lights?'"

The brain shuts out so much memory in times of trauma but Jamie can recall the sensations of that fateful night at Ipswich in '87.

"I can remember leaving the start line, then ending up in hospital with no leathers on and a sling around my left arm and a brace on my neck. I tried to get up and was physically sick."

He explained his feelings as the crash unfolded: "When I went over the handlebars, for a split second you see the bike, you see the sky, then the gravel. All I felt was calm and peace and it went on forever as far as I was concerned. It was a really weird and yet quite nice feeling. No pain, no nothing."

Remarkably, he was back riding in a month.

"I never told the doctors how I felt or anyone around me what was going on in my head, or not going on. Maybe in hindsight that's what I should have been doing. I did look into ice pads and how electronic chemical reactions work in the brain but I could never really understand it."

Unsurprisingly, Jamie struggled at the higher level and found himself back in the National League with Rye House in the latter part of the '87 season.

"I qualified for the NLRC but Paul Woods was a good friend of mine. He'd been with the Rockets

Long way from home . . . Jamie signing for Edinburgh in a £10,000 deal.

Press day at Middlesbrough in 1991, his final season.

all year and had done his 20-30-odd meetings, so I let him take my place. I used to love Rye House, though. It was a bumpy and fast track for its size."

Riding was off Jamie's agenda that winter but Edinburgh persisted and after a £10,000 deal he and brother Jeremy, who had joined him at Wimbledon from Arena-Essex in 1985, were off up to Scotland. It was a surprise move by Monarchs to go for a couple of southern-based riders.

"Well, I was born in Kent, so you can't really get more southern," says Jamie. "I moved up to Edinburgh to live and I really got on with everyone there. Powderhall had such a great atmosphere. I loved Edinburgh, loved the city. I used to go to nightclubs and there are great restaurants and shops. It's a nice city with good architecture and classic buildings, nice people and a lovely place to be."

In 1988 Jamie pushed former World No.2 Les Collins all the way at the top of Monarchs' averages with final figures in excess of 8.5. A return to Rye House produced an 18-point maximum and he was voted Monarchs' rider of the year.

Success with the Scots was short-lived, however. His Monarchs' career ended after just two matches in 1989 – ironically, back at Foxhall Heath.

"At Ipswich I wasn't happy. It was shedding it down with rain, people were falling off and I was thinking, 'this ain't the lifestyle for me'. I just told (co-promoter) John Campbell I wasn't coming back. I was dreading driving back up to Scotland through the night to get back in time for the following night's meeting at Powderhall. I said, 'I'm retired, had enough, I'm going home', so I just got in the van and went home.

"The next day John rang to say that if I didn't ride that night I'd be sacked. When I didn't arrive for the meeting they put it in the paper that I'd been sacked. But that wasn't true. I'd retired, so I thought I'd wind them up as much as I could.

"You know how you get little voices in your head telling you whether or not to do things, like buying a house or a car? Well, I told the paper that God had told me to stop racing, just to get back at the lies."

Jamie with his model girlfriend Sam.

Even so, he was back racing with Middlesbrough by the end of the '89 season. Persistence by manager Ken Knott, who arranged for Jamie to live on Teesside and provided bikes for him to ride, eventually paid off. So, why the change of heart?

"I'd gone back to Kent and was dealing in cars but I was bored," he explained.

Jamie saw out two reasonably successful seasons with Bears but niggling injuries were taking their toll. Injuries to friends also began to trouble him.

"I'd been up to see Paul Whittaker in a Newcastle hospital, where he'd been taken after smashing his elbow to pieces. He had so much morphine he could barely move. I decided I didn't want to lay there like that anymore."

His racing career finally ended five meetings into 1991, when Jamie took a tumble at Newcastle.

"Paul Bentley's dirt shield hit my head and ribs, two of which broke, so I was back in hospital. I lay in bed thinking, 'this is enough, I've had enough pain'. When you get hurt you can't see your body shake but inside you feel everything shaking. Your lungs hurt, your heart hurts, your ribs hurt. Sometimes I've been in so much pain that I'd rather have been dead when the pain's been too intense. So I had to stop putting myself through it."

By then his car-dealing had grown to a point where he was driving thousands of miles a year in addition to speedway – and the car sales business was paying well.

"I was making five times more money doing that and if I could apply myself more I could earn lots of money," he says.

Jamie developed the car business before selling it at the height of its success, as his 'flippant' trait once more re-emerged. Since then interests in hairdressing, property and even antiques mean that Jamie no longer needs to work.

"From a sportsman's point of view, the accolades of being a speedway rider were greater than the financial rewards.

"In 1987, after that crash, I knew I wasn't going to be World Champion. I could have ridden for another 10 years but that didn't mean anything to me. I know that sounds shallow but it was what I wanted."

Naturally, Edinburgh weren't happy about losing such an expensive investment so soon and an online article on Jamie describes him as "tending to a prima donna."

"I *was* a prima donna in Edinburgh," he admits, "but some of the decisions they made towards me weren't in my favour or to my liking and I can be the most stubborn person you can ever meet in your life."

Over the past few years Jamie has carved out a career in photography, working with a wide portfolio of glamorous models and his business, J Project Photography, is in demand. His creative work is now highly visible online, via the eye-bulging galleries to be found on the Facebook social networking website (log on to www.facebook.com, search for 'Jamie Luckhurst-Photography' and join 4,000-plus members already appreciating his efforts!).

He explains: "Eight years ago I met my girlfriend Sam, who was 17 back then, and now she models for me under the name Cocoa Blush."

Jamie also has an 18-year-old daughter, Chloe, from a previous relationship. As well as attending college, she also models as well as sing.

His parents, Reg and Gloria, now spend most of their retirement years in Tenerife.

So how does Jamie sum-up his career in speedway?

"At the time it was the only thing I wanted to do and most probably the only thing I was capable of doing. My opinions on accidents and pain have totally changed since I stopped riding. Then it was acceptable but it's so very unnecessary. What I've done over the past 10-15 years outweighs what I did in speedway."

At 46, Canterbury-based Jamie Luckhurst spends his time taking photos of a glamorous 25 year-old girlfriend and other models . . . which does tend to invite the ironic question once famously asked by a hotel porter of George Best, when the football genius and his girlfriend 'Miss World' were found on his bed, bathed in £20 notes and with a bucket of expensive champagne on ice beside them: 'So where did it all go wrong, Jamie?'

"Maybe I'm a chameleon?" he replies. "Maybe I will be for the rest of my life?"

BRIEF ENCOUNTERS WITH... Robert Pfetzing

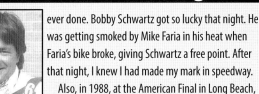

What were your first impressions of the UK?

Bricks! I remembered driving in London and just being amazed that everything was built out of this beautiful red brick. Over here in the States they are a rarity – only the really expensive fancy houses have so much brick. I just assumed everywhere in the world looked like Southern California.

How different were the tracks and the racing in the UK and how did you adapt to them?

Night and day. I remember walking up to Wolverhampton the very first time and being a little relieved, thinking: 'Ah, that's not too big'. I don't think I ever really adapted to them. I was still learning how to keep speed up in the turns. I needed another season to get it figured out. I was there three seasons total.

Did you make as much progress as you'd hoped to in the UK?

Nope. I should have been more of a consistent top contender. I was getting there.

Were there any other stand-out moments in your racing career?

Finishing second in the US National Championships in 1986 was my arrival. I had scored 14 points in the championship-style format, something very few guys had

ever done. Bobby Schwartz got so lucky that night. He was getting smoked by Mike Faria in his heat when Faria's bike broke, giving Schwartz a free point. After that night, I knew I had made my mark in speedway.

Also, in 1988, at the American Final in Long Beach, I beat every one of the top Americans at the time except Sam Ermolenko. Lance King, Rick Miller, the Morans, Faria, Schwartz, John Cook . . . I was on it. That night I was 'drag racing' Shawn Moran down the back straightaway. He dove in mid-track and I drove it in fast and hard to the cushion, went around him and pulled away. That doesn't happen too often, so it is easy to remember.

And the low point?

Ah, low point was not getting to come back with the Wolves – that was a bummer. I had purchased a house and expected to be there a few years at least. I did get an offer from another team but I didn't know the promoters that well, and I just couldn't commit. I should have.

What was the funniest or strangest thing that happened to you during your time in the UK?

Rick Miller looks sweet, but he is trouble. I heard about him and his entourage putting old TVs behind their vans on a 30ft rope and driving around at night watching them break apart. So we followed them one night. I must admit, it is pretty funny, especially when you come to a roundabout and the TV is swinging all over the place, with lots of sparks too.

BERWICK AWAY DAYS

Doug Nicolson recalls the early 70s, when hair was long and time was short. Petrol, for a time in these halcyon days, cost a mere 6/8d (33p) per gallon and this encouraged fans of first division Glasgow to make the Saturday afternoon trip down to Berwick, where they watched their juniors in second tier meetings . . .

COATBRIDGE Monarchs' licence was sold to Wembley at the beginning of the 1970 season, which meant Glasgow supporters no longer had the opportunity of a second helping of speedway action in a weekend at Cliftonhill, a short train journey from their Hampden Park home.

The best alternative was a Saturday afternoon trip to Berwick to watch second division racing, involving a pleasant car journey of more than 100 miles. Even so, a number of Tigers fans made the effort to keep tabs on how our junior riders were faring.

My debut drive down to Bandits' Shielfield Park home was the first time I saw John Louis. Despite a fall and an engine failure, he looked one for the future, although none of us would have expected such a meteoric rise to the extent that 'Tiger' would qualify for the World Final at Wembley just two years later.

Berwick seemed in good shape in the early weeks of the season, having won challenge matches at Workington and Middlesbrough. Bandits had also top-scored in a four team tournament at Doncaster before beating Dragons at home in the first round of the KO Cup. Throw in a narrow 40-38 defeat

Riders roar into the third bend at Shielfield Park.

at Long Eaton and you could understand why the locals believed their third season of BL2 action in the Borders promised to be their best yet.

The next time I saw Bandits was when they lost narrowly in non-league Newtongrange's opening meeting. However, successive home defeats by Canterbury and Romford saw Maurie Robinson, Peter Kelly and Ken Omand all carrying injuries and both Roy Williams and Alistair Brady struggling for form at Shielfield. Worse was to follow when the in-form Andy Meldrum sustained nasty facial injuries in a horrific spill at Ipswich.

Kelly had announced he was retiring and planned to emigrate. He signed off with a fine 10+1 in the KO Cup semi-final against Canterbury and received warm applause on his farewell lap.

The attractive Young England v Young Sweden Test match was in doubt right up to start time. Captains Eric Broadbelt and Tommy Johansson both had trial laps before agreeing to start the meeting. A brave decision but it should have been cancelled. The Swedes, already missing injury victims Tommy Jansson and Lennart Michanek, put up a fighting performance in the mud. Tommy Johansson and Kalle Haage were untouchable with 18 and 17 respectively, while Young England lost the services of Dave Jessup who looped at the gate in his first ride and never rode again. This allowed Andy Meldrum and Al Brady – both Scots – to get on track and their scores of two and three respectively were crucial in the 54-54 draw.

After Jimmy Gallagher's fine performances, Berwick fans were clamouring for him to be given a chance in the team, and he didn't let them down with 7+2 on his home debut against Long Eaton. However, Jimmy's enthusiasm was to be his downfall. The following week he crashed out in his first race and didn't ride again as Bandits disappointingly lost at home to Doncaster.

BANDITS 1971 – Standing, left to right: Bobby Campbell, Maurie Robinson, Andy Meldrum, Doug Wyer. Front: Alistair Brady, Alan Paynter, Peter Kelly.

Doug Wyer dropped only 14 points at Berwick in 1971.

His approach to machine maintenance always left a lot to be desired, with some of his temporary repairs defying description. He never regained a team slot that year.

The KO Cup Final against Ipswich was looming large and promoter Mrs Elizabeth Taylor signed the hitherto unknown Doug Wyer to stiffen Berwick's tail end. He first came to their attention when riding at Newtongrange earlier in the season. He made his debut with a fine 7+2 score at home to Bradford in mid-September and this no doubt took some pressure off the Berwick promotion, who had said they were on the point of signing a new heat leader – widely believed to be Taffy Owen, who ended up joining northern rivals Workington instead.

In the cup final, Wyer top scored with 11 from five rides in a 47-31 defeat at Foxhall. Bandits made a brave, but ultimately fruitless, attempt to claw back this deficit at Shielfield, winning by just 42-36.

Jimmy Beaton suffered serious arm injuries.

Flyer Wyer

BERWICK started the 1971 season like the proverbial steam train. Doug Wyer, Maury Robinson and Al Brady were firing on all cylinders, the latter having put the mechanical problems of the previous year well behind him by purchasing a bike from Wayne Briggs. Peter Kelly (whose plans to emigrate fell through) was his consistent self and Andy Meldrum was fast regaining his confidence after the injuries that had ruined his previous season. New signing Bobby Campbell was taking his time to find his feet but that wasn't a problem as Bandits were carrying all before them – at home at least.

At Shielfield, visitors were toiling to break the 30-point barrier but it was a completely different story away from home. Bandits won 40-38 at Teesside in the North-Eastern Trophy in April. However, a 36-42 defeat at Birmingham was their best effort in BL2. They were probably quite popular visitors, with Wyer and occasionally Robinson giving the local heroes something to think about and generally putting up a good show before going down. BSPA statistician and *Speedway Star* columnist Bryan Seery reported that Berwick were the only team to have gone through a season unbeaten at home in the league while losing all their away matches.

Bandits were always keen on signing Jimmy Beaton but Glasgow had initially refused to loan him out. However, it soon became apparent to Tigers' management that Jim would benefit from regular league racing and eventually a loan deal was agreed.

By early July he had gained a team spot at Alan Paynter's expense. Berwick were obviously taking a long-term view here, because Paynter's figures looked as good as Beaton's and Campbell's.

Paynter subsequently asked for a transfer and later retired, got married and returned home. There was no animosity over his departure, though, and he wrote a farewell letter to the programme thanking the supporters, management and riders.

No-one knew it at the time but Maury Robinson's spectacular tangle with the safety fence during the Danny Taylor Memorial Trophy event would be his last appearance in Bandits' colours.

Wyer was undoubtedly the success story of the year and his exploits are fondly remembered to this day. There were high expectations of him at the start of the year and it must be said that he met them in full. He dropped only 14 points at home, at least six of which were attributable to engine failures, and notched double figures in 25 out of 33 league and cup meetings.

Double tragedy

IT was virtually all-change for the 1972 season. As expected, Wyer had gone full-time with parent first division club Sheffield and Peter Kelly's retirement was no real shock either. However, Maury Robinson's non-return was more surprising. Doug and Willie Templeton had planned to retire from speedway at the end of their time with Glasgow but were persuaded to turn out for Berwick, which led the travelling Glasgow fans to take even more interest in Berwick affairs.

Bandits opened the campaign in some style with a 44-33 win at newcomers Hull in a North-East Trophy fixture, while a draw at Sunderland a couple of weeks later clinched that particular title.

The Templetons had settled in quickly and, along with Andy Meldrum, formed a solid heat leader trio. Bobby Campbell asked for a transfer when he was dropped in favour of the returning Jim Beaton. Hec Haslinger came to Berwick at the end of April but three disappointing second-half rides ended their interest in him.

At this time, Berwick were winning at home and making a fist of it away. In fact, their win at newcomers Scunthorpe in early May was their first away league success since 1969 at Plymouth.

However, their inexperienced tail was beginning to show. George Beaton and Geoff Davies were now permanent members of the side and obviously needed time to gain experience, particularly at away venues.

BANDITS 1972 – Standing, left to right: Willie Templeton, Geoff Davies, Andy Meldrum, Kenny Taylor (team manager), Jim Beaton, George Beaton, Alistair Brady. On bike: Doug Templeton.

The KO Cup tie with Bradford was the defining meeting of the season and one that is still remembered with some anguish and emotion. A horrific Heat 3 crash saw Jim Beaton go through the fence midway down the back straight, sustaining such severe arm injuries that there were initial fears over whether his arm could be saved. It was a tribute to the skill of the surgeons and Jim's courageous determination which would eventually see him return to race nearly five years later.

Controversy still rages over this incident to this day. Was it an unfortunate accident or the worst kind of foul riding? I tend to believe it was the former but have to say that my vantage point on the back straight near the second bend afforded little view of what happened.

In the following heat, Jim's brother George looped at the gate and sustained a badly broken arm. In the second-half, Mick Beaton (no relation) was also hurt in a crash.

With Geoff Davies also missing for a few weeks, Bandits had to replace the bottom end

Jimmy Gallagher was much missed when he left to join Coatbridge in 1973.

of their team virtually overnight. John Lynch (ex- Sunderland), local junior Mark Perram and East Anglian Graham Jones were enlisted, although only the latter showed sufficient promise to be retained.

Just when things seemed at their darkest, Berwick pulled a rabbit out of the hat by signing Glasgow's Jimmy Gallagher, stimulating renewed interest in Berwick meetings among travelling Tigers fans. Jimmy's determined riding shored up Bandits, who managed to see out the season with a near perfect home record, although away wins were still a pipedream. Crewe were the only team to take anything from Shielfield, where they managed a 39-39 draw that went quite some way to securing them the league title.

The final meeting of the '72 season featured the usual speeches, pranks and mechanics' race which included the spannermen of Messrs. Jones, Meldrum, Jackson and Willie Templeton. The latter's bike ended in a severe state of disrepair after crashing into the safety fence. It is understood the 'mechanic' in question was Jim McGregor . . . who went on to become a referee!

All good fun but the tears of laughter turned to tears of anguish when it was learned that George Beaton had been killed in a car accident near his Blantyre home a few days after the season ended. A number of Berwick fans travelled to Glasgow for his funeral.

Helmet history

WITH Jimmy Gallagher going full-time in the first division following Glasgow's switch from Hampden Park to Coatbridge, Berwick had a gaping hole in their line-up for 1973 and, in truth, one they struggled to fill all season.

Bandits' home defeat in their opener highlighted their lack of depth beyond their spearhead of Andy Mcldrum and the Templeton brothers, although it has to be said that, before the month was out, Dennis Jackson, Graham Jones and Chris Quigley were all scoring nicely.

In early May, Peterborough were seen off comfortably with a fine 49-29 win but home defeats to Boston and Eastbourne were followed by a string of heavy away losses, during which Jackson retired to be replaced by a young Rob Hollingworth.

Geoff Davies was the next to retire. Initially he was replaced by Coatbridge's John Wilson, which at least gave West of Scotland fans something to cheer about. However, he soon lost his place to Ipswich junior Denny Morter. Berwick's team settled with this squad and managed to hold their own at home, although at times it was a struggle.

In the closing weeks of the season an injury to Quigley gave Coatbridge's South African Ettienne Oliviere, fresh from his eligibility squabble with the authorities, a run out.

Meldrum capped a fine season by taking over the No.1 position and wrested the Silver Helmet from Workington's Mitch Graham at Berwick, becoming the first Bandit to hold the match-race title. Sadly, his reign was short-lived, losing it at the first time of asking to Mike Broadbank at Chesterton.

Berwick brought the curtain down on their '73 season with a challenge between Andy Meldrum's team and a Jack Millen Select. Unbeknown at the time, this would prove to be Andy's last meeting for Bandits before his close season transfer request.

Tigers favoured Lions' roar

THE winter brought the sensational news that Coatbridge's first division licence had been sold to Hull, with Tigers taking Vikings' place in the lower league. All of a sudden, Bandits were now the Tigers' equals. And after Berwick's shock away win in the Cliftonhill opener in Division Two, it could be argued they were now their betters!

Away days to Berwick would never be the same.

BANDITS 1973 – Standing, left to right: John Robertson (team manager) Andy Meldrum, Graham Jones, Chris Quigley, Dennis Jackson, Willie Templeton, Kenny Taylor (co-promoter). On bike: Doug Templeton. Kneeling: Geoff Davies.

But the real blow for travelling fans was the exponential rise in the cost of petrol following the Gulf crisis. 'Divvying up' petrol money, once a casual, rounded-up affair, was now the subject of detailed scrutiny and some scrimping and saving to fund it. "Happy days have gone again!"

I managed a few meetings in Border country, in particular those featuring the marquee match-races between Jim McMillan and Scott Autrey and the George Hunter-Ole Olsen contests.

The former came after a protracted meeting against a disaffected Crewe side that took forever to run. As a consequence, the planned buffet reception for the two British League stars was cancelled by the local hotel's owner.

The real nail in the coffin in terms of travelling down across the border on Saturday afternoons came in 1975, when Paisley Lions opened their doors to Saturday night racing – a closer, and consequently cheaper, alternative speedway night out.

Over the years my trips to Berwick have dwindled, the last being some 20 years ago and best remembered for Tigers' Robbie Nagy coming and speaking to my children at the Harthill services on the way home. My young son was so excited he couldn't sleep that night.

Now the proud possessor of a bus pass, maybe this year I'll get back to Shielfield and relive the Berwick Away Days of my youth. I certainly hope so.

On 2 Minutes With...
GARRY MAY

Do you remember getting your first bike?

I bought it from Simmo for £300. It was a two-valver and I took it to Iwade, Weymouth, Eastbourne and some other tracks to practice. Then I got a chance in the Weymouth team in 1976.

How did your career progress?

In the winter before I started riding for Weymouth I won the Training School Championship with a 15-point maximum. I rode in some junior matches and they put me in the team. It was hard. You needed to pay good money for good equipment, too, and sometimes you don't have that.

So I moved to Crayford in 1977 and loved it. I struggled to start with, because I'd come from the big Weymouth track, but Len Silver, who was promoter at Crayford, said to me one day: 'Garry, open that throttle up, turn that bike and off you go round the corner. Get round it once and you'll get round it all the time'. After that I rode really well there.

I broke my wrist at Crayford in 1977 and that put me back a bit. I nearly got a maximum the week before against Glasgow – three wins and a one, I just didn't catch Mick McKeon on the line, so I just missed out.

I was back at Weymouth in 1979 when the Reading promotion took over and although I was in and out of the team again, it was good. But in 1980 I couldn't get in the team, I was struggling with bikes and other things. I went to Poole for a second-half but crashed and put my spine out of line. That done me.

Which team-mate did you most enjoy partnering on the track?

Martin Yeates and Laurie Etheridge were both good. You could always go and ask them things and they'd tell you because they were older riders and they could help you out. And there was Vic Harding, too – he was a good mate of mine. I used to live that way in London and he lived on Canvey Island, so we travelled a lot together.

What was your worst crash or injuries?

The one I had at Poole. I went to go wide to cut back inside someone but another rider just T-boned me and I went into the fence legs-first. My legs hit the fence and pushed my back right up, which put my spine out of line at the bottom. I hurt all over. I went away from speedway after that.

GORDON
KENNETT

NUMBER two in the world, a share of the World Pairs Championship and an England regular for the best part of 10 years, Gordon Kennett has plenty to shout about, although you would never know it from his always pleasant demeanour and a boyish shyness that has remained part of his charm since he began racing at Eastbourne more than 36 years ago.

The shaven-headed man at the door of his Bexhill-on-Sea semi-detached looks younger than his 53 years. But a jogging vest revealing his trademark muscular torso and a firm handshake are reassuring signs that I've arrived at the right place.

An oil painting of Gordon in spectacular action hangs on the wall at the foot of the stairs and, if you look hard enough, in a glass cabinet in the lounge is a red and white rosette from the 1978 World Final bearing his portrait. Next to it is a gold key, about three inches in length, which he received from the FIM for finishing second to Ole Olsen in that Golden Jubilee final at Wembley.

Gordon says he still has an old two-valve Jawa tucked away in the garage but apart from a couple of old speedway body colours from his days as undisputed No.1 at Eastbourne and White City, there's little to show for a brilliant career that spanned 26 years until it not so much finished as petered out at Wolverhampton in 1995.

His pride and joy these days is an impressive looking, bright red Ducati 749 road bike that he wheels from the garage onto the patio area at the back of the house. He still enjoys the adrenalin rush of high speed machinery on two wheels.

Hardly a rebel, but Gordon did briefly experiment with a bleached blond look at Oxford in 1973. This shot of him relaxing was taken on the centre green at Eastbourne, where he'd gone to watch his former team.

Physically, he's in great shape and looks no different than he did in his racing days. "I'm about 11-and-a-half stone, the same as when I rode speedway," he confirms.

He looks after his health to the degree that he performs up to 200 sit-up exercises at the end of each day, as well as running between five and eight miles, three or four times a week.

Gordon's on-track achievements and his general wellbeing are a remarkable testimony of his dedication to fitness and make a mockery of an illness that proves so debilitating to millions of others.

It was in 1979, a year after his best ever season in the sport, that he discovered he had type one diabetes. He has hazy memories of much of his career – "it all seems a long time ago" – but thinks he can pinpoint the time, place and events that triggered the condition that has meant having to inject himself with insulin twice a day for the past 27 years.

First division action for Oxford at Cowley.

"I fell off at Ipswich and broke my coccyx," he recalls. "I think the shock from that injury might have sparked the diabetes, because I'd been fine until then. It really hit home to me a short while afterwards, when I rode at Vojens in Denmark and could hardly hold on to the bike because I was so tired. During the drive home, I must have drank gallons of water and lost about a stone in weight. It took them two weeks to confirm I had diabetes.

"Being a diabetic definitely had an adverse effect on my racing. I would feel tired towards the end of a meeting and having to eat at certain times of the day didn't help my preparation either. Normally you wouldn't want to eat much before racing but I always had to get something inside me about two

In his second spell with Eastbourne, Gordon leading team-mate Steve Naylor and Coventry's Ole Olsen in 1979.

With his World Pairs-winning partner Malcolm Simmons in 1978.

hours before going out to race, to give the food time to circulate around my system.

"I've got used to it over the years – I can even inject myself while driving now! – but that's why I pay so much attention to keeping fit. Being in good shape helps me to control the diabetes."

If Gordon's blood sugar levels dropped enough to drain him of energy, it rarely showed throughout his career. He spent most of it as No.1 at Eastbourne, where he first broke into the team in 1970 and is, without doubt, the most successful rider to ever emerge from Arlington youth academy. The Golden Eagle himself.

"Those early second division days were a lot of fun and we had a very strong team that had a blend of youth and experience – the likes of Jimmy Squibb and Reg Trott helping us kids along. Reg used to turn up for meetings in a caravanette, with his wife, daughter and their dog. I actually went out with Reg's daughter for a while.

"It was Arthur Nutley, our team manager, who spotted me riding for the Kent Youth Motorcycle Club and brought me and a few others to Eastbourne. Arthur was a great character, a big chap. He would sometimes drive three or four of the Eastbourne riders to away meetings, with their bikes on a big trailer."

The man Kennett respects most for helping him to scale world class heights is Bob Dugard, who was just finishing his own riding career when Gordon and his elder brother Dave were starting theirs as key members of Dave Lanning's 'Kamikaze Kids'. Front man Lanning was the perfect publicity machine but Eastbourne Speedway is synonymous with one family only – and that's the Dugards.

"I think Bob rode for Eastbourne a couple of times in his last season and knocked off a few Canterbury riders. Their fans wanted to lynch him!" laughs Gordon.

"I remember his father, Charlie, and then there was Bob's brother Eric and, later, I also rode with Bob's son, Martin."

Bob and his wife Margaret are still part and parcel of the scene and Gordon added: "They always make me feel welcome whenever I go back to Eastbourne and I'm very grateful for that."

After three seasons of promising progress at Eastbourne, Gordon made the jump into the top flight with Oxford – also run by Bob Dugard along with Danny Dunton – in 1973. Again, three more seasons of steady improvement, in which he gave decent support to successive No.1s Hasse Holmqvist, Bob Kilby and Dag Lovaas, saw him establish himself as a British League heat leader.

"I liked the Oxford track which, like Eastbourne, had tight turns which suited my style," says Gordon. "I felt sorry for their supporters when the Rebels team left and moved on to White City in 1976. I know some of them reckoned Bob had fixed it for the team to switch to London but I don't think he did.

"Bob had a short fuse but he was great for his riders – he always stuck up for us no matter what. He was a bad loser but he was behind us 100 per cent and I also liked the fact that he always tried to bring in young, English riders. I never really fell out with him in all our time together."

The No.13 body colour didn't prove unlucky for Gordon in the 1978 World Final. He's seen here on the inside against Jerzy Rembas and (below) on the Wembley rostrum with Ole Olsen, third-placed Scott Autrey and Miss World Mary Stavin.

Mementoes from the night he finished World Final runner-up.

One of Kennett's great qualities as a rider was his versatility. It's not often that a small track specialist can adapt very successfully to much bigger circuits but Gordon made the switch to the wide, open spaces of White City's Wood Lane track in west London with ease. It was probably the making of him as a rider.

"White City was long and fast but it also had tightish turns and I found that if I missed the start, I would often nip past people on the inside coming out of the second bend. That was the best place for me to pass."

Gordon emerged as Rebels' No.1 in 1976 and a year later, when he broke the 10-point average barrier for the first time, he led White City to the BL championship. Gordon received most support from Steve Weatherley, Pole Marek Cieslak, Kai Niemi ("one of the best friends I made in speedway") and Trevor Geer, while the link with National League Eastbourne proved

Happy to be at Wimbledon with Kelvin Tatum and John Davis in 1984.

Gordon (fourth from right) in his successful third spell with Eastbourne, parading the NL KO Cup in 1986.

crucial as Eagles' stars Mike Sampson and Paul Gachet contributed match-winning performances.

"I had a lot of extra rides that year," says Gordon, who doesn't believe that Rebels received all the credit they deserved for winning the title by operating the rider replacement facility all season for the absent Dag Lovaas, who had retired. "We still had to win the matches and the extra rides we were given to cover for Dag," Gordon points out.

What he does not dispute, however, is the advantage White City had – through the Dugard connection and their close proximity to the factory – over their rivals when it came to snapping up Weslake engines and parts that were in increasingly short supply.

"I wasn't honestly aware that we were getting engines and bits and pieces that others couldn't get," he says, "but I lived only 10 minutes away from the Weslake factory at Rye and I never had a problem getting anything from them. I'd go there and collect anything I needed – I guess they put it on Bob's account? I think Bob's machine tool-making factory supplied Weslake with engineering parts, too, but that still shouldn't take anything away from what we achieved that year."

Despite winning the 1977 championship, White City could never attract sufficiently good crowds and after tumbling all the way down to 15th in the final table for '78, Rebels disbanded. Most returned to Eastbourne, where Dugard took the gamble to enter senior league racing for the first time in 1979.

For Kennett, the next four years saw him reaffirm his status as Eagles' No.1, although the first season back in the blue-and-gold racejacket was overshadowed by the career-ending injuries to Steve Weatherley, who was paralysed in the crash at Hackney that killed Hawks' Vic Harding.

Kennett, who was far away from the tragic scenes in east London that night, explained: "Steve took my place in the four team tournament because I was riding in Germany that weekend. I got a call on the Saturday morning to say what had happened and drove all the way down to see Steve. It was a double tragedy for me, because Vic was an old mate from our junior grass-track days."

Gordon in 2006 with one of his White City racejackets and his road bike that still provides an adrenalin rush.

Gordon describes Eastbourne and White City as "good family set-ups." He says: "Danny and Lee Dunton were also nice people to ride for and from the Oxford connection, I already knew Richard Hellsen and Richard Greer, as well as those who joined us from Eastbourne."

Kennett fancied trying his luck elsewhere in 1983 but describes joining King's Lynn as "a big mistake," adding: "I felt I needed to ride for a bigger track after spending so long with Eastbourne and although Lynn was a good track to go to once or twice a year, I just couldn't get the hang of it on a weekly basis."

In 1984, a move to Wimbledon saw his form dip even further, failing to even make heat leader grade. When the south London club opted to drop into the NL in '85, Gordon made a dozen appearances for senior league Swindon but returned to Eastbourne, where he regained No. 1 status as Eagles entered yet another new era in their turbulent history. "I needed to go back there to regain the confidence I'd lost at King's Lynn," he explained.

Eastbourne were league and KO Cup winners in both 1986 and 1987 and only once in the period up to 1990 – when Martin Dugard scaled the heights in '87 – was top Eagle Kennett knocked off his lofty perch at Arlington.

"Martin was a very good rider but he should have achieved more for all the talent he had. I had three good winters riding in Australia and I think it would've done him a lot of good to have gone there when he was younger."

The first half of the 90s saw Kennett lead Milton Keynes before an unhappy spell at Exeter and, finally, a disappointing end to his illustrious career back in the top flight with Wolves.

"I was going well there for a spell and actually rode at No.1. I got on well with Sam Ermolenko but No.1 position proved too hard for me by that stage and in the end they dropped me to bring in Andy Grahame. I don't think they could fit me in because of the points limit, or something like that.

"I never heard anything from Wolves again and as no other track phoned to ask me to ride, I just stopped without actually deciding to retire. I thought I could've ridden for another couple of years but I've never ridden speedway since.

"I wouldn't change any of the past, except I'd rather have won the 1978 World Final instead of finishing second!" says Gordon, still as reluctant as ever to steal the limelight.

Nothing like a Dane

ALTHOUGH Gordon Kennett was an England star for most of the late 70s and early 80s, he didn't always get the recognition he deserved.

In fact, at one stage he became so fed up about being overlooked by England that he seriously contemplated taking out a Danish licence and riding for Denmark – the birthplace of his first wife, Heidi.

Gordon met her, then 18, when he was riding for Oxford and she worked as a local *au pair*. She went along to Cowley one night to watch the Great Dane Ole Olsen riding for Wolverhampton against the Rebels but the feisty blonde caught the eye of home rider Gordon, who bought her a drink in the stadium bar after the meeting.

Ironically, Olsen and the first Mrs Kennett were to feature as central figures in the career and life of Gordon by the late 70s, when he was nearing his peak.

He explained: "It was Ole who was behind talk of me possibly taking out a Danish licence. He was all for it at the time, I think it was his idea.

"I even rode with a Danish flag sticker on my bike and my leathers were black with red and white flashes. I'd seen the 'flash' design on a visit to Australia and, I suppose, with the 'Flash Gordon' character in mind, I tried to incorporate it in my leathers. It didn't really catch on, though. "

The Kennett brothers, Barney, Dave and Gordon, on Eastbourne's 1971 visit to Romford.

Ironically, the shy, quietly spoken Kennett was anything but flash. He rarely blew his own trumpet, although Heidi – who spoke perfect English – was never slow to remind anyone who would listen, including the England team selectors, just how good her husband really was.

She knew that Gordon needed to push himself more if he was ever to realise his full potential, especially when it came to gaining more open bookings at home and abroad. And despite their divorce five years ago, he acknowledges her supportive efforts in this respect.

"Heidi handled all my bookings and did the paperwork and my accounts," revealed Gordon, "and I agree that she was good for my career – she was very upfront and outspoken, as Danes tend to be. She even acted as my mechanic at a few meetings and tried speedway once herself!"

Gordon played leading roles in championship-winning sides at first and second division level, with White City and Eastbourne, and won other silverware with the latter, but he never managed to put it all together on one night when one of the major individual titles was on the line.

Yet no-one could ever accuse of him of giving less than 100 per cent for club or country. He and American Kelly Moran – who would become team-mates at Eastbourne in the early 80s – contested one of the most courageous, hard-fought battles in appallingly wet and mucky conditions at the end of the 1979 World Team Cup qualifier at Reading. Midway through the race, with the rain beating down, Kennett pulled off his goggles to try and improve his vision – but still wouldn't shut off the throttle as the pair went at it tooth and nail on the Smallmead slurry. It remains one of the most enthralling races I've ever seen.

Kennett reached his pinnacle on September 2, 1978 – his 25th birthday – when he went to Wembley as the least fancied of the four English contenders (Mike Lee, Dave Jessup and Malcom Simmons were the others) and ended the night a point away from a run-off for the world title.

Olsen won his second World Championship with 13 points, one more than Kennett, whom he had beaten in a thrilling Heat 4. On a Wembley track superbly prepared by Len Silver, Kennett, Olsen and Ivan Mauger raced wheel to wheel for a couple of laps before Ivan, whose bike was losing speed against the other two, got a nudge from Gordon and went down by the pits gate. Another referee might have excluded the White City star but Tore Kittilsen allowed Olsen, who nipped round the outside, to win what turned out to be the decisive race and one of the best in World Final history.

Second places behind Ila Teromaa and Scott Autrey in his third and fourth rides proved costly for Kennett, who in the end had to settle for the silver medal after a last race win over Jessup, Anders Michanek and Lee.

The drama didn't end there, though. The outspoken Heidi was convinced that Olsen benefited from 'favours' from one or two others before clinching his third world title.

She even went as far as to use the Danish press to accuse her fellow countryman of skullduggery.

Of course, her claims could never be proven and her outburst rebounded on her husband. Kennett said: "That didn't do me any good, it didn't help me in speedway and a few people had a quiet word with me afterwards to say that we'd been out of order for what was said.

"I didn't get on with Ole after that but we couldn't prove he'd done anything wrong," added Gordon, who was beaten fair and square by Olsen when they met.

"I think that sort of thing went on a lot in speedway back then, although only once did I try to 'buy' myself a point. It was in a qualifying round at Hackney but, despite agreeing to help me, the bloke in question went out and beat me anyway!

"I suppose I was happy with second place in the World Final at the time, because I wan't expected to even go close to winning. Second's not as good as first, though, is it?

"Although people tell me that I should feel proud of being a World Champion by winning the Pairs title in Poland with Simmo that same year. Simmo was brilliant. He even lent me a bike to get us through the meeting at Katowice.

Malcolm Simmons, who scored 15 points compared to Kennett's nine and retained the World Pairs title for England by defeating New Zealand's Ivan Mauger in a run-off, said: "Without Gordon's points, we wouldn't have won, so I appreciated his efforts in helping us both to become world champions that day."

Before they split, Heidi introduced Gordon and their three children, son Nikolai (25 this year), and daughters Katrina (19) and Sophie (15), to the local church. Kennett had a two-year period of learning the virtues of Christianity, although he is now unconvinced and no longer attends

He says his parting from Heidi was "amicable" – she went for someone younger," he smiles – and he is delighted to have regular contact with their children, who followed their mother to live near Alicante in Spain.

Oh, brother

WHILE middle brother Gordon was easily the biggest achiever of the three Kennett racing brothers who all started their careers in the early 70s, David, the eldest, and Brian (or 'Barney' as he is universally known) also made their mark on the sport.

Dave made his debut for Eastbourne in 1970, the same season in which Gordon – 17 months his junior – began with the Eagles. A bad crash while riding for Hackney early in '73 proved a massive setback but he returned to feature in White City's league-winning team of '77 and returned to Eastbourne to enjoy further success at NL level.

In 1971, Barney – who is 17 months younger than Gordon – began a long and successful career with Canterbury, where he established himself as a loyal and long-serving Crusaders legend.

Gordon relaxing at home with some essential reading matter.

Gordon laughs when asked to compare himself to his brothers: "Dave is definitely the most lairy and loudest one of us! I think I knocked him out once when we rode together for Eastbourne.

"Barney was a nutter who also liked a fight. He was fiery and would wind up the crowd. He was a good team man. He trained as a plasterer after he left school and still does it now.

"If ever I had any problems with other riders, my brothers would be straight on the scene.

"I've always been the quiet one. I'm more like Tracy, our youngest brother, who never rode speedway. He manages an ATS tyre service now and we talk quite often on the phone."

The brothers always had visible support from their parents, Connie and Dick, who, sadly, have both passed away in the last 10 years. "Mum was particularly helpful and would drive us everywhere for grass-track meetings in the early days," says Gordon.

"She was only 65 when she died of a brain tumour. I think Dad passed on about six years ago – he smoked too much."

Of course, the Kennett speedway connection is maintained today by Dave's son, 20-year-old Eastbourne and Rye House star Edward, who is one of England's most promising prospects.

"I think he'll make it, he has the right temperament and is more laid back than his dad! Edward has done well, he has a nice style and I'll be there for him if he ever needs my help," added Gordon.

Where did you get your first bike and how much did it cost?

My first speedway bike cost me bugger all. My dad owned Norm Askew Motorcycles at Bankstown (Sydney, New South Wales), which 'Cowboy' Bob Sharp built, and he bought an old Staride JAP bike. He only got it for the motor, to

go into a Hagon grass-track bike wanted by a customer. So the Staride frame lay outdoors, propped up against Dad's workshop, before I put my 4B JAP engine into it, which I'd used in short circuit racing since I was 17.

My first real speedway bike – an 890 Jawa – cost $645 in 1973, when Dad took on a Jawa agency.

My father died in 1985, aged 57. When I was getting started, he wouldn't sign my racing licence form because he thought speedway was dangerous and I was very wild when I was younger. By the time I started riding speedway at the age of 21, I'd calmed down a fair bit.

Who helped you most in your early days?

Dennis Alderton – father of the late Brett – came to Nepean to advise me on how to ride and soon he said I should get a new Jawa. Trevor Sheridan (who rode at Stoke in 1973) and I would go to Dennis' two or three times a week and just talk speedway. Geoff Curtis was a family friend and he was going to get me in at Crewe and I was going to hang out with him in 1974, but, sadly, things didn't work out that way. Geoff was killed at the Sydney Showground in 1973 – the same night Jim Airey retired.

Favourite track?

I just loved Oxford. In Australia, it was the smaller Liverpool.

Track(s) you never looked forward to visiting?

Even though I did ride well there, I reckon Berwick. You just never knew what it was going to be like. In Australia it was the Sydney Showground. It was fun to ride but I nearly lost a very close mate, my little brother Steven, at the Showground. He was a very talented youngster who was destined for a big future before breaking his leg in a high speed crash at the Showground in 1977. He didn't ride again.

Which team-mate did you most enjoy partnering on-track?

The guy I enjoyed riding with the most was Pip Lamb at Oxford. Pip did knock me off once or twice but, generally, he

would ride the outside while I stayed on the inside. This worked well. I really liked the guy and he was full of life, enjoying his speedway.

I recall the time (June 1979) when Pip broke his back. It was the final race of the night, so all the prize money was split. I was a fair way behind, as I was testing a two-valve Jawa for my mechanic. I was the closest one to him, at the back, as he tried to go inside George Hunter and Les Rumsey, when he hit a hole on the inside. He went into the fence. He was still sat on his seat when he crashed, so took the full impact, and I clipped his feet on the way through.

Worst crash/injuries?

At Hull (May 1977), I got knocked off by Joey Owen and then run over by Frank Auffret while riding for Birmingham. I spent the night on life support even though I didn't break a bone. Instead of breaking my collarbone, I ripped it from my breast bone. It took ages to heal – soft tissue damage takes a lot longer than broken bones – and the crash shook me up pretty bad.

Then, at the very end of the same season, I broke my ankle at Mildenhall.

Career highlight/proudest moment?

In my first two seasons with Birmingham we won the BL2 championship in both 1974 and 1975 – and in '75 we won the KO Cup, too.

My career highlight was that I survived, I can still walk. John Langfield said to me, after seeing me ride at the Showground, that if I wanted to survive I would have to change a few things. I think luck was on my side.

Given what Rob Hollingworth had to say about you in a recent *Backtrack,* what is your reaction to the general view that you had a bit of a 'reputation'?

I was just over-keen to win, or at least beat the other guys. Youthful exuberance, I reckon, nothing malicious.

I did once start a race at Oxford with my team-mate Kevin Young and we were against Jack Millen and Tim Nunan from Stoke. After two re-runs there was just me and Kevin left. I reckon I was lucky to get away from that one with my front teeth! Both Tim and Jack had a reputation for being 'knuckle men'.

My nickname in speedway was 'The Spear' but not many people call me that these days.

OLE
OLSEN

THERE are many facets to Ole Olsen – the first superstar of Danish speedway, probably the best team manager the sport has ever seen, top promoter at one of the finest tracks in the world and, for the past dozen years, Grand Prix supremo.

Olsen's brilliant 17-year racing career, in which he won three individual World Championships during the golden era of the 70s, ended with large crowds paying emotional farewells to him at Coventry and Vojens – the track he built – at the end of 1983.

But the man who put Denmark on the speedway map with his first title win in 1971 was never going to disappear quietly into cosy retirement. His on-track brilliance provided the inspiration for the next generation of Danes to try and emulate his fine achievements and he did much to ensure

Planning ahead . . . Ole studying the programme in the Cradley Heath pits during a 1970 Black Country derby with Wolves.

his countrymen dominated the sport throughout the 80s, firstly as captain and then as the team boss whose man-management and motivational powers earned the respect of even his most fiercest rivals.

In 1995, Olsen realised another dream when the FIM finally answered his call to abandon the traditional one-off World Final and introduce a Speedway Grand Prix series to determine the No.1. In his powerful role as SGP Race Director, he has taken international speedway to another level and, though he has ruffled a lot of feathers and been criticised for building a GP empire partly at the expense of a declining domestic scene in Britain, Olsen commands respect.

His relentless commitment to the continuing development of the SGP (and its team World Cup associate) quickly became obvious when we first set up this interview. "I don't like to look back," he said. "Who's interested in reading about me winning the World Championship all those years ago? I prefer to look forward."

"Yes, Ole, I appreciate all that, but at *Backtrack* looking back is what we do!" I explained, trying desperately to retain his interest. He still seemed unconvinced about the merit of talking to the sport's retro magazine but agreed that I should visit him at his beautiful converted farmhouse at Sommersted, just 20 minutes drive from the town of his birthplace at Haderslev, in the south-east corner of Denmark. "Well, if you think it would be useful to come here, then come!" he added, helpfully.

Any fears I held that this mission might be hard work were quickly dispelled. Ulla, Ole's wife, showed me into her husband's large office, a long room built above a disused swimming pool in the grounds of the two-acre site where the couple have lived for more than 20 years. It's from here that Ole runs his company, Speed Sport.

There's a large desk where the managing director plots his SGP strategy and, in the corner, a modern computer where hundreds of emails pour in each week. In the middle of the room is an impressive oak boardroom table, where Ole sits to face me. Behind him stands a 7ft-tall trophy cabinet stretching almost the full length of the room, containing some 600 trophies and mementoes (with hundreds more stored in his loft) that remind you of his immense stature in the sport. The walls are decorated with innumerable framed awards from Danish royalty, the FIM and other organisations who have been quick to recognise his achievements.

Olsen is now 61 but dresses – casually in smart shirt and jeans – and sounds like he could pass for someone 20 years younger. When he gets into full flow, talking excitedly about his ambitions plans, he has all the zeal and vibrancy of a teenager.

The SGP may have little or nothing to do with what this magazine is mainly about, but Ole can't look back for too long without looking forward. And what he does so successfully now is in itself a product of where he came from and everything he has learned from being at the forefront of the sport.

To appreciate his current status as probably the most powerful man in speedway, you have to appreciate how he got there . . .

'Bloody idiot' who climbed to the top

YOUNG Ole Olsen was sitting on his moped outside a car workshop and petrol garage in Haderslev one day when he was alerted by the sound of a DKW motor bike. Within seconds, an unknown rider came roaring out of a side alley and threw the machine into a broadside on the station forecourt. He skillfully manoeuvred his bike around a petrol pump in an arcing movement that resembled a speedway rider negotiating a tight first turn.

A curious Olsen was captivated.

The young man on the bike was Henry Bork and if he hadn't immediately grabbed young Ole's

Innovative Olsen had the 1972 Wolves racejacket design woven into his leathers.

attention in the way he did, we probably wouldn't now be looking back on the glittering career of speedway's first Great Dane.

Born on November 16, 1946, Olsen recalls: "Before and after school each day, I used to deliver newspapers and groceries on my moped for a local shop in town. I pulled up outside the garage as Henry was doing his thing. He came over and asked me if I was interested in bikes. When I replied 'yes', he suggested I went to Haderslev Motorsport, where in 1967 the Danish Motor Union (DMU) had started running two meetings a year for novices with 175cc bikes.

"I told my parents what Henry had said to me and informed them that I wanted to buy a bike. But they thought I was a bloody idiot and wouldn't buy me one. They couldn't find the money for it and they were against me riding, so I saved the money myself and bought a 175cc Husqvarna road bike, which had already done around 80,000 miles when I got it.

"My friend, Hans Hansen, who rode at a track not far from Kolding, had a copy of *Speedway Star,* which was printed in black-and-white then, and we were looking at it together one day. I thought, 'Jeez, what's this speedway?' We couldn't believe that it only seemed to be happening in England. Nobody could get there in those days – you had to have three legs to go there, or so it seemed to us!"

With his parents, Grethe and Henry, initially unable to finance their son's passion for two-wheeled power, Ole had to earn the money to pay for his early thrills and speedway's education.

"When I was 16 I did an apprenticeship as a car mechanic and bought my first speedway bike – a brand new 500cc ESO – in 1965. It cost 4,800 Danish crowns and my father guaranteed the money. I had to pay him back at a rate of 112 Crowns per month."

Olsen travelled to England for the first time in 1966, when he qualified for the British-Nordic Final at Sheffield. Understandably, he was out of his depth at Owlerton that night, scoring five points in a qualifier dominated by Barry Briggs and Ivan Mauger, but he vowed to return to England – and he did, early the following year.

Diamond who just needed polishing

SPEAKING about the man who gave him his first big break in British speedway at Newcastle, he said: "Mike Parker was a great man, a fantastic promoter. There were a few who didn't like him but, then again, he was criticised because he wanted to change things in the sport and make British speedway better."

Little did the pioneering Parker realise it then, but he'd found a kindred spirit in Olsen. "He tried to get speedway going in Spain and he was a man of vision," Ole added.

"He had good ideas, such as contacting the DMU and getting them to send eight of us young Danes over there for a training school he set up at Belle Vue, which Ivan ran for him in February 1967."

Ole didn't stand out as the best rider on view at Hyde Road that winter's day – Kurt Bogh impressed the most – but he had the best command of the English language, which enabled him to communicate with Mauger, the then Newcastle No.1. After testing each of the young Danes' bikes, Ivan came to the conclusion that Ole had plenty more to offer if only he had better machinery.

Olsen's big chance came on April 24, 1967, when he made his belated debut for the Diamonds in the home BL match against Cradley Heath. Mauger had recommended the 20-year-old to Parker as a replacement for Brian Brett, who announced his sudden retirement just days into the season, but the signing was initially blocked by the Speedway Riders' Association who took a dim view to replacing a former English world finalist with a little known, inexperienced foreigner who needed a work permit.

Picking the brains of his mentor: Ole and Ivan Mauger before the 1972 Laurels at Wimbledon.

Olsen soon justified his place in the black-and-white racejacket, however. After finishing second to Jack Scott in his opening ride at Brough Park, he added three more second places for a match-winning debut eight points in Newcastle's 40-38 victory over the Heathens.

By the end of his first BL season Olsen had achieved a 7.54 average – second only to mighty Mauger in Diamonds' scorechart. It was a similar story in 1968, although Olsen raised his figures by almost two points a match. When Mauger left Newcastle to join Belle Vue in 1969, Olsen became Diamonds' No.1 in his own right with an outstanding 10.40 CMA, amassing almost 400 points from 34 official matches.

Olsen has never been slow to acknowledge the debt he owed Mauger for setting him on the path to greatness. Over the course of those two seasons spent together at Newcastle, Ivan drove them all over the country and it was during those long hours on the road that the eager young Dane never stopped picking the master's brain. Ole smiled: "I'd ask him the same question three times and if he gave me three different answers, I made up my own mind. But if two answers were the same, I thought that was pretty close to the truth!

"We spent so much time travelling together and I liked Ivan very much. I modelled a lot of what I did on him. He was at the top, so if you want to get to the top it makes it a bit easier to look at and ask the people who are already there, or who have been there.

"Ivan knew me backwards, which was a big advantage to him. But I learned later how to sort him out, too. We've always had a fantastic relationship. We had this ritual of shaking each other's hand before important meetings. He would say to me: 'All the best. I hope I win but if I don't, then I hope you do instead'. We said the same thing to each other before all the big meetings."

Even after Olsen dethroned Mauger as World Champion in 1971 and became his most formidable rival throughout the early 70s, their mutual respect never diminished. Watch the videos of World Finals won by either legend and you'll note how, momentarily suppressing their own personal disappointment, one would invariably be the first to congratulate the other at the end of the night. "We always had great respect for each other," Ole added. "I would say that Ivan, or 'Sprouts' as I call him, did more than anybody to change the sport in his time."

If anything, the master taught the pupil too well, as Mauger would discover as the 70s unfolded. Ole has an impressive record of having beaten Ivan from the back in important races and none more so than towards the climax of the 1971 season. He took him from the back in both the European Final at Wembley, where only a freak machine failure denied Olsen the title, and a few weeks later, when he surged past the Kiwi on his way to winning his first world title in Gothenburg.

As well as taking inspiration from Mauger, Ole says he was also inspired in his younger days by Swedish legend Ove Fundin, who won the last of his five world crowns in the year that Olsen began his BL career. Ole places two identical black-and-white photographs side by side on the table in front of us and points out the striking similarities between the image of Fundin, sitting alone on the steps next to the Wembley pits, and one of him in exactly the same spot in the famous tunnel during that dramatic European Final four years later. Fundin is covering his eyes with his hands, a model of concentration, while Ole cuts a forlorn-looking figure, contemplating the broken rocker arm that moments earlier had robbed him of glory.

"Igor Plechanov (the greatest ever Russian rider) sent me these pictures from Russia," says Ole. "Ove told me that after he retired, his favourite spot on those steps in the Wembley pits would become mine. Ove has always been good to me. There were a lot of times when we caught the early six o'clock flight out of Gatwick together before racing in a Scandinavian meeting. I've always had a lot of respect for him. He was my hero.

"When I got to know Ivan, he became my mentor. I remember sitting up in the stand and seeing

Denmark's first motorsport world champion, Ole after his first title success in Gothenburg, with Ivan Mauger and Bengt Jansson taking the minor medals. Below: The pressure of the huge Wembley occasion never troubled Olsen, seen here leading Ray Wilson on the way to his second crown in 1975.

Ole had nothing but the greatest respect for Coventry supremo Charles Ochiltree. Young Jakob watches his dad sign his last Bees contract in 1983.

him ride for the first time in the 1966 World Final at Ullevi, which Barry Briggs won from Sverre Harrfeldt."

Ole doesn't agree with my point that it was harder to win a one-off World Final in his era compared to a GP series today. Even allowing for his inevitable bias towards the GP elite, his response is unconvincing. "You say that there were more top riders capable of winning it when I rode, and on paper there was, but when there were 80,000-90,0000 at Wembley, a lot of them s*** their pants, if you'll please excuse my language. They couldn't take the pressure.

"In my experience, a lot of English guys struggled when they went outside England, where they couldn't get their cup of tea or bacon and eggs in the morning. Maybe I'm exaggerating a bit but you know what I mean? Their attitude towards different tracks and handling foreign cultures and languages was not what it might have been. That's where Mauger was so very good.

"Today, the top guys still have to be good over a whole season and be able to come out on top on different tracks. The modern bikes are easier to ride than in our day, when we had to have more throttle control, but the skill some of them have today, on equipment that grips so much, still makes it very tough for anyone to become World Champion."

Wolves' spark of genius

OLE explains that it was his desire to relocate to the Midlands that led to his transfer from one Mike Parker track to another, from Newcastle to Wolverhampton, at the start of 1970.

"Wolves fans didn't like me when I first signed for them. I had replaced their favourite, Hasse Holmqvist, who was the big local hero a couple of years before me. But then Cradley came over one night with Bernie Persson, who usually cleaned everybody up at Monmore Green, and I beat him twice from the back. I was a 'Wolf' from that day on!" Ole laughed, reflecting on the first of his 71 maximums in the gold-and-black body colour that he wore with distinction.

After scoring an impressive 13 points on his World Pairs Final debut (alongside Bent Norregaard) at Stockholm in 1969, followed by his individual World Final bow a year later, in 1971 Olsen made history by becoming the first Wolverhampton rider to win the World Championship.

It was during his six seasons with Wolves that Olsen first met Peter Adams, who would become one of his closest allies for the rest of his racing days (Adams gives his assessment of their special relationship in *Backtracking Volume 1*).

"Pete was a great Wolves fan, and obviously still is now he's their team manager. I met him for the first time after a spark plug problem caused me to stop in one meeting.

"I don't know why but for some reason we couldn't get the type of spark plugs that I liked to use and Pete read about this in a newspaper article. The next thing I knew, he knocked on my door one day at our house in Holmes Chapel and handed over a few of the spark plugs I'd tried everywhere to get hold of.

"We got to know each other very well. He's a very clever boy – a civil engineer. I would confide in him a lot. He actually produced all the architectural drawings for the stadium we built at Vojens in 1975.

"Peter was brilliant and had a great influence on me. I'd say he was England's answer to Arne Bergstrom in Sweden – someone who did so much for speedway in that country. Pete studies and understands it.

"He should have been the England team manager. But maybe he didn't take the job because, in the back of his mind, he had concerns about the attitude of some of the English riders . . ."

Olsen's friendship with Adams blossomed into a successful marriage of sharp minds both eager

Olsen on the outside of Hans Nielsen, the man who would succccd him as Denmark's No.1.

to shape the sport's future. Adams, whose intelligence somewhat belies his dour public persona, succeeded Midlands-based national newspaper journalist Mike Beale as Olsen's business manager in the mid-70s.

In 1978, Olsen and Adams introduced a ground-breaking Master of Speedway series – effectively, the forerunner to the SGP that dominates the sport today. Peter Collins was the inaugural winner of the series, staged over four rounds (two at Olsen's Vojens track, plus one meeting each at Bremen in Germany and Gothenburg, Sweden), for which the Belle Vue and England ace earned a hefty £10,000 cheque – the biggest prize in speedway at that time, which put the FIM's World Championship pay-out to shame.

"The Masters series was always something I wanted to do, although it was a culmination of both of our ideas," recalls Olsen, whose hopes of staging a round at Coventry were rebuffed by the BSPA, much to Bees' promoter Charles Ochiltree's dismay. "They fought against it and the FIM was also a bit concerned that it was looking too much like the real World Championship. They took that stance in the belief that they were sitting on something they thought was going to last forever.

"Pete and I put all our ideas together to make it work, although I wouldn't say that it crossed my mind back in 1978 that the World Championship would evolve into the GP we run now," says Olsen, whose Masters series lasted only four years. It took him another 14 years or so to finally convince the FIM that the traditional World Championship format should be scrapped and run as a GP series.

Olsen's last season at Wolves was marred by the tragic death of Gary Peterson, a highly rated Kiwi who died at Monmore Green on October 17, 1975 after hitting a metal lamppost during the Midland Cup final clash with Oxford. If the much-acclaimed air fences which prevent so many serious injuries today had been around then, Peterson would almost certainly have survived the crash. But Olsen – who had to go out and ride in the next race immediately following his team-mate's fatal spill – doesn't feel bitter about the hazards riders of his generation had to contend with. "I never thought about the steel posts around the edge of the track. I didn't go stupid, of course, but those lampposts were never in my mind while I was racing," he says.

"What happened to Gary really shocked us. He'd previously had a couple of bad crashes, including one that left him with a broken jaw.

"It was another very sad day for the family. Gary's sister, Jan, had been killed in a car accident on her way back to New Plymouth the year before after having dropped Gary off at Auckland airport. I had actually arranged to pick him up on arrival in England.

"He'd ridden for me in the opening meeting at Vojens, just three weeks before his death. Ulla and I knew Gary very well – he'd come over to our place for Sunday dinner. He was more like a brother to Ulla. He was a caring, fantastic human being."

Within days of Peterson's death, Olsen – who withdrew from the '75 BLRC as a mark of respect to his good friend – had also gone from Monmore Green.

Hull can go to hell
EXPLAINING his protracted transfer to Coventry, Olsen says: "I was World Champion in 1975 and I said to Mike Parker that it would be my last season with Wolves, as I wanted to move to Coventry in '76. He knew I would be moving on and that Coventry was where I wanted to go.

"In fact, I told Mike that I wanted to leave Wolves at the end of '74 but I agreed to stay for one more year.

"I had a couple of meetings with Charles Ochiltree and we shook hands on an agreement for me to join Coventry. Everything was set before I went away to Australia and New Zealand that winter."

Team-riding with Tommy Knudsen against Cradley Heath pair Phil Collins and Alan Grahame in 1983.

In those days, instead of using a maximum points limit to try and equalise team strengths, a Rider Control Committee – made up of BSPA management committee members – would shunt riders around from track to track on an arbitrary basis. Some riders with less influence had no option but to go where they were allocated, although others, like Ivan Mauger and Olsen, dug their heels in and would only accept moves to their satisfaction.

At the end of the 1974 season, Rider Control tried to shift Olsen from Wolves to Oxford but he wouldn't budge and the Rebels were allocated Reading's Dag Lovaas instead. In the winter of 1975-76 the RC committee decided Olsen should be sent from Wolves to Hull, who were badly in need of a boost after finishing one place off bottom spot in the '75 BL. Hull had, in turn, agreed to release Tommy Johansson and Jimmy McMillan (who wanted a move to the Midlands) to Wolves.

Go to Hull? Olsen told the authorities to go to hell. He made it abundantly clear that he would much prefer to have been sent to Coventry.

"Charles phoned a couple of times while I was in Australia and informed me that I had to join Hull instead of Coventry but I told him that there was no way I was going there. I didn't have a written deal with Charles but we had a handshake, which was good enough for me and, as I was very pleased to hear him say later, good enough for him, too.

"I told Charles that if I couldn't ride for Coventry, then I wouldn't ride anywhere in Britain.

"So I went to America, where I had a visit from Hull co-promoters Ian Thomas and Wally Mawdsley. They phoned me in California and invited me out for a meal to discuss a proposed move to Hull but I told them that there was no deal to be done. I wasn't going to Hull. They tried to get me drunk on rum and Coke, in the hope that I'd change my mind and agree to sign for them. They kept going up and up on the money, too but I kept telling them: 'I ain't going'.

"Then they said that they had an agreement to sign me. I haven't read Ian Thomas' book but, apparently, he wrote in there that he had a deal to sign me. But I never, ever did any deal with anyone to go to Hull.

"When I came back from the States, I had a meeting with Thomas and Charles at a motorway service station, although I told Charles that I didn't want to have the meeting in the first place. There was no point. I think Thomas started by asking for £20,000 for me but I told Charles: 'Don't pay him a bean because I ain't going there'.

"If I couldn't have joined Coventry, I would have retired from British speedway there and then. In fact, around that time, I was approached by the Broadspeed company, near Oxford, who wanted me to drive for them in the British Touring Car Championships at Silverstone. Who knows how my life would've turned out?

"In the end, Charles agreed to pay Hull £15,000 for me. It's the easiest money Ian Thomas ever made. It was a joke and I never liked the fact that Coventry ended up paying so much. It was totally unfair on Charles but he stood by his word to sign me and I appreciated that."

Thomas wrote in *Wheels and Deals* that he would have settled for a £12,000 cheque from his Coventry counterpart but increased his demand for an extra £3,000 after Olsen insulted him by calling him 'A Little Man'. "OK, that was probably right. I probably called him a little bastard as well!" smiled Ole.

In the spring of 1976 Olsen finally got his wish to join Coventry, where he proved the catalyst that transformed the Bees from also-rans to champions. The great lengths Charles Ochiltree went to were more than justified by Olsen's will and skill in taking the Midlanders to the top.

"I'd like to talk about Charles, because he was a fantastic promoter who taught me a hell of a lot," says a respectful Ole. "He was also one for making radical changes. I came in and said 'this is no good and that's no good' and he accepted what I told him and was happy to act on my advice.

"I used to have meetings with him in his office – his wife Linda would bring us cheese rolls and

Still the Great Dane, Ole racing clear of Tommy Knudsen and Hans Nielsen in the second-half of the World Team Cup qualifier at King's Lynn in 1981.

a cup of tea. Charles would be sitting on the other side of his desk and write down everything I said we should do with the team. He used to say: 'So you are telling me that's he's no good?' and write it all down on his notepad.

"We used to walk the Coventry track together. Everything was nicely laid out and chalked up, the pits and the dressing rooms were always perfect. It was such a good stadium to bring sponsors to.

"I'd just built Vojens in '75 and I learned a lot from Charles about promoting. He taught me things about the different attitudes of riders and how they could affect him as promoter. He gave me good ideas on how to run the operation, produce the programme and other ways of promoting the club.

"A deal was a deal with Charles, he was fantastic. I never had any problems negotiating with him. As a matter of fact, he always gave me more than I'd expected in the first place!

"He had a very good approach to riders' insurance. He sat me down and after we'd agreed my basic deal for the season, which would include a bonus for where we finished in the league table, he'd ask what insurance cover I had in place. When I told him, he pointed out that as I was earning a lot of money, I needed higher cover in case of injury. He stressed how important it was that my income from the insurance was in the same region as the money I'd be earning if I was riding, injury-free, all the time.

"So he would make arrangements to pay a higher premium – at his own additional cost – to ensure I had even better cover. He paid out thousands of pounds in that way for all the Coventry riders.

"It was a very sensible approach, as most riders think it's more important to spend their money on a new carburettor or back wheel than on extra insurance cover.

"I saw another example of his generosity after I'd won the world title at Wembley in '78. All we got for winning it then was £500 and yet there was a record (speedway) crowd of more than 93,000 inside the stadium that night. The Sunday Mirror doubled the prize money, so I received a cheque for £1,000.

"But when we went back to Coventry the following week and they had a parade with me and the trophy, Charles gave Ulla a thousand quid as well. He said to her that she deserved it after I'd focused so hard on winning the title. It was a tremendous gesture. Charles really looked after us. Ulla and I would go for meals with him and Linda to a little pub for a good talk. I never had a dispute with Charles about anything.

"Apart from speaking to Charles about different riders, I also told him Pete Adams was the person we needed as team manager."

After Olsen signed and Adams replaced Mick Blackburn as Coventry team boss, Bees went from strength to strength. Back-to-back BL champs in 1978 and '79, apart from eight place in 1977, they never finished lower than fifth in Olsen's eight seasons at Brandon, where he coaxed and cajoled some riders of comparative limited ability to believe in themselves and succeed beyond all expectations.

"They had good riders there when I arrived, including the likes of John Harrhy, but they were really only semi-professional, so it was difficult for them. We needed to be fully committed to speedway to be successful," he explained.

As well as having a major influence on new signings and team selection, Olsen also arranged for his mechanics – Aussie Cliff Anderson, the former Crewe rider, and his Danish spannermen, Benny Thomsen and Soren Klünder (Ole's brother-in-law) – to check the mechanical set-ups on all the Coventry team members' bikes.

"I would tell the other boys that they had to have a new front tyre and, for an important heat, to put on a new edge. Some of them didn't want to do it because they had been used to using only one tyre a meeting. But if they wouldn't do it, they were soon out. That's why we won things – we made sure of the details, like ensuring they had a good chain and their clutches were set up right.

"I think I created a good atmosphere at Coventry. It's all about knowing your product and, above all, to think humans. You have to keep thinking about the people around you and what kind of buttons you need to push to get them going and do what I'd wanted them to do. It's no good shouting at them. You have to say, 'look mate, if you do this or that, you're going to earn a lot more money'.

"They would give me a funny look when I asked which gate they wanted – I think they thought I would always choose the best gate for myself. They usually liked to be on the outside of me because they knew I could look after them around the first corner. I was able to do that a lot with Alan Molyneux, who was a good gater."

The smooth Brandon track was never less than immaculately prepared during Ochiltree's 50-year reign at Coventry. Some visiting riders, who had to weave their way through the traffic, would grumble that the circuit was a little too slick at times but Olsen always looked comfortably in control on any type of surface.

He says: "It never used to worry me what state the track was in. If it was a bit rough, I used to think to myself: 'That's good, now I've only got to beat three riders,' whereas before I'd probably have to beat 10 others. They would switch off, mentally. Riders sub-consciously programmed themselves into a negative way of thinking.

"If the track was wet or a bit rough, I used to think it was beautiful. I said the same to Erik Gundersen before the 1984 World Final at Gothenburg. When we opened the hotel window on the morning of the final, it was pissing down with rain. Erik said: 'Oh s***, man, it's raining'. And I said: 'That's good for you. You're a good gater, so you'll get out of the start before the others'. I turned it around so that it became a positive thing, an advantage to him instead of a disadvantage."

Olsen's motivational powers lifted Denmark to an unprecedented level of international domination through most of the 80s. But Olsen doesn't brag about his personal glory or how much success many of his fellow Danes enjoyed due largely to his leadership as captain and, later, as team manager. When he finally brought down the curtain on 17 seasons in the saddle just days after competing in his 11th World Final in 1983, he turned his attention to new challenges that have consumed him ever since.

Danish divide

IN 1984, just months after he had brought down the curtain on his own illustrious racing career at the age of 37, Olsen's powers of motivation and his psychological techniques played a major role in helping Erik Gundersen to become the first Dane to win the world title since the maestro won his third at Wembley six years earlier.

He took almost a patriarchal interest in Gundersen's pursuit of the big prize and there was more reflected glory for Ole when the impish, little racer from Esbjerg retained his crown at Bradford in 1985.

Unfortunately, by firmly nailing his colours to the Gundersen mast, Olsen increasingly alienated himself from several of the other leading Danish contenders, notably Erik's main rivals Hans Nielsen and Tommy Knudsen. To compound the feelings of unease within the Danish camp, Olsen became Denmark's team manager in '85 and the simmering discontent between him and Nielsen came to the boil when he named him as reserve for a Test match against England on Hans' home BL track at Oxford. Even the most ardent England followers felt embarrassed for Nielsen that day and Oxford fans let the Danish team chief know exactly what they thought of his shabby treatment of their main man by unfurling banners in protest.

More than 20 years on from that unseemly feud, when many felt Olsen had abused his position of

Danish delight: Olsen's last World Team Cup title as a rider, at Vojens in 1983. Standing, left to right: Erik Gundersen, Jorgen L. Jensen (team manager), Hans Nielsen. Front: Finn Thomsen, Ole, Peter Ravn.

authority, Gundersen candidly admitted to *Backtrack* (issue 23) that he could understand Nielsen's feelings of resentment that Ole could represent one rider one moment and the team the next. To add further insult to Nielsen's wounds, his main rival was also appointed Danish skipper by Olsen.

Olsen and Nielsen have long since buried the hatchet, although Ole doesn't share his former protégé Gundersen's view that his dual roles of personal guru to the Danish captain and that of national team boss were incompatible.

"I read what Erik said in your magazine but I think he is wrong. I would do anything for *anybody*. In those days someone had to pick the team and two riders to represent Denmark in the World Pairs. Everybody had to be pulling together.

"There was a lot of talk about this in Denmark and I've always given the example I gave to Denmark's famous sailing champion Badelowski, a lawyer, who was asked to chair a meeting of the Danish Motor Union when I was called to explain my position over the Nielsen-Gundersen situation. Eight committee members gathered at a hotel and I finished them with what I said to them that day.

"I wanted to help all the riders but, as I explained to the committee, Hans wanted me to line up all the riders and tell them the same thing. I could have done it that way but it doesn't work very well.

"You have to get into them as individuals. Tommy Knudsen had to be treated differently to Erik Gundersen. Erik needed a kick up the pants sometimes but then another time you had to cuddle him and let him cry on your shoulder a bit. It's a team but the riders all have different individual needs.

"Anyway, before the big discussion with the DMU began, I gave them an imaginary scenario where I had both Erik and Hans in the back of my car. I said to the committee: 'I'm driving in my car and I approach a red traffic light. I say to them: 'Boys, when that light goes to amber, shortly after it

Caught in the middle: Ole between Hans Nielsen and Erik Gundersen at the 1986 BLRC at Belle Vue.

will turn green and we can go like a rocket'.

"And then Erik says: 'Oh, that's really beautiful, I know that now and believe it to be true'. But Hans says: 'Well, are you sure, will it really happen like that?'

"Obviously, I was trying to present to the committee how both riders would typically interpret the same situation differently and the message I was trying to put across to them. That was the thing with Hans – he doubted me and seemed to question whether I was really telling him the truth and if I genuinely wanted him to be as good as the other man, whereas Erik was much more receptive. It's what I call 'mastermind', where it's .3 in the law of success. One + One = Three. It means that two brains in harmony creates a third where the sum is bigger than the two put together.

"In other words, because Erik and I were working towards the same goal, we would create more and lift it. But Hans and me weren't quite in harmony. He didn't understand me and didn't want to do things the same way, so we were pulling against each other."

Did the antipathy between them in the mid-80s pre-date to a racing incident when they were on-track rivals? Apart from Bent Norregard Jensen's shock victory in the Danish Championship of 1974 (when injury ruled Olsen out of the meeting), Ole had reigned supreme as national champion every year from 1967 until Nielsen ended his monopoly (10 titles in 11 years) in 1978.

Ole couldn't recall any specific incidents that might have provoked any ill feeling between him and Nielsen or any of the other emerging younger Danes who were determined to emulate him, although I recall the occasion he stuffed Bo Petersen into the fence on the first bend at Hackney, which left the Hawks star fuming. Olsen says: "Those boys all wanted to beat me and I wanted to beat them. I accepted that, it's the way it was. But, hey, they weren't going to get it for nothing. I was going to give them a run for their money.

"One problem I did have with Hans was over his appearance money at Vojens. I thought he was very tight – that's his choice and he has done very well for himself, but he always wanted more money and it was all one way. He wanted an increase every time he rode at Vojens and we had words about that. Then he would talk about the cost of inflation and say he wouldn't ride.

"I would offer him the chance to earn more money, but it was based on a bonus incentive where he earned more for finishing in the top three. But he didn't want that and there was not enough give and take on his part. Hans always wanted guarantees.

"I loved Hans, though. He is a great man and he was a great rider and all that," says Olsen of the rider who, ironically, won the first-ever World Championship GP series in 1995 and remained the Main Dane until his retirement and Nicki Pedersen took over as the top Dane.

Olsen revealed that, at one stage, he was set to help Nielsen at the 1982 World Final in Los Angeles, where the then Birmingham No.1 was Denmark's lone representative after Gundersen, Bo Petersen and Ole himself had been eliminated in the penultimate round at Vetlanda, Sweden.

"I offered to help him at the final in '82 and he said he'd like me to do that. In fact, I think he asked me to help him, and I agreed I would. But then something came up and in the end he decided to go his own way.

"He might have been a bit afraid that I didn't really want him to win it. I think he had those thoughts in the back of his mind for some years."

If you still consider Ole to be in denial over the rift that drove a giant wedge between the leading powers of Danish speedway in the mid-80s, then it is hard to refute his next observation. His mere presence in the Gundersen pit corner was a massive motivating factor in itself for Nielsen, whose desperate attempts to reach the top were finally fulfilled at Katowice in 1986, when he ended Gundersen's hat-trick bid.

Olsen said: "I did more for Hans Nielsen than anybody else has ever done for him. He had been in several world finals and not really done anything but after I stopped riding and became Danish team manager, then that little bit of rivalry between him and Erik came into play and it lifted them both.

"Hans wanted to beat Erik just to prove to me that he was the better rider. Because of my involvement with Erik, I gave Hans a very, very strong reason why he wanted to be World Champion.

"Between them, they won every World Final for six years in succession. But without the rivalry they had, I'd bet you anything that they wouldn't have won as many titles as they did.

"I'll give you a classic example of the point I'm making. Hans always wanted to be the No.1 Dane. After Erik suffered his bad injuries and had to retire in 1989, in '90 Jan O Pedersen got hurt and had to miss the final at Bradford. Hans was going very well that year and most of us thought he was going to be World Champion again.

"But I'll never forget talking to Erik about it, just before the '90 final. After Jan O broke his wrist go-karting, I said to Erik: 'Hans won't win it now'. But Erik disagreed, saying: 'He'll walk it, there's no-one to challenge him'.

Swede Per Jonsson's brilliance in winning at Odsal must be recognised here but Olsen insists that it was the absence of a Danish rival that weakened Nielsen's bid to claim a fourth world title, which he had to wait three more years to achieve.

"Hans finished up fourth or something at Bradford," continued Ole. "Without Jan O to challenge him, he thought it was just a question of turning up to win it. If Erik or Jan O had been riding that night, Hans would have really gone for it because he wouldn't have wanted either of those two Danes to beat him. He had to be the best Dane. It's like the younger Poles now all want to beat Tomasz Gollob, and in my day they all wanted to beat me. Having something big to aim for lifts them.

"So I feel that I've done a hell of a lot for other Danish riders. Erik and Hans wanted to beat each other and then it got even better when Jan O came along to rival those two.

"I have a very good relationship with Hans today, as I do with all the Danes. Hans contributed a few bits and pieces to my biography and he says that he was probably wrong in some things that happened in the past and I was wrong on other occasions. I would agree with him there."

At home with sons Jakob (far left) and Torben, wife Ulla and Jakob's daughter Sarah in 2008.

Writes and wrongs

AS Gundersen pointed out in issue 23 of *Backtrack*, it suited the national daily newspapers in Denmark to perpetuate a rift between the rival Erik/Ole and Hans camps.

The three main Danish speedway protagonists were back page news. Whatever was written about them – true or false – it sold more papers.

Although it has to be said, most of the publicity was also good news for the respective riders, who benefited from bigger sponsorship deals in their homeland, and Olsen, as the master of all he surveyed in Danish speedway and the promoter of Denmark's No.1 track. They weren't going to let the truth get in the way of a good story.

Offering an insight into Danish sports media politics, Olsen explained: "We were caught in the crossfire of what the different newspapers in Denmark were reporting about us. *Jullandsposten,* the biggest selling newspaper, took Hans' side a lot of the time, while the tabloid *Ekstrabladet* was on mine and Erik's side.

"Some of the things that came out were incredibly wrong, though. Once, it was falsely reported that we gave a Czech rider a brand new Jawa for letting Erik beat him in the 1984 World Final at Gothenburg, which was a load of rubbish and really hurt me. He won that fair and square and had he not had his bad injury, he would have won a lot more titles. Erik was a great boy and still is."

Gundersen revealed to us that he did not pay Olsen anything for working as his svengali during his peak years, although Ole pointed out that he still has something tangible to show for his considerable efforts. "Erik must have forgotten, because he did offer to pay me, but I said 'no'. All I asked him for was the helmet he wore at Gothenburg in '84. He gave it to me and I still have it at home.

"I can tell you, when Erik won his first world title that year, I felt the same joy I would have if I'd won another title myself. I was so thrilled at the way I worked with that boy, mentally, the way I was able to change his attitude and get him thinking about things psychologically . . . I knew it could be done if we did things the right way. It was all up in the head, so for me it was, like, 'wow!'. I still get goosebumps just thinking about it.

"I remember the sing-song we had with Erik on the boat coming home from Sweden, when two German girls were playing the Snowman song on their guitars. The whole boat was singing along with us – it was bloody great!

"I didn't need the elation I felt after Erik won in '84, because I'd had my time as a rider. But it was just the feeling that we'd worked so hard to achieve it, as I'd done myself to win the title in '75, that made it so good. It was another milestone in my life."

Jan O Pedersen, who followed in Gundersen's footsteps at Cradley, won his one and only individual world title at Ullevi in 1991 before, like Gundersen and Per Jonsson, suffering a career-ending injury.

But Tommy Knudsen, the Danish youngster Olsen brought to Coventry in 1979, never got closer than losing a run-off to Olsen for the silver medal at the Wembley World Final in 1981. Knudsen was fortunate to walk again after breaking his back in a crash in Australia and it was much to his dismay that Olsen, who had nurtured him through his early BL days at Coventry, couldn't give him the attention he gave Gundersen in the mid-80s.

"What gets me a little bit is when Tommy says that I could have made anybody a World Champion if I'd wanted to and that I promised to turn him into one," says Olsen.

"I did tell him that when he was younger but he then said that I chose to help Erik instead of him, because he (Tommy) was injured and I couldn't wait for him to get fit again. That's not correct. Erik asked me to help him, so what Tommy said about that hurt me a little.

"I've always had a great respect for Tommy and I would've helped him too but he did get badly injured a couple of times and it slowed him up. If Tommy is saying I promised to help him become World Champion, which I admit I did, then he hasn't had a strong enough reason *why* he wanted to be No.1. If he had, he should have been sitting on my doorstep every day, pestering me to help him.

"But for him to just sit back and say, 'well, I ain't going to do it because Ole isn't going to assist me and he's helping Erik instead' . . . it's the wrong attitude for him to take.

"Some people think that life owes them something. But it doesn't owe any of us anything, so let's get on with it."

As well as advising Gundersen throughout the first two of his three individual World Championship-winning campaigns (1984 and '85), during his time as a rider and manager Olsen guided Denmark to five World Team Cup victories (1978, 1981, 1983, 1984 and 1985) and two gold medals in the World Pairs (1979 and 1985). Nielsen shared in all five WTC wins and Gundersen the last four. Hans partnered Ole to Denmark's first pairs title at Vojens in '79, while Ole was team manager when Erik successfully combined with Tommy Knudsen six years later at Rybnik, Poland.

So one way or another, the three biggest legends of Danish speedway, Ole Olsen, Hans Nielsen and Erik Gundersen, contributed considerably to each other's success.

Giving it his best shot
OLE has been married to Ulla since April 3, 1969 but, in truth, as Ole himself admits, he remains in love with speedway, too. He still talks about it with a boyish enthusiasm and, regardless of whether you agree with what he says, you cannot but respect and admire his devotion to the sport in which he has wielded so much influence.

His brain is still bursting with ideas and while some have accused him of being a control freak and a ruthless dictator who always likes to get his own way, no-one can question that he has been very successful at almost everything he has ever set out to achieve.

Having said that, during a relatively quiet period in January, he was clearly delighted for some brief respite from the pressure of work, to receive a visit from his sons, Jacob (35) and Torben (25) who, coincidentally, happened to turn up at their parents' home on the same day. And it was a very proud grandfather who hugged and kissed Jacob's three-year-old daughter Sarah as the Olsens all gathered together in Ole's office.

Ole never seems to relax but on the rare occasions that he does switch off from speedway, there is nothing he enjoys more than going hunting with Torben and friends. Ole showed me into the room where he keeps three rifles and the walls are adorned by the antlers of deer and moose he shot during previous trips to other parts of Scandinavia and Siberia.

"This is a total contrast to what I'm normally doing in speedway, away from the noise and the excitement. When I get away in the winter, I like to smell the woods and see the sun rise in the morning," he says.

After happily posing for more pictures with his rifle, Olsen returns to philosophical mode as he reflects some more. As you will have gathered he is well-read and is fond of quoting famous sayings.

"I don't have any regrets, either in my career or in life itself," he says. "The failures I experienced have just been part of the process in reaching my goals. What I have learned and the experience I've gained from these things has been tremendous.

"I read somewhere that inventor Thomas Edison made over 10,000 experiments before he had one that was successful. The journalist interviewing him asked what it was like to have so many failures, and he said: 'I never had one. But I found 10,000 ways it could not be done'.

"The same also applies to me and the things I've done in speedway," added Olsen.

Shooting star: Ole at home in 2008 with his hunting rifle and 'trophies'.

Where did you get your first bike and roughly how much did it cost?

It cost about £600, but Steve Schofield's dad, Peter, bought it for me. I had no money and I couldn't afford to ride, so it was a Godsend really. I think he bought it so he had someone to keep Steve company! We'd go to the Hackney training school on Saturdays and the Eastbourne training school on Sundays. And I didn't have any transport either – so not only did he buy me a bike, he actually took me there too. I'd got to know Steve because he lived round the corner from me and I'd seen him ride past with a Bell helmet on. I'd been doing grass-track and I had a 250cc BSA – it wasn't going right, so I took it round to him.

Who helped you most in the early days?

If it hadn't been for Peter Schofield, I'd have never got started. Lew Coffin at Weymouth was a big help too – I think he helped everyone, didn't he? It was Weymouth where I started off and I made my first team debut for them in 1983. The year before, though, I'd ridden a couple of junior matches for Wimbledon – in our team were people like my brother Gordon and Kelvin Tatum, and when we rode at Belle Vue we were up against the likes of Martin Scarisbrick and Andy Smith.

Best promoter you've ridden for and why?

To be honest, they were all great. Mervyn Stewkesbury at Weymouth was very good and so was Colin Hill at Exeter. People said Colin was a bit of a strange one but I got along very well with him and you always got paid every week. But if I had to pick one promoter it would be Peter Thorogood at Arena-Essex. He was a great guy and very loyal – he wouldn't throw you out of the team if things weren't going well, he'd give you a chance. I don't think you get loyalty like that in speedway these days.

Favourite track?

Canterbury. It was a big track, which I liked. I always seemed to have a good meeting there and I enjoyed going to Kingsmead.

Tracks you never looked forward to visiting?

There weren't any – I enjoyed them all. There were none that scared me and even if I didn't do particularly well at certain places, I still enjoyed going there. Take Mildenhall – it was the sort of place where you'd be leading for three-and-three-quarter laps and then one of their riders would go round you and the other one would go underneath you. You just couldn't shake them off there.

Worst crash/injuries?

The one that actually led to me retiring was damage to the cruciate ligaments in my left knee. I first did it at Arena in 1988, when Martin McKinna came inside me and Martin Goodwin and we both came off. I didn't think too much of it but a similar thing happened when I was riding for Exeter at Powderhall in 1992. I was going really well at the time, my average was up to something like 6.7, but doing my knee again really set me back. It was taking me longer to strap it up before a meeting than it did to ride, so I knew it was time to stop. I've had seven operations on it to sort it out.

Which team-mate did you most enjoy partnering on the track?

Andrew Silver and Martin Goodwin at Arena. 'Hi-Ho' was phenomenal in 1987 and breaking track records everywhere. We'd get a 5-1 and he'd be half-a-lap in front! But unless he was up against someone really good, he'd give me the choice of gates. Martin was the same – he was very generous too. They both helped me out a lot.

Career highlight/proudest moment?

It might sound strange but it would have to be the first time I rode in a league match at Plough Lane. I'd been a Wimbledon fan as a kid and always lived near the stadium, so to walk out onto the track just like the riders I'd watched was something special. I would have loved to have ridden for Wimbledon. They were in the first division when I was starting, though, and guys like Kelvin (Tatum) were pretty quick out of the gate – it wasn't a place for guys like us!

STEVE
FINCH

WOODLAND in West Yorkshire led to the sun-kissed shale of Italy for Steve Finch, who went on to go within one point of beating two budding speedway superstars to a major international prize.

Despite his career speeding round the longer tracks of northern England, Steve wasn't averse to the challenge of the trickier venues.

"It all started with us taking our bikes down to the local woods in my home village of Middlestown," said Steve. "We had a few famous people living locally, such as road-racer Mick Grant and Nigel and Eric Boocock. Charlie Monk also used to stay with the Booeys' father when he was over from Adelaide too – he was literally just 200 yards down the road."

Just like Partington across the Pennines where the Collins' and Mortons attracted many other locals into racing, so this Yorkshire village just outside Wakefield has its own place in speedway folklore.

Steve explains: "Lots of people from our village went to the speedway at Halifax and so from messing about in the woods we started going to the training schools at the old Belle Vue on Saturday mornings back in 1973. Some weeks we headed down to Boston instead."

Long Eaton manager John Bailey saw Steve's potential in second-halves at Halifax and invited him to join the Archers halfway through 1974, when the Rangers reverted to their traditional nickname

The back straight at Ellesmere Port, where gate four was Steve's favoured choice.

for one final season. As their No.7, he supported stars such as Geoff Bouchard, Phil Bass and Alan Molyneux. Steve's stay in the East Midlands was brief, though, with the Derbyshire team going into hibernation at the end of that year and a move to Berwick beckoned for him in 1975.

"With Berwick being a Saturday track I missed out on Halifax but it was the only way to get a guaranteed place," he recalls.

By the end of that first full year Steve had raised his average to nearly seven points and while he was happy with the Bandits' promotion, the travelling was taking its toll on the youngster.

"Elizabeth Taylor and her son Ken, who ran Berwick, had a logging company up in Northumberland and were an old-fashioned family who had had to cope with the loss of the father, Danny. They were straightforward, straitlaced people but it was a 350-mile return journey for me and the roads weren't as good as they are now. The 'local' derby was Coatbridge – and from here that's 250 miles away!"

Steve (left) with Ellesmere Port team-mate Chris Turner and Newcastle's Joe Owen in 1976.

Steve found his way to Ellesmere Port and a doubling-up role with Halifax in the British League alongside characters such as Chris Pusey (described by Steve as "laugh a minute"), Charlie Monk and Dutchman Henny Kroeze.

"Despite knowing Charlie, he'd never speak to you but when he ended-up in the National League (with Barrow) you couldn't shut him up. Then he used to come up to me and chat. He kept himself to himself but it wasn't that Charlie didn't want to help, more that he'd got 'the secret'. And since he'd come halfway round the world to earn a living, he was protecting himself by not letting it go."

Steve's first season at Ellesmere Port saw him steadily move up the Gunners' ranks to star status, recognised by a first international cap for a NL England side led by Tom and Joe Owen against Australasia at Stoke.

By 1978 Steve was an established star at Thornton Road and was nominated for the European Junior Championship, the predecessor of today's World Under-21 title. Success in the qualifier at Rodenbach, Germany saw the young Yorkshireman take his place in the final at Lonigo, Italy, where a third place in his first ride was followed by a second and three heat wins. Alas, he missed out on the title to Denmark's Finn Rune Jensen – now a top engine tuner – by one point. His total of 12 was good enough to earn him a run-off for second place against fellow Brits Kevin Jolly and Neil Middleditch.

Steve says: "Neil niggled me in that race – he came hard underneath me on the last bend of the last lap and his front chain came off but the referee excluded me.

"But I did come back from Italy full of confidence, on top of the world. I felt I could beat anybody."

Fourth place was no disgrace considering the next two places were taken by a fresh-faced pair of young Danes named Erik Gundersen and Hans Nielsen, although Steve reveals that he had help from a high level.

"You weren't allowed to use a four-valve engine and, on a big track like Rodenbach, really needed

Gunning for gold. The 1979 NL Four Team Tournament winners. Standing: Joe Shaw, Pete Ellams, Steve Finch, Richard Park. Front: Eric Monaghan, John Jackson, Louis Carr.

a long-track motor, so Ivan Mauger loaned me one for the qualifier."

Steve's links with the legendary Kiwi had been forged a couple of years earlier when they rode together in one of Ivan's meetings in Austria, while Gunners' promoter Ernie Park had also supported Ivan financially, playing a role in the multi World Champion's move from Exeter to Hull.

The 1978 season also saw Steve combine with John Jackson to give Ellesmere Port their second victory in the NL Pairs Championship, this time defeating Newcastle's Tom Owen and Robbie Blackadder in the final at Halifax.

"That was special, if only to prove to some of the Halifax people that I could actually ride the Shay track," he says. "The problem was that it was at NL level, using standard bikes, and the locals expected me to win every race there in the British League after that.

"We did our own tuning but used standard bikes. You couldn't spend a lot of money on machinery and in the British League you really had to have sponsorship."

So what was it like riding alongside a National League legend such as John Jackson?

"Jacko was a quiet lad – a bit like Charlie Monk until he got older, then he came out of his shell. He was like so many . . . they all had that 'secret'.

"At the end of one season as things opened-up between us, we went on holiday with our families to Crete. John had occasionally made a sarcastic comment in the pits and we all had a laugh. In his earlier days he did ride for himself – the aim was to simply be as far ahead as possible after four laps and he wasn't interested in helping his partner. But as he moved down the order, he started to lose the 'secrecy' and would join in with the rest of us."

Steve gave an insight into the Cheshire track: "Gate four was the best gate to go from. The referee was at the back of the stand so while he could see your helmet, he couldn't see how far you were up to the tapes. Not many broke the tapes off gate four there.

"I thought the line to the corner was better from gate four and if you could get a couple of yards clear, you could really chop up the others.

"It was like a mini Halifax but dead flat. If it had been banked, it would have been so much faster. The Thornton Road track was great to ride, though. There were a lot of big tracks about then (Ellesmere Port was 424 yards), such as Peterborough, Berwick and Coatbridge, which was like Halifax with steeper banking.

"I could get round the small tracks as well," he points out, "and if you could do both big and small, you were OK. I used to love Crayford (a 265-yard tiddler) even though it was a bit awkward. There was a technique but I always enjoyed it most when Lew Stripp was refereeing."

Steve explains: "Well, everyone used to hate Lew. They'd look at the programme, see his name and say: 'That's it, we've lost!'

"But I liked the way he wouldn't allow any messing at the start – and that's how it should have been. If you're competing in the Olympic 100 metres, you don't get to mess around in the blocks."

Gunners claimed the NL 4TT title at Peterborough from Mildenhall and the local Panthers in 1979, while Steve took the Showground track record away from home favourite Ian Clark in a year that saw him reach the top of the Cheshire side's averages and secure sixth place in the NL's overall top 10.

Many would suggest that this was the time to make the step up into the British League but it was finance, or rather the lack of it, that prevented him from making the leap.

He says: "I've often thought about that over the years but it really comes down to money. You had to invest a lot to make it work. When I was training at Boston Michael Lee was there, always with immaculate equipment. He had a skill and worked hard but his father had a moto-cross background, had good contacts and could find sponsors. Peter Collins' father didn't have much but they had the backing of sponsor Jim Rawlinson.

"Our family had no motor sport background but my dad backed me, just as he used to do when I was winning swimming trophies in Halifax before taking up speedway, but we just didn't have the money to plough in. I used to go to Eric Boocock's shop in the daytime to help him but there was no magic wand.

"To make it in the BL you had to have skill but you also needed backing and confidence.

"Take engine tuning. Dave Nourish was tuning Weslakes then but if you put in an order it was 12 months down the road before he could tune your motor. But obviously, if it was PC, it would be done tomorrow."

In 1980 Steve hit the top of the NL averages with figures just below 10 points and finished on

Halifax Dukes of 1983. Left to right: Eric Boocock, Steve Finch, Steve Baker, Kenny Carter, Dennis Gavros, Martin Dixon, Doug Wyer, Gianni Famari.

the podium in the NLRC at Wimbledon, where Berwick's Wayne Brown won and Steve lost out to Weymouth's Martin Yeates in a run-off for the silver/bronze medals. Ironically, Steve was getting BL rides for Wimbledon at the time but struggled to adapt to the Plough Lane track – a problem that cost him in the crucial race with Yeates.

"The Thursday before the NLRC I was at Wimbledon but had problems with the third and fourth bends, which were shaped like a triangle. The line was to go out wide and cut back but I was doing the opposite and Martin Yeates got it right on the night. Neither the Wimbledon riders, nor manager Cyril Maidment, had pointed out what I was doing wrong. I only worked it out for myself much later while watching a video.

"I talked with Martin Yeates after Wimbledon and we agreed that there was no point in giving up a living scoring 10s and 12s in National League when, say, Yeatesy could go up the road, score a couple of points for (BL) Poole and get no money.

"National League produced good racing, too, and we all used to go to watch it rather than BL. Take Paul Embley (a former Gunners team-mate). He'd be great for three laps, then fall. You'd get riders falling and rows over whose fault it was. That was the National League. It was fun.

"I made money and could earn a week's pay in one Friday night at Ellesmere Port. As Eric Boocock used to say: 'Why work all week when you can make it all in one night at Halifax?'. I had four bikes at one point and did have a 'small track bike' but, to be honest, if it felt all right, you just stuck to the one bike while it was still running well."

Steve recognised how important psychology was in the sport, saying: "99 per cent of it was in the head and many were psyched-out before they started. I took a bike I'd ridden at Ellesmere Port on the Friday to Milton Keynes on the Tuesday and was flying. But many riders fiddled with compression to suit the various tracks, especially Charlie Monk who often used to burn the midnight oil to get it right for the next track."

Steve's success at NL level continued unabated and he has fond memories of fellow heat leader Louis Carr.

"What a star, we used to say of him. He would travel with his father Jack and his grandad and their car never seemed to get there and back from Weymouth. One night they were stranded by the roadside and spent the night in the car with candles, one of which must have set fire to grandad. That joke went on forever within the Gunners set-up.

"Louis used to spend more time riding other people's bikes – we were always being asked by Richard Park or Joe Shaw: 'Have you got this to lend to Louis?' Jack Carr didn't have a lot of money but he put in what he could. If Louis and his brother Peter had been taken under someone's wing, they could have been world class."

Times were getting harder for speedway and Ellesmere Port was certainly not sheltered from the storm.

"We'd lost Ernie Park, who was one of the nicest people you could meet. His life revolved around his potato business but his passion was speedway. After his passing, his son Richard and his mother tried to keep it going but there was another son, who wasn't interested in speedway, who was also entitled to his share.

"Things were getting expensive, so John Jackson, Eric Monaghan and I, having done OK as riders and brought the track on, we wanted a little bit more out of it. But Richard Park called our bluff and closed the place."

That was in the 1982-83 close season, a time when the NL was trying to impose a pay policy.

"Nobody can tell me Ian Thomas wasn't paying the Owens extra money at Newcastle and it was widespread – what went on the pay slip was being topped-up. Joe Shaw was so straight and believed it was working, although Richard Park was a businessman and knew the truth. But the pay policy was a useful get-out for him when negotiating with riders."

With Thornton Road closed, Steve finally went full-time with Halifax in the British League in 1983 but by then his attitude to speedway had changed.

"Eric Boocock and I had started an electro-plating firm in Halifax and speedway became more of a Saturday night business. One day I started work at 7.00am, drove down to Poole, carried on working when I got back, then had to sleep on the Thursday afternoon. It wasn't a happy time at Halifax and by the end I hated it."

After two lean years in the top flight Steve returned to the NL in 1985 – to the short-lived Scunthorpe promotion who pulled their team out of the league in May. "I still haven't been paid," was Steve's bitter memory.

"Later in the year, Edinburgh's promoter Tony

In action at Halifax in 1984.

Frankitti was on the phone but I wasn't too interested and did something I'd never done before. He asked me to name my price and I did – it was a lot. He agreed! It was more than I'd ever asked for.

"Halifax let me go on loan and Tony even paid for a mate to take Friday afternoons off work to drive me up there. I had a hell of a good season. Sadly, he lost money and interest and in 1986 I was off to ride for David Fairbairn at Berwick."

Until then Steve had avoided significant injury but that run came to an end with the Bandits. In his Gunners' days only the two European Junior Championship meetings in 1978 had stopped him recording a record run of nearly 300 appearances but a broken shoulder forced him to miss much of 1986.

"It was my own fault. I got it wrong, landed badly and broke the soft part of the shoulder. We had a strong team led by the McKinnas and Steve McDermott and I'd even been down at No.7 at one point."

The end of a 14-year career came in May 1987, when Steve suffered a badly broken leg in a World Championship qualifier at Middlesbrough.

"Halifax junior Peter McNamara wiped me out on the first and second bend. I knew it was bad as soon as I hit the post and heard the leg break. McNamara was squealing like a pig and I was worried that he'd impaled himself on a post. There was too much 'furniture' around some tracks, especially the dog track venues such as Hackney. I knew as I lay there that after two bad injuries, that was it."

Now 52 and married to Yvonne, Steve has long since swapped two wheels for four.

"Dave Thomson, the old Glasgow promoter, was with the British School of Motoring and he got me involved in driving instruction. And 22 years later, I'm still doing it," he explained.

SAD SOREN LEFT HIS MARK

Soren Sjosten was one of the finest Swedes to grace the British League. Here Richard Bott recalls the highs and the lows of a spectacular and popular racer . . .

SOREN Sjosten, Sweden's mighty atom, self-destructed and died from alcohol poisoning in his homeland in April 1999 at the age of 61.

But he had endeared himself to so many in a long and distinguished speedway career, particularly in his adopted home of Manchester.

And, particularly, to someone who was to follow in his tyre tracks and become a Belle Vue legend in his own right. Chris Morton, MBE.

"Soren was my hero," says 'Mighty Mort', still deeply involved with the Aces since his own retirement from racing and committed, as co-promoter with David Gordon, to taking the world's most famous speedway club into a brand new stadium just a stone's throw from their current home in Kirkmanshulme Lane and their late, lamented Hyde Road circuit.

"I was seven-years-old when I first went to Belle Vue, so it's all a bit misty and I don't really

Soren in his early days at Belle Vue.

Peter Craven was a big influence on Sjosten.

Soren (right) on the World Final rostrum with Ivan Mauger and Barry Briggs at Wembley in 1969.

remember seeing Peter Craven ride before he was killed in 1963," says Mort.

"But I had a fixation with Soren from the start, although I had to wait a couple of years to satisfy my yearning for his gutsy style of riding because Swedish riders were not allowed to ride in the new British League in the mid-60s.

"Then he came back (in 1967) and I just loved watching the things he could do on the track because he was such a clever rider. I think riding with Peter Craven had influenced his own style because they were both small and had fantastic balance.

"It was the way Soren hung off the bike and made those big turns that was so entertaining. He was still riding for the Aces when I got into the team in 1973 and that was like a dream come true for me.

"In 1975, his last season with the Aces, he was banned from driving and I used to pick him up at his home in Salford and take him to the away meetings.

"He was just a great bloke who enjoyed his speedway and didn't really know anything else. But he had such a sad demise. He had a few bad years when he struggled for points, his father died and his younger brother Christer died after a track crash in Brisbane. Drinking was Soren's solace and it got him in the end.

"Interestingly, he influenced my career in both a positive and negative way. The positive was that his riding style rubbed off on me.

"On the negative side, I remember watching him ride as he was getting to the end of his career and was struggling like hell to score points. I thought, 'you shouldn't be riding any more' and I vowed I wouldn't let that happen to me. It is important to know when to stop.

"But he had been one of the best . . . a world champion for Sweden in pairs and team racing and

113

twice third in the individual, as well as helping the Aces to become British League champions three years in a row. That is what I want to remember him for, not his demise. And he will always be my favourite rider."

In 1972 Belle Vue won their third consecutive league title when they broke so many records and also lifted the Knockout Cup, beating Hackney in the final. Known as 'the Belle Vue steam roller', the Aces finished 12 points clear of joint runners-up Reading and King's Lynn, having won all but three of their 34 league fixtures. Their points total of 63 was the highest-ever in first division history, shattering the 39-year-old record set by the all-conquering pre-war Aces, who boasted the likes of Eric Langton, Frank Varey, Max Grosskreutz, Frank Charles and Bill Kitchen, in 1933.

Team managed by the late, great Dent Oliver, Belle Vue's 'magnificent seven' of 1972 finished the campaign with the staggering combined CMA of 56.45: Ivan Mauger (11.42), Soren (8.81), Peter Collins (8.63), Chris Pusey (8.29), Eric Broadbelt (6.83), Alan Wilkinson (6.68) and Ken Eyre (5.79).

Ken Eyre, still a regular in the pits at Kirky Lane, is another admirer: "Soren was brilliant. He had a wonderful riding style, very similar to Peter Craven's, and he was great fun. Sometimes, on the way back from a meeting, he used to pull up alongside me on the motorway because he had a left-hand-drive car.

"He would wind the window down and shout, 'now we have a race, yes?'.

"When I first got into the Belle Vue team, Soren used to come over and ask: 'Have you got any insulating tape?' Well, I always had a big roll of it with me. He said: 'I borrow it and I bring it back in a minute or two'. But when he brought it back there was only a bit left.

"The next meeting when he asked to borrow some insulating tape, the same thing happened and I thought, 'what is going on?' And it happened a third time. He took the whole roll and only brought a small bit back. I found out he was using it to tape up his boot because with him being short-legged it was in the clutch all the time.

"He was still a great rider and he is in the history books as a member of Belle Vue's treble champions. But he didn't get on with Tommy Roper!

"They were team-mates at Belle Vue and often used to be together in Heat 13 or the second-half final. Neither of them liked being beat and often they used to come back to the pits, jump off their bikes and knock seven bells out of each other."

Ring of confidence

SOREN Willy Ernfrid Sjosten, born in Avesta, Sweden, in December 1938, had already been associated with the Aces for 10 years when they won that third successive league title in '72, having first joined them from his second Swedish club, Vargarna.

It is probably a little-known fact that he was a champion Greco-Roman wrestler before his speedway career took off, winning the Marine Cup at flyweight during his national service in the Swedish Navy.

Writing in *Speedway Express* magazine in November 1976, columnist Ray Lambert revealed that speedway was Soren's 'second choice' in sport.

Wrestling's loss was speedway's gain when, in 1961, he made the transition. He had come to England for the first time that year, with the Swedish Test squad, and caught the eye of the Belle Vue management, who promptly signed him up for the 1962 season.

"When I asked him about his wrestling career, he said: 'That's going back a bit. I was wrestling five years before I started doing speedway'. Soren also became a weight-lifting champion during his national service," wrote Lambert.

His other passion was game fishing and he once caught a 26lb salmon in the River Esk. He also loved taking part in a kangaroo chase on his trips Down Under although, as far as I'm aware, he never succeeded in snaring one.

Soren first showed a penchant for speedway riding with his local club Folkare, in 1957, and within two years he had given up his job on a building site and become Swedish Junior Champion. He then joined major league club Vargarna, captained by Bjorn Knutson, and helped them to second place in the competition. He also topped the averages in his first year.

International recognition followed quickly with a call-up by Sweden for

Partnering Christer Lofqvist at Hackney in 1973.

their UK tour in 1961. He immediately impressed with a stand-out performance when he beat the legendary Kiwi Ronnie Moore in his first race and went on to score nine points.

It was more than good enough to convince Belle Vue manager Ken Sharples to sign Soren for the Aces and his faith was fully justified when the little Swedish fireball, then 23, scored a 15-point maximum against Wimbledon on a rain-sodden night at Hyde Road.

In fact, Sweden's rising star reached the first of his six individual World Finals in 1962, the year Peter Craven triumphed for the second time – the last English World Champion until Belle Vue's Peter Collins won in Poland 14 years later.

And he helped Sweden to lift the World Team Cup in Slany, Czechoslovakia, that same year, going on to pick up two more team gold medals, in Abensberg in 1964 and at Wembley in 1970.

Soren finished a creditable ninth, with eight points, in that 1962 Wembley final and was back there in 1965, scoring nine points, and again in '69 when he got on the rostrum in third place behind Ivan Mauger and Barry Briggs. Briggo denied him a silver by beating him in a run-off for second place.

Soren never quite managed to hit the heights on World Final night but he was fourth in Wroclaw in 1970 and picked up a second bronze medal in Gothenburg in '74, where he lost out on the silver in a run-off with Mauger.

All in all, though, he had a record to be proud of in World Championships and in Sweden's colours. But very early in his burgeoning track career it was England that became his 'home'.

That doyen of northern speedway journalists, the late Frank Maclean, writing in Soren's 1975 testimonial brochure, recalled: "Soren travelled with Peter Craven and Dick Fisher to most away tracks in his first season with the Aces and gives Peter most credit for his quick grasp of the English language.

"He told me: 'Peter used to point to things as we drove along and I would wrestle to find the English word for it'. Soren considered Peter to be the greatest of British riders, past or present, although his all-time favourite was his fellow countryman Ove Fundin.

"Soren's speedway career started on a closed-down track high in the forests of Avesta, about 120 miles from Stockholm, but he never expected to become a Test or World Final star. He bought a speedway bike for fun, to ride on the track at weekends, and it was only when other riders came to join him that he was persuaded to try his luck at league racing."

Another contributor to Soren's testimonial brochure, in 1975, was the then-Belle Vue PR and advertising guru Norman Roland, who enjoyed a long association with the track.

Sjosten told Roland: "Peter Craven not only taught me how to adapt to English circuits but helped me to overcome the language problems. Peter was my first real friend in England and is the man to whom I owe whatever success I've had in speedway.

"But it is a fallacy that small riders find it easier to win races. Peter was an exception. If I hit a bump I have hardly sufficient weight to keep me in the saddle, so rough and bumpy circuits make things particularly tough.

"Track maintenance people could learn a lot from Belle Vue," said Soren, recalling his 1974 World Pairs title triumph at Hyde Road with fellow Swede Anders Michanek.

"Everything went right for Michanek and me. The circuit was superb."

Settled in Salford

SIX years earlier, Soren had married a Manchester girl, Yvonne Waugh, which helped him to rejoin the Aces while the ban on Swedish riders was still in force. I interviewed Yvonne for a chapter entitled 'What the wives say' in my seventh *Champions Book of Speedway* (published in 1976 by Stanley Paul & Company).

She revealed: "I never thought for a minute that I would marry a foreigner. He didn't actually

Captain of the weakened Swedish team that was hammered 5-0 by England in the 1975 series on UK tracks. This was taken before the first Test at King's Lynn. Left to right: Soren Karlsson, Tommy Nilsson, Bengt Jansson, Christer Bergstrom (team manager), Tommy Jansson, Thomas Petterson, Olle Nygren, Kennet Selmosson.

The Folkare Jet . . . Soren in action for Sweden during the 1975 World Team Cup Final at Norden, Germany.

propose, as far as I can remember. Why did I fancy him? I don't know. I suppose the accent had something to do with it.

"We met in a bar at Belle Vue one afternoon. I knew he was a rider because I used to go to Belle Vue on Saturday nights with a gang. It was a bit of a laugh because I couldn't speak a word of Swedish and he didn't know much English.

"Every time he went home to Sweden I thought that was the end of it but he took me over for Christmas in 1964 and I had never seen so much snow.

"The wedding looked like causing a few problems and we thought of having it in Denmark, to be neutral. But his mum and dad had never been to England and since it was my parents' silver wedding, we decided to have it over here.

"When we first got married we had a flat in Manchester during the British League season and then moved everything over to Sweden for the winter. I soon got fed up with that. Then Soren wanted to take Steven (their son) and me to Australia one winter but I said I would rather spend the money on a house, so we bought our home in Salford.

"He's away a lot, flying home to race in Sweden, but I can always find something to do because I am very house proud. And I can watch what I like on the telly."

Sadly, the marriage ended when Soren's drinking problems began to overwhelm him and his racing career petered out.

They were exacerbated by the death of his brother Christer, following a track crash in Brisbane in 1979.

Shortly before leaving Belle Vue, Soren receives the Northern Trophy in 1975 from Halifax boss Eric Boothroyd, while Jack Fearnley pours the champagne. Paul Tyrer is in the background.

Hard to pass

BY then, Soren's British League career was over. He had left Belle Vue in 1976, having one season each with Birmingham, Wolverhampton and Bristol. Soren had captained the Aces in the 1975 season, his last at Hyde Road, and his 'boss' was former Halifax and England star Eric Boocock, who had pulled down the curtain on his own riding career the previous year and accepted a management role with Belle Vue.

Booey recalls: "Soren had had a fantastic career with Belle Vue and in the years when we used to race against each other he was the hardest man to pass I ever came across. It was as if he had 20 mirrors on his bike, like one of those Lambretta scooters.

"He used to go into a corner very slowly and you tied yourself in a knot trying not to run into him. Then, he would make a fast exit.

"The very last time I raced against him was in the BLRC at Belle Vue and I loaned him a spark plug. We met in the last race and I needed to win it to win the meeting but Soren made the gate and I couldn't get past him to save my life. If I went out, he went out. If I cut in, he cut in. He had everything covered.

"He couldn't win the meeting, so I should have told him to keep out of my way. But he beat me fair and square.

"Soren had a reputation for being very hard and he was. But all the Swedes were like that.

"I still liked him a lot. Unfortunately, towards the end of his career, when he was getting on a bit, he kept getting the worse for wear with drink although, in fairness, he never turned up drunk before a meeting.

"But Jack Fearnley, who ran Belle Vue Speedway and was very good to Soren, wasn't happy with the situation. So we were facing a dilemma in that 1975 season. I said to Jack: 'If we don't get rid of Soren now, while he's still got a career, we will feel obligated to run him while he drops down the riding order and becomes a liability. And Jack said: 'You are absolutely right'.

"So Soren got fixed up at Birmingham, then Wolverhampton and finally at Bristol, where he probably did a lot better, financially, than if he had stayed at Belle Vue.

"It wasn't nice having to tell him to go but, whoever you are, your career has to come to an end some time. But the drinking got worse and he used to turn up in a terrible state sometimes after he had retired. I believe he was even drunk when he got off the plane in Australia to go to his brother's funeral.

"But I have seen what drink can do to better people than Soren and it is such a sad way to go."

Speedway tour operator James Easter, of

Before the 1976 Inter-Continental Final at Wembley.

After leaving the Aces' pack, a season with Birmingham in 1976. Soren leads team-mate Lou Sansom from Wimbledon's Barry Crowson.

119

With the Wolves in 1977.

Showing bulldog spirit at Bristol in 1978.

Travel Plus, recalls: "Once I was organising air tickets for the Swedish riders and had to arrange for Soren to get from Sweden back to England in time to ride for Belle Vue at Ipswich one Thursday night.

"He flew into Heathrow but had no idea how to get from there to Ipswich by train. Several hours later we sent someone to pick him up from Ipswich railway station. It was about 5.00pm and they found Soren asleep on a station trolley, clearly the worse for wear. But he still rode that night."

Tragic demise

SIX times World Champion Ivan Mauger also has mixed memories of Soren's time at Belle Vue – his undoubted contribution to the glory years at the start of the 70s and his rapid decline a decade later.

"Like me, Soren used the Belle Vue workshops and we got to know each other quite well. He was a likeable guy, always jovial, and his wife Yvonne, who he met when he first came to Manchester, was a lovely person."

Soren maintained his own bikes but his favourite machine, which housed an engine given to him by Peter Craven, was stolen at Coventry in 1965. The thieves removed the bike and spares from his car boot but didn't take the vehicle.

On another occasion, while driving in Russia, he crossed a double white line in his haste to overtake a slow-moving lorry. He was flagged down by the militia and ordered to pay a fine of one ruble (about 20p). Explaining that he had no Russian currency, he was instructed to change a traveller's cheque while the police hi-jacked his team-mate and car passenger Alan Wilkinson as a guarantee until he paid the fine. "I have often wondered whether I was being over-generous paying 20p for Wilkie's release!" said Soren later.

But Soren deserved every penny and every pound he grossed from his testimonial meeting at Belle Vue in April 1975.

Back to Ivan's recollections . . .

Captains Soren and Peter Collins follow Eric Boocock and Frank Varey on parade before the Swede's well-earned testimonial in 1975.

"Soren was a really sharp rider and very good from the start. His style was to go very fast into the corners, come to a bit of a stop in the middle of the bend, make a turn and then exit the corner at speed – a bit like Hans Nielsen would do in the 80s and 90s.

"At lunchtime he often would go to the local pub and have a few pints, although never on race days. Sadly, after he finished riding he became an alcoholic and used to hang around with all the winos in central Manchester, often sleeping under bridges. After he went back to Sweden he died of alcoholic poisoning."

A tragic demise indeed. But all of us should remember happier days and golden nights when Soren's track craft and personality won the hearts of so many fans and established him as Chris Morton's sporting hero.

Interview & tribute by Tony McDonald ● Issue 37 & 38 (2010)

KELLY
MORAN

THE familiar voice on the other end of the line sounded amazingly chirpy given the circumstances. "Kelly's office!" said the American, answering my call from his bed. While I wouldn't exactly describe his demeanour as bubbly, he seemed a whole lot livelier than I'd expected.

It was Kelly Moran, one of the most popular and spectacular riders ever to grace the world stage, taking my call. Not from his California home, but from the hospice where he was being treated for a very serious illness.

Just days earlier, the former Hull, Eastbourne, Sheffield and Belle Vue favourite, had been found semi-conscious and barely alive in his trailer home where he lived alone in the small desert town of Thermal.

In January, 2010 he had been rushed to the JFK Memorial Hospital in Los Angeles, where medical staff didn't expect him to survive much longer, or even make it through the night. He was in such a bad state that Kelly's family and closest friends were contacted and advised to visit him for what looked like being the last time.

After years of habitually abusing his body with cigarettes and alcohol, his lungs and liver had taken far too much punishment and were on the brink of packing up altogether. Doctors who examined

Young, fresh-faced kid who landed at Hull in 1978.

Kelly and younger brother Shawn in their schooldays.

Kelly racing in California in 1977, before taking the plunge in the UK.

him said his lungs were working to 20 per cent of normal capacity.

Kelly spent four days and nights in the intensive care unit before he had recovered enough to be able to move out of the hospital to the Odyssey House Hospice at Palm Desert in early February. It was there, on February 10, that we first spoke on the phone.

Happy to be interviewed for *Backtrack,* he said: "A specialist at JFK hospital told me that he and his colleagues were very concerned when I came in. They weren't sure if I was gonna make it – especially when they saw that my lips had turned blue. Well, I'd be concerned too, if my lips were blue!"

Typical Kelly. Rather than wallow in self pity, he laughed at how close he had been to death and tried to make light of a desperately dire situation. I asked him to tell me the moment he felt short of breath and we'd break off the interview. But he was soon in full flow and sounded keen to tell his story, warts and all.

"After I came through those first few nights, the doctor said that it proved I was a fighter who wasn't going to give up. Then I thought to myself, 'he doesn't know the Jellyman . . . you can't give up. You don't give up on the track and especially not in life itself. Winners never quit 'cos quitters never win.

"Since I've been in hospital I've felt no inkling to have a (alcoholic) drink or a cigarette and it feels terrific. The doctors and nurses have warned me: 'Wait till you get outside again, it's a different world. See how you go then'. But I've been watching TV while I've been here, seeing all these people partying, and I think:

'I know how you're going to feel in the morning because I've been there'."

That's the trouble, he's been there far too often. Friends who have his best interests at heart have been saddened and concerned by his visibly deteriorating health in recent years. But trying to persuade Kelly Moran to stop smoking and quit boozing is like telling kids that chocolate isn't good for them.

Nurses and doctors at Hackney Hospital help their star patient celebrate his 18th birthday.

Ron Preston, who rode with Kelly for the USA and Eastbourne in the early 80s, became so concerned about his former team-mate's condition last year that he arranged for him to move into caravan-style accommodation on a friend's desert ranch, where it was hoped the fresh air would help ease the strain on his lungs.

Kelly had previously been living in a small apartment in Adelanto with his younger brother Shawn (interviewed in *Backtracking Volume 1*) and their mother Sharon, who both share his liking for a drink, before moving out out to stay with friends near San Diego, where his health continued to go noticeably downhill.

"They gave me a chest x-ray and found out I had emphysema," explained Kelly. They said: 'You're going to have to quit smoking or at least cut down'. Cut down? I'd been smoking Marlboro Reds in America, so I switched to Marlboro Lights and in the end I was smoking up to seven cigarettes a day. I was also using an inhaler, like asthma sufferers use, for shortness of breath. Now I'll be on oxygen for the rest of my life.

"But what really got me was when I had a COPD (Chronic Obstructive Pulmonary Disease) attack, and I thought: 'No, that's irreplaceable'. My lungs can't ever be repaired and the only way they will remain as strong as they are now is if I don't ever smoke again. No problem! I've given up. I don't even have a craving for them.

"As for alcohol . . . my friend (American speedway promoter) Jason Bonsignore called me at the hospital from New York and asked if I was having withdrawal symptoms. I told him: 'No shaking or cold sweats,' which is really nice. If I really wanted a drink I could get a mate to bring me some in but I don't want it."

Cannabis is a way of life for millions of Americans but the only drugs Kelly is taking today are the prescribed meds that have become part of his daily routine for the past two months. "I've been taking 18 pills every morning," he says. "They're only tiny ones and after eating breakfast I swallow them down with Cranberry and apple juice.

"I'm feeling 140 per cent better than when I first went into hospital. I'm putting on a bit more weight. I'm eating well – breakfast consists of eggs, bacon, toast, pineapple juice, milk and coffee – but I've had to cut down on my salt intake. I've still got my chicken arms, though, so there's some way to go."

To boost his spirits, a 'Kelly Jellyman Moran' group was set up on Facebook, now the biggest global social networking site. Within days it had recruited more than 2,000 members, friends and fans of Kelly, from all over the world who have flooded the site with their prayers and messages of love and support.

The stark evidence of his condition was graphically illustrated in new photos that appeared on Facebook and a couple of short videos, filmed soon after he moved to the hospice and introduced by a rather solemn Bruce Penhall, that have since been viewed by thousands on the YouTube internet website. As Bruce says, the amateur footage was shot so that Kelly could thank everyone who has sent him messages of support.

At the end of the first film, Kelly sits upright on his bed and delivers a warning that he knows he should have heeded himself many years ago: "Don't smoke and don't drink."

Most who have seen the film clips were shocked and moved in equal measure by his frail appearance, which made him look quite a bit older than his 49 years, but there was a positive side, too. The sad sight of this once little pocket dynamo confined to bed triggered a staggering worldwide response that left the patient overwhelmed.

"People have been telling me what's been appearing on my Facebook page . . . yeah, it's humbling, I don't really know how to put it into words but I'm awestruck by it," he says.

One of the first to rush to his stricken mate's bedside was Ron Preston. An appreciative Kelly says: "He's been invaluable and so, too, has Carol Stock, a girl I've known since 1978 when I broke my back at Hackney. When I was first admitted to hospital, she and Ronnie spent alternate nights in my room, curled up on a tiny couch. They were taking messages and writing down notes for me.

Receiving advice from Ivan Mauger, his Hull team-mate, during practice for the 1979 World Final.

A Birmingham Brummie in 1980.

There's no way I could ever repay them for their help and kindness."

It's fair to say that the old fun-loving, live-for-today Kelly had intimate 'encounters' with more than his fair share of female admirers, most of them casual acquaintances probably too numerous and brief to remember. His engaging personality, cherubic looks and fun-loving spirit served as a magnet for many who wanted to be with the irresistible little guy who loved to live life to the full, always on the edge and who was proud to wear hats with the slogans 'Bad Boy Club' and 'Life's a Beach' emblazoned on them.

But Carol, a former West Ham supporter from east London, is very different to the vast majority of women who have fallen under Kelly's spell. He could not have wished for a better friend or kinder, more caring person in times of trouble than her.

As well as visits from the vigilant Preston, Penhall and his brother Shawn, Kelly has been equally delighted to be reunited with a number of other former USA Test stars and American-based riders who, in some cases, have made long journeys to be there for him in person. Our readers will recognise familiar names such as 'Captain America' Bobby Schwartz, Lance King (who flew in from Arizona), Keith Chrisco, Dennis Sigalos, Rick Miller, Brad Oxley and Gary Hicks, plus Dubb Ferrell, Doug Nicol, Bob Tocca and the Faas brothers from States-side. To see this illustrious group together again at the hospital evoked memories of the early 80s, when the Morans were very much at the forefront of the explosion of American talent in British speedway.

When he has not been receiving a steady flow of visitors, his bedside phone has been virtually ringing non-stop, hence his opening quip of 'Kelly's office' when *Backtrack* first called him up.

He says: "I had Ivan Mauger calling me from Aussie and stuff. A couple of days later Egon Müller phoned from Germany. Some friends phoned from South Africa and Australia." Add other speedway names like Andrew Silver, Gene Woods, Mike Bast, Steve Colombo and Reg Fearman to an endless list of concerned callers.

"It makes me realise how fortunate I've been throughout my racing career and my life as a whole," Kelly added with genuine humility.

Kelly's illness has also brought the Moran family together again. Sharon and Tom Moran, who both played a big part in their sons' early speedway development when they ferried them to and from mini bike meetings and then their initial forays on the small tracks of Southern California, divorced when the boys were young and, sadly, Tom died some nine years ago. But as well as Sharon and Shawn, the Morans' stepmother, Beanie, and her three daughters (Kelly and Shawn's stepsisters), Kelly-Shannon, Kasey and Kristy, have also been at Kelly's side.

The biggest surprise of all for Kelly, though, was when he was reunited with his ex-wife Lorna and their 18-year-old daughter Chelsea, who flew in unannounced from their native Yorkshire when they heard how ill he was. Lorna admitted in a video interview she did with Bruce Penhall that she was shocked and saddened to see Kelly the way he is, but she added that it was a trip she was glad to make.

Kelly said: "I thought I was having a dream, under the influence of my meds or something, when they both suddenly walked into my room. It was such a great surprise – I hadn't seen them both for about seven years, although Lorna and I have remained friends and I've kept in touch with the family through her mum, Mrs Brindley, who has sent me pictures and stuff. I tell ya, she used to cook the best Yorkshire roast dinners you could ever wish for!"

Let the party begin . . .

KELLY Michael Moran was born in Huntingdon Beach, California on September 21, 1960 – 14 months ahead of his brother – and he was first introduced to the delights of Yorkshire when he left America behind in March 1978 to join unfashionable Hull.

After three nondescript seasons in the top flight, the Vikings were looking to become a major force and it was very soon after they signed reigning World Champion Ivan Mauger from Exeter that Moran appeared on their radar.

Kelly admitted at the time that he was so thrilled at the prospect of being in the same team as Ivan, whom he'd watched as an awestruck kid on the Kiwi's annual visits to California, that he hadn't even given the much-maligned Boulevard track a second thought. He could hardly have chosen a circuit more unpopular with British-based riders or alien to the small oval tracks he had grown up on at Costa Mesa (where he made his competitive speedway debut in 1977), San Bernardino and Ventura. This was like comparing the set of *Bay Watch* to *Coronation Street* but, as we all quickly learned, nothing ever fazed him.

Despite his chronic illness, Kelly's mind and his sense of humour remain as sharp as ever. Retracing his eventful career also reminded me how articulate and intelligent he can be when he is fully focused and sober.

"I loved that track, although not many visiting riders did," he recalls as if it were yesterday. "Bryan Larner and the fella who prepared the track used to throw 4x2 inch bits of wood onto it and then set

With Bob Dugard during happy days at Eastbourne.

light to it with petrol. The away riders would arrive, see our track in flames and wonder what the heck they were letting themselves in for. But Bryan would just tell them that it wasn't a problem – he was just drying out the surface!

"Hull had long straights and tight corners – a bit like walking down a narrow hallway and turning left into the dining room – but it was great for us home riders."

He wouldn't say the same about Hackney, though. Enjoying a fine first BL season in which his average just exceeded seven points, Kelly's '78 campaign ended abruptly in August when he crashed with teammate Robbie Gardner and suffered multiple injuries. "I celebrated my 18th birthday in hospital," recalls Kelly, who broke three vertebrae and had to have his shattered left leg pinned below the knee.

"I was in there for seven-and-half weeks. I've had so many injuries but that one, the broken back . . . well, when they say you're never gonna walk again.

"I overheard doctors telling this to my dad, so I thought, 'OK, I'm gonna have to prove these guys wrong'. Getting over that injury was a big thing for me."

Although Kelly claimed that he was left in traction too long, causing his left leg to be slightly shorter than the right one, he made a remarkable recovery and within a year had upped his average to almost 8.5 and qualified for his first World Final.

No-one gave America's lone contender much hope but his 11 points earned him fourth place overall and also helped Ivan Mauger to win a record sixth world title.

Again, it's typical Kelly. When asked for his stand-out memories of his World Final debut in front of nearly 100,000 fans at Katowice, rather than recall how brilliantly he rode to keep Mauger's main rivals at bay, he chuckles and says: "I just wanted to get to the party afterwards! Ivan had a van full of champers, although I don't like champers. I just wanted to go and celebrate with a beer. I wasn't thinking about anything else. I thought, 'Man, this is fun, I wish all the crowds were this big'.

"I didn't know how good or bad I was expected to do in Poland. I went out and rode to the best of my ability.

"Then, back in England a couple of days later, my mechanics Bernard Harrison and Keith Rosini told me: 'Oh yeah, you've got a broken valve spring'.

"I said: 'So, what's that? They go: 'Well, you've got four springs and one of them is broken'. They suggested to me that maybe this attributed to my bike picking up traction because it wasn't revving as much as it should have on the slick track.

"And I said: 'So what are you both telling me?' They just looked at each other and said, 'never mind'."

It's fair to say that the featherweight youngster in white leathers left an indelible mark on Hull co-promoter, the late Ian Thomas. Kelly drove Ian to distraction with his off-track antics, including apparent attempts to break the land speed record in a sponsored Lada car, but he was idolised by Vikings fans in his two seasons on Humberside.

After Hull had been pipped to the league championship by Coventry in a memorable finish to 1979 – the closest Kelly ever came to winning major domestic team honours – and the Hull hierarchy tired of the ill-disciplined American's transgressions away from the track, he looked like staying home in California in 1980. Eliminated from the World Championship in the qualifier held at Anaheim at the end of '79, he didn't return to England until June '80, when he moved to Birmingham.

Although he'd missed the revival of the thrilling England v USA Test series held earlier that spring, he immediately brought more colour and spice to a multi-national Brummies team, where he gave solid support to Steve Bastable and finished his half season at the old Perry Barr with an average of around eight points.

"I dealt with Jeff May, the co-promoter, and our team manager was John Harrhy," says Kelly. "I wasn't there that long but I really liked the Perry Barr track."

Compared to Hull, the tight turns at Birmingham were much more like speedway California-style, as were those at his next destination – Eastbourne's Arlington raceway, where he replaced Wimbledon-bound Kai Niemi and spent the 1981 and '82 seasons. Although Kelly couldn't quite dislodge Gordon Kennett as Eagles' long-standing No.1, his final CMAs of 9.28 and 9.62 underlined his continuing progress towards the top for club and country.

Putting on a show

IN '81, he began to establish himself in the American Test side and played a starring role in the Yanks' 3-2 series victory in '82, the year of his second World Final appearance. The natural exuberance and flamboyance of the Americans wasn't everyone's cup of tea but their camaraderie was as infectious as it was effective.

One of my abiding memories is watching a Swindon Test match from the pits and seeing the Moran brothers, seemingly linked by an invisible umbilical cord, flat out and hanging off their Weslake machines as they hurtled round the third/fourth bends on one wheel while waving and gesturing to the crowd. It was audacious, and maybe looked a bit flash to the Brits, but you had to admire their sense of showmanship that made them so popular – even among many British fans.

"I was waving to the boys in the pits – not taking the mickey out of anyone or trying to discourage the English riders or supporters," explained Kelly, anxious that his and Shawn's extrovert actions wouldn't be misconstrued.

"I think there was a picture in your paper *(Speedway Mail)* around that time showing me sticking my right leg out during a qualifying round at White City. The caption read: 'Spot the Ball competition' – but I was actually pointing my leg at my brother and Cookie (John Cook, another natural showman) who were sat on top of a van parked in the pits."

Of all the Americans who illuminated the BL scene in the first half of the 80s, none were as universally popular as the ever-friendly Morans, who always made time for their supporters. As you would expect from a couple of very lively descendants from the Dublin area of the Irish Republic (as young kids, Kelly and Shawn both raced in green and white leathers carrying the shamrock emblem), they liked to enjoy the craic at every opportunity.

Even Kenny Carter, reckoned to be the biggest Yank-hater of all and Penhall's nemesis, liked Kelly. So much so, he named his daughter, Kelly-Marie, after his American buddy.

Gravity-defying moment from the 1982 World Final practice at the LA Coliseum.

"Shawn said that he didn't get along with Kenny as well as I did but he was a very dear friend of mine, on and mainly off the track. We had a blast together, man. I used to wind him up about Bruce and he'd say, 'yeah, you reckon?' and I'd say to him: 'Yeah, this is what you gotta do to him'. He thought it was funny and we both laughed about it."

Another England star, Michael Lee, also became a good friend of Kelly's. Lee quickly empathised with Kelly and other American riders, who were similar in age and outlook to him, more than the comparatively strait-laced members of his England team.

"Michael was more easy-going, whereas Kenny and the people around him made speedway more into a business, which was a smart thing to do," continues Kelly. "Kenny had that Yank-style motorhome and stuff. He was a terrific rider but away from the track, me and him would talk about anything but racing.

"Away from the track, Michael was still Michael. When he dropped a point it wasn't the end of the world for him. Why go and throw your helmet? It's not your helmet's fault!

"Gosh, Michael was one of the best, that's for sure. He was consistently good – not just in England but also on the continent. He had a cool demeanour and he still does to this day."

Bruce Penhall's victory in the 1982 World Final, the controversy surrounding his bitter clash with Kenny Carter and his dramatic sudden exit from speedway, announced on the podium just minutes after retaining the title at the LA Coliseum, largely overshadowed the fact that Kelly had again finished fourth with 11 points on the biggest night of all. Maybe his time would come?

Self-inflicted damage

WITH Bruce heading for Hollywood, it was anticipated that Dennis Sigalos – third behind Penhall and Les Collins in LA – and Kelly would vie to become the next US No.1 on the world stage and perhaps go all the way to the top. A bad ankle injury soon put an end to Siggy's hopes but Kelly's ultimate decline as a genuine title contender was inevitably self-inflicted.

In his second season with Eastbourne, Kelly fell foul of the authorities and his promoter Bob Dugard when he missed a meeting after cancelling his original booking on a flight back from the States. On another occasion he turned up at Eastbourne unfit to ride. The Wimbledon team and management were so convinced that Kelly was attempting to race while under the influence of alcohol that they demanded he be examined by the track doctor. Kelly had fallen off at the first bend in each of his first two rides against the Dons . . . but then went out again and won his next race, as if to prove his accusers wrong.

But when Eastbourne visited Belle Vue later that season, Kelly was barred from competing after the track doctor ruled him unfit to ride. He was also fined by the Control Board.

Dugard couldn't have done any more to accommodate his biggest crowd-puller. Much as Manchester United boss Matt Busby gently cajoled wayward football genius George Best in the late 60s, Dugard put an arm round Kelly's shoulder, tried his best to curb his star's worst excesses, indulged him more than a few times when he did get out of control and disciplined him when his tolerance level had been pushed to breaking point. But Best, who died an alcoholic, never changed and neither would Kelly Moran.

Bob and his wife Margaret even tried to take care of Kelly's financial affairs, by paying his earnings directly into his bank account, but it never stayed there long. As fast as they were paying it in, he was at the cashier's window drawing it out. There was fun to be had, some fast living to be done and no time to waste on trivial issues like saving for a rainy day. Kelly (and Shawn) should now be enjoying their post-racing lives in nice, big houses paid for by their speedway earnings, but it's not to be.

Kelly has no hesitation in describing his two years with Eastbourne as the happiest of his British career – and not just because of the enjoyment he had while living at the Dugards' home in Brighton. "It was definitely my best time in England," he confirms. "Being an ex-rider, Bobby Dugard knows the ins and outs and what it's like for a rider. I still have the utmost respect for him."

Kelly is also now regretful about the manner in which he left Eastbourne. He decided to remain in the States for the 1983 season and wouldn't race in the BL again for another three years.

"There was no fall-out with Bob and at first I had every intention of going back to Eastbourne. What happened was, I was racing in a meeting at Long Beach and I blurted out that I wasn't going back to England, saying I'd be racing in America the following year instead. Next thing you know, it got picked up in England and I thought: 'Oh boy, I should have called Bob and told him first, explained everything to him and apologised'. It was my really big mess up."

West coast wonder

THE drastic decision to stay home was not taken lightly, though, and it was the prelude to the most rewarding period in Kelly's career on the West Coast. With Penhall gone, he was the most highest ranked American in the sport at the start of 1983. The '82 season had also seen him collect his first World Team Cup winners' medal after contributing 10 points in his country's maiden WTC victory at London White City.

He had led the Americans' World Team challenge with a maximum in the first round at King's Lynn (where he was only beaten by Peter Collins in a thrilling run-off to decide the meeting winners), followed it with 10 points in their Inter-Continental qualifier win at Vojens and then completed a fine campaign by equalling top scorer Penhall's 10-point haul in the final.

"From 1983 I was sponsored by STP, Oakley Goggles and Arai Helmets, so I was making good money even when I wasn't on the track," said Kelly. "Once I became US National Champion that year and I was still at home to defend the title, my pay cheques were doubling. And because I was very well sponsored, I wasn't paying for anything.

"Plus the crowds in California back then were still good – anything from 6,000 to 9,000. What do

No wonder Kelly preferred to stay home in California during the mid-80s.

they get at Costa Mesa now – 1,200 maybe?

"Heck, it was a good time for me. And look at the weather I had to deal with back home . . . poor Kelly!" The sarcasm is accompanied by a cheeky, knowing smile that tells you he had a blast back home, where his natural sense of fun and showmanship endeared him to fans who, first and foremost, went to the speedway to be entertained, not fill in programmes and fret about averages and points limits.

"Racing all the time in California in the mid-80s affected me, though, when I rode in a World Championship meeting in Europe. You didn't have to worry about sharpness at a place like Costa Mesa because I could always pass riders from the back there. I couldn't give anything away to the top guys in the World Championship events."

Even so, Kelly still managed to qualify for his third, and last, individual World Final at Gothenburg in 1984. And just as he had in both 1979 and '82, he finished fourth in the scorechart with another tally of 11 points. It wasn't a bad return for a rider who, according to Barry Briggs, his advisor in the Ullevi pits, wasn't as fully focused as he should have been on winning the meeting. Instead, it was another American, Cradley Heath's Lance King, who joined new champion Erik Gundersen and his Danish rival Hans Nielsen in the top three.

Kelly remains typically philosophical about finishing one place off the medals in all three of his World Finals.

"Stuff like that happens, you know? I was on my way to a fourth World Final until my motor seized up and Gert Handberg hit me up the back over in Germany (1991), but what's meant to be is meant to be. That's especially true when I think about what I've gone through in the past few weeks. Whatever the big guy upstairs has got planned, no-one's gonna change it."

Four times World No.1 Barry Briggs is less inclined to believe that the destiny of the sport's biggest prize is decided by fate alone. "I'd talk to Kelly and he'd listen – and I never doubted his talent and ability for a moment. But then the next minute I'd turn around and he'd be talking to his brother or somebody else in the pits instead of worrying about himself and what he needed to do," said a frustrated Briggo.

Bob Dugard had his many frustrations too but, much to Kelly's relief, his former boss was again ready to forgive him.

"When I returned to England for a Test match or something, I met up with Bobby again. I know that look in Mr Dugard's eyes and I thought, 'I have it coming, to me, no problem'. But he just put out his hand and said: 'Hello, Mr Moran' – and with his other hand he offered me a cigarette. To those of us who know him well, that just shows what a gentleman Bob can be. I love him.

"I've recently read about him maybe wanting to pull out of Eastbourne. If he's reading this, one thing I'd like to say to him is this: 'Bob Dugard . . . if you retire or step back from Eastbourne Speedway, I'm gonna come over there and you'll have to be my carer for the rest of my life. That means an enema once a week!" The thought of it makes Kelly burst into laughter again.

Then, just as quickly, he puts on a more serious face and offers up an interesting analogy: "If Bob ever left Eastbourne Speedway, it would be like Colonel Sanders pulling out of KFC. It couldn't possibly be a success without him."

Brothers reunited

KELLY ended his self-imposed British exile at the start of 1986. He recalled: "I won two National championships in three years but after I broke six bones in seven months in '85, I thought: 'Mmmm . . . maybe I'll talk to our kid about riding for his club at Sheffield'.

"He spoke to (promoter) Maurice Ducker and the next thing you know, I'm back in England riding for Sheffield. Although I knew all the tracks from before, it felt like I had to learn to ride them all over again. There were also new motors, like Goddens and GMs, coming on the scene by then, so I had to get used to them too."

Shawn had replaced Kelly at Hull in 1980, his first season in England which ended with a move to Sheffield after he too fell out with the Vikings management, and though they were paired together for their country, there was something special about seeing them line up together in Tigers' colours.

"We'd often ridden as a pair in the Test matches and, years before that, when we rode mini bikes as kids, so it was just like old times when we were partnered together for Sheffield," says Kelly.

"Basically, 'Shooey' preferred the inside line while I was happy to stay on the outside, or go wherever I needed to. We seldom switched race lines when we rode together and if we did, it was to catch somebody out. It sounds big-headed but it worked in our favour and because of the understanding we had on track, I think we only messed up about twice in 100 times."

After Ducker pulled out of Sheffield and the Tigers closed temporarily shortly before the start of the '89 season, the brothers moved across the Pennines to Belle Vue, where they both remained popular with Aces' fans for the next four seasons. The only losers in this were their adoring fans at Sheffield. Oh, and the Owlerton stadium owners who saw their bar takings plummet.

Some of the parties Shawn and Kelly threw at their almost adjoining houses in the High Green region, just outside the steel city, are the stuff of legend – for those who can remember them. The now demolished Pinegrove Country Club (its demise had nothing to do with the Morans!), a once popular nightclub-cum sports bar near Sheffield, was a regular haunt of the brothers, who became popular local celebrities.

Kelly's first season at Belle Vue, in 1989, got off to a bad start when he broke his finger in Shawn's testimonial meeting at Kirky Lane. It went much better the following year, when he achieved a small piece of family history that he never quite managed at Sheffield – by beating Shawn to top spot in the team averages with figures a shade under 8.5.

He also proved he was far from a spent force on the international stage with an inspirational match-

Fast and fair battle with Ipswich's Jeremy Doncaster at Sheffield in 1987.

Always game for a laugh but too many cigarettes took their toll.

winning performance in the 1990 World Team Cup Final at Pardubice in the Czech Republic. After a point-less first outing, he won all of his remaining four races to lead the USA to a three-point victory over England. It was the greatest of many successful and proud days for him in the star-spangled racejacket.

Another favourite memory is the astonishing balance and throttle control Kelly showed in a compelling, wheel-to-wheel battle with Gordon Kennett in atrociously wet conditions during the WTC qualifier at Reading in 1979. He couldn't quite pull it off in a run-off against Hans Nielsen to decide the World Pairs title at Pocking, Germany in 1986 after he and Sam Ermolenko had tied with the Danes, Nielsen and Erik Gundersen.

Despite never having attained a final double figure average for any of his six clubs, Kelly had the character and ability to rise to the big occasion and he could handle high pressure situations with ease. Three fourth place finishes in the World Final, two World Team Cup gold medals, a silver in the Pairs . . . he didn't do too badly for a 'crazy kid' who loved to fool around and didn't appear to take anything too seriously.

But you have to look beyond cold, hard statistics to measure the true value of Kelly to his teams. He would undoubtedly have recorded higher averages and scored many more points in his career if he hadn't always approached each race with the same selfless attitude that characterised his career. He'd readily give up the best gate positions to his less accomplished race partner and be prepared to sacrifice his own points return in an effort to team-ride his mate home. For him, the team always came first.

Even in his final British season and at the age of almost 32, Kelly played his part for his country and actually captained the USA team that defeated England at Swindon in September to complete a 3-0 series whitewash in 1992.

By then he had joined struggling Swindon on loan from Belle Vue – a surprise early-season move that paved the way for Shawn to end his self-imposed retirement and return to the Manchester club in place of his brother. John Perrin, the outspoken Aces boss, had his moments with both Morans but he kept re-signing them year after year because of their points-scoring ability and the entertainment factor.

The promoters on America's East Coast must have recognised the same qualities in Kelly when they invited him to end his near 12-year retirement from racing and compete on tracks in upstate New York in 2004. A week after an improving Kelly had won the main event at Owego, he was also looking good in a meeting at the Action Park track when he suffered the injury that would finally end his career.

He explained: "I was coming out of turn two when the bike lifted and came down on my leg. The frame, which I later found out had been re-welded, snapped again and the weight of the bike broke my ankle. You should never give a rider a re-welded frame to use," he sighed.

No-one was more disappointed for Kelly and the painful manner in which his career ended than his biggest fan. Yes, the ever-loyal Carol Stock had flown from London to NY especially to see what became her hero's last speedway race.

For a true racer such as Kelly, a race was never over until the check flag came down, which is why he now bemoans the slick conditions that blight too many meetings he watches on television these days. A fan of the traditional one-off World Final, he says: "With most GPs I saw last year it was a case of 'gate and go' – it's ridiculous and a rip-off for the fans. They're paying good money, especially the way the world economy is now. I can see why people would rather stay at home and watch it on telly – you're closer to your refrigerator for a start!"

Given his own spectacular, attacking riding style, it won't surprise anyone to know who Kelly enjoys watching the most of the current stars.

"I love watching that Russian kid (Emil Sayfutdinov) on telly. As long as he stays away from injuries, he's gonna be a big star of the future. Man, I'd like to be able to do some laps with him, it would be fun.

"I don't know anything about England's new boy for 2010, Tai Woffinden, but I knew his dad, Rob, and was really sorry to hear that he passed away. Shawn knew him since his early days at Sheffield. At least he lived long enough to fulfil his last wish of making it past Christmas."

The party's over

WHICH brings us back to his own immediate battle to regain a level of health that will at least prolong his life even though the long-term damage to his lungs and liver appears irreversible.

When I phoned Kelly again on March 10, roughly a month after our first chat, he was cheerfully looking forward to leaving the Palm Springs Health Care Center in the desert city of Palm Springs,

'Bad Boys' Kelly and Shawn before a 1988 Test match at Bradford.

where he'd been transferred on February 25, and moving into another assisted-living facility in suburban Orange County – not far from where he first wowed US speedway fans as Rookie of the Year in 1977.

"Bobby Schwartz and a few others have arranged this move for me – it's a team effort really – and it means I'll be much closer to my family and friends, who won't have as far to travel to see me.

"I realise it's going to be a hard road ahead for me. I can't walk far without getting out of breath and I'll have to carry oxygen with me if I go out anywhere.

A guy called Frank Ray Parker has been in touch to say that he's going to donate me a three-wheel scooter that I hope to get about on. And no, I won't be attempting to do anything silly on it, like pull wheelies or drive it to the pub!"

Those carefree days of fun and recklessness are now well and truly behind him. They have to be if he is to have any quality of life in the future. Sadly, he can't turn back time but admits he would if he could.

"With the attitude I have now, oh yes, oh yes . . . there would have been no parties and stuff. But then again, who knows if I'd have been the same Jelly Man? I think the answer to that is a resounding 'no'. Gee, I'm not too good with hindsight."

What Kelly is now clear about, however, is that his past lifestyle brought him to this crisis point. "I've had plenty of time lately to reflect on everything I've done – hey, I've got 35 years to catch up on!"

Easy now, Kelly. Trying to rewind your whole life story, re-living the escapades, dramas and scrapes you got yourself into, would stretch anyone's nerves to breaking point! He should certainly skip that day, in 1986, when only the quick thinking and reactions of Chris Morton saved him from probable death after he'd slipped and his left arm went crashing through a plate glass window in a Polish hotel, where they were staying after the Edward Jancarz Farewell meeting.

With blood pouring from Kelly's severed artery, Mort quickly applied a tourniquet to avert disaster, although lucky Kelly still had to undergo microsurgery to repair damaged nerves and tendons when

Chucking it sideways at Belle Vue, ahead of Coventry's Tommy Knudsen in 1991.

His last individual victory in Britain, Kelly receiving the Peter Craven Memorial Trophy from Brenda Craven in 1991.

Kelly and wife Lorna at their daughter Chelsea's christening in 1991.

he returned to England.

Kelly struggles to recall that narrow escape but admits: "I was partying enough for two or three people some nights and still able to race the next day. My head and my body didn't like it but I still got on with the job. I loved life and was full of testosterone. Yeah, I did some silly things but it was fun at the time. I wasn't looking to the future, only the then and there. That's hindsight.

"I would always accept any open meeting bookings in London because it meant I could go to the Hard Rock Cafe (in Piccadilly) after meetings at Wimbledon or Hackney for proper Yank-style burgers, mustard and lagers.

"I had a great time, man, and by the look of what's been written on Facebook, it looks like a lot of other people had a good time with me as well!

"I loved racing bikes, I got to fly round the world and I got paid for it, so what a great job to have had.

"You know, I don't miss those partying days now. Heck, I'm done. I'm very lucky to have survived all the stuff I've been through and I'm not going to live my life so loosely in the future. I see things from a different perspective now.

"The big guy up there gave me a second chance and I am not going to mess up," he added, striking an uncharacteristically serious tone.

Our conversation was just about over and after exchanging best wishes, he suddenly put aside his own problems to ask: "Hey, by the way, between you, me and the operator, Alfie Weedon is still around . . . isn't he?"

He sounded somewhat relieved when I confirmed that although speedway's veteran snapper hasn't been in the best of health in recent years, Alf was still looking forward to his 90th birthday in July. "Well, would you please pass on our regards to him from Shawn and me," he added, before gathering up his belongings and moving out of his 'office'.

C'YA!

KELLY MORAN'S long battle with illness finally ended on April 4, 2010, when he passed away peacefully in his native California. But as Tony McDonald – the last journalist to interview Moran – reports, the colourful and lovable American didn't die in vain...

WE all have our own different memories of Kelly Moran – incredibly talented and thrilling speedway racer, born showmen and irrepressible party animal all rolled into one.

We've seen him at his brilliant best and his exasperating worst.

But we always forgave him his over-indulgencies and the occasional 'fun' things he did that weren't actually funny because . . . well, he was Kelly Moran. A unique character.

It was impossible to change him and, God knows, enough people have tried.

When the sad news that Kelly was entering his final hours filtered through from Southern California on Easter Sunday, April 4, few who knew him best and who were aware of how serious his condition had become were shocked by his impending departure from our world. For all the renewed hope of his rehabilitation in various hospitals and care homes since the turn of the year, he was on borrowed time.

One of the last pictures of Kelly. He hoped others would learn the lessons of his fatal excesses.

Thirty-odd years of smoking and hard-drinking had damaged his lungs and liver beyond repair. The doctors and nurses who treated him since he was rushed into hospital in January did their best but the horse had already bolted and the stable door almost closed.

Deep down, despite brief hopes of getting himself well enough to work at Keith Chrisco's car racing engineering business, Kelly knew it, too.

When people talk about Kelly and reflect on his carefree lifestyle, words such as 'waste' and 'regret' inevitable re-surface. When he spoke to us from his hospital bed in February and March, for the final interview he gave in the last issue of *Backtrack*, I was even a little surprised to hear him say that he really did regret not having looked after his body over the years. It was a refreshing admission by Kelly and one that should also serve as a stark warning to young speedway riders of today who might be led off the straight and narrow.

But as Kelly himself then pointed out just as soon as he uttered those remorseful words: "Had I lived my life differently, I wouldn't have been the same Jelly Man."

The common notion that we like our heroes to act as role models is an unreasonable burden we like to apply to them often out of pure selfishness. There was never anything sly or underhand about Kelly Moran – he always did what it said on the tin. And many of us loved him all the more for it.

He should have had much more to show for all the enjoyment he provided and the success he achieved. But he didn't die in vain. By extending his life an extra few laps, at least it gave him the chance to say his proper 'goodbyes' or, as he put it: "C'ya, C'ya, Cya!"

He had just enough time to properly thank the people who cared most for him in his darkest hours of need – the likes of Ron Preston, the ever-loyal Carol Stock, who was by Kelly's side when he drew his last breath at 11.40am on that Easter Sunday (7.40pm BST), and former Team USA skipper Bobby Schwartz, who arranged the hospice facility at Palm Desert where Kelly stayed to the end.

And by refusing to hide away and bravely facing up to the video cameras, he was able to express his sincere appreciation to the thousands of fans, many of them total strangers to him, who have been touched by his fighting qualities via his appearances on YouTube and Facebook. Within days, the Facebook group created and managed by Mike Donaldson became the platform for a non-stop outpouring of 'get-well' messages from all over the globe as 2,000-plus members reached out to their computer keyboards and typed the words they prayed would help to keep the Jelly Man going. Although they weren't enough to save him, he died knowing just how much people loved him and that his incredible skills aboard a speedway bike had enriched the lives of so many all round the world.

And let's not forget what he did achieve. Three individual World Final appearances (11 points and fourth place each time), two World Team Cup gold medals and two treasured victories in the US National Championship, plus innumerable other lesser highlights that gave him pleasure and enabled him to have the money and magnetism to live his life just the way he wanted to.

So not bad for a Californian kid who, according to some, wasted his life. There are countless riders who would love to have 'wasted' their life in the same way!

Not that winning and accumulating silverware was ever his be all and end all. Can we honestly believe that Kelly had any less pleasure from his speedway career than, say, Ivan Mauger or Bruce Penhall?

Though shocked and saddened at how the diminutive body of this once vibrant teenager had aged to that of a man looking way beyond his true 49 years, his supporters also got to experience the good that Kelly did before he was ready to pass the chequered flag for the last time.

Apart from the countless great memories he left us, those spectacular, gravity-defying on-track manoeuvres that delighted thousands from Costa Mesa to Katowice, San Bernardino to Sheffield, his greatest legacy will be the poignant message he asked to be read out and published following his passing.

Here we repeat his last words:

Kelly's final words

"DURING the time that I've been at JFK Hospital, a Facebook page was created for me that allowed my fans, family and fellow racers to post comments and pictures and videos about me and my racing career. The response has been overwhelming to me, and at times a burden with all the phone calls.

"The one message that my page has proven and given me is that we CAN put down our Guns and Swords and get along. When Ivan called me, he said that because of my page, he's now talking to people he never gave a second look to in the pits at his races back then. And because of my page, there are riders from all over the world creating their own Facebook names and writing really neat stuff to me, and re-connecting with other riders all over the world. I'm humbled that this has happened, it's like the Lord made me sick so this could happen.

"My wish, after I'm gone, is that they will continue to communicate and expand on it. In other words, I want more riders and their families to talk to each other. I don't care if it's on my page or not. But if Ivan can talk to people he used to dislike, then don't you think we should follow his lead?

"In the words of that guy during the LA Riots . . . can't we just all get along? I'm especially appreciative that my boys, from the US Team, have all gotten back together.

"Thank you for all the great messages, I love all of you!
"C'ya C'ya C'ya!

"(Oh yeah, one more thing . . . Don't Smoke and Don't Drink!)."

BRIEF ENCOUNTERS WITH... Wayne Forrest

How did your move to the UK come about?

During the 1972 season I was approached by the then King's Lynn rider Bob Humphreys to see if I was interested in going to the UK to ride there. Several telephone calls were made to Cyril Crane regarding me going to Lynn for the 1973 season. Cyril had a trip organised to Australia and during that time I met with him after a meeting at the Sydney Showground, where arrangements were made for me to join the Stars.

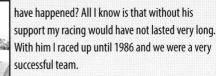

Which clubs did you ride for in the UK?

King's Lynn (1973) in British League Division One and second division Crewe (1973 and 1974).

What was your first impression of the UK?

Cold! I could not believe how such a small country had such densely populated areas and after short drives I was in a country setting. Also, how green the countryside looked. And I couldn't believe how many speedway meetings there were. Basically, every night there was a meeting somewhere. That was something quite different from Sydney, where meetings were generally at Newcastle on Friday nights, Sydney Showground/Liverpool City Raceway on Saturdays and Kembla Grange every second Sunday.

Did you have an English 'dad' or did you have to fend for yourself?

No, I didn't have an 'English dad'. My father left my mother when I was approximately seven-years-old. I have always thought how much easier it would have been for me if I did have a father to support and help me during my speedway career. This is something I have always dwelled over. I had to do it all alone, which at times was very difficult. I found out later in life that my father was at meetings when I rode in Sydney but he never tried to contact me to help or guide me.

Later in my career I had a good friend, John Liestins, who became my mechanic/driver and advisor. John would spend hours on my bikes and not miss one meeting. If only I'd had John at the beginning of my career, who knows what could

have happened? All I know is that without his support my racing would have not lasted very long. With him I raced up until 1986 and we were a very successful team.

Any regrets?

I think everybody has some regrets in life. My speedway regrets? I should have spent many more seasons racing in the UK and had the belief that I was as good as any rider going around. I always had some disbelief in my own ability.

I proved I was good enough when I used to ride in Australia. Every year after I decided not to return to the UK, that was my choice.

Peter White started a tour to Queensland and the Northern Territory with the stay-at-home NSW riders. I did many of those tours and was very successful and at times unbeatable.

I had many offers to return to the UK with several different clubs but declined each offer. Why? I can't answer the question even now.

What have you done since speedway?

Since retiring from speedway I have had a family – two daughters, Kischa, now 30, and Kara, who is 24. I worked at Motorcycle Accessories for many years up until 1986. I took up a job as a correctional officer working at Long Bay Gaol in Sydney, a position I still hold.

I have had very little to do with speedway since retiring apart from a short stint as a referee. I only attended minimal meetings. It was just too hard – I got the urge at every meeting to try and give it a go again but with age and the old weight gain, that was just not possible. I still occasionally throw my leg over a speedway bike whenever I get the opportunity but that is very seldom.

I would love to have a ride on the modern speedway bikes, which I believe are so much better.

Speedway was very kind to me. I made some very good friends and with modern technology, I'm making contact with people from my past more often.

MARTIN
YEATES

MARTIN Yeates went through the whole of his 16-year speedway career without suffering a single broken bone.

And yet the career of the man more deserving of the moniker of Mr. Weymouth Speedway than any other nearly came to a very abrupt, early end in 1974 when he nearly drowned in a bizarre incident on the Eastbourne centre green.

Yeates explained to *Backtrack:* "There was a well on the centre green at Eastbourne from which they used to water the track.

"It was the last meeting of the season and there were all the usual high jinks of that period, messing about with flour bombs and all that stuff. The cover came off the well and the next thing I knew I was thrown into it as a prank.

"These were the days before kevlars, so I was wearing heavy duty leathers. And not only that, I was also unable to swim!

"I don't think it was until I bobbed up for the second or third time that my team-mates realised that I was in serious trouble and got me out.

Martin in his first season, at Eastbourne in 1974.

"It was actually one of the scariest things that ever happened to me."

His speedway career had first kicked off a couple of years earlier, in 1972.

Martin recalls: "I was riding in a grass-track meeting and Brian Collins, who rode for Poole, was there. He saw me in action and suggested I go along to Matchams Park, which was the Poole training track near Ringwood.

"I'd seen meetings at both Poole and Swindon as a kid but I'd never really considered turning my hand to speedway – I guess I considered it to be a bit out of my league.

"I didn't have a speedway bike, so I went along to Matchams Park and rode around there on my grass-track bike – and it all went from there.

"I signed a junior contract at Poole. Charles Knott was running the speedway at the time, while his brother Jim ran the training schools. The tutor at Matchams was Mike Broadbank.

"In those days, there were decent opportunities. Not only was there a training track where you could practice all day, but, time permitting, they also fitted in a few junior races at Wimborne Road on a Wednesday night."

The 18-year-old Yeates made his British League debut for Pirates in 1972, failing to score in three appearances.

"To be honest, I was just making the numbers up," he admits. "I was quite outclassed. I was drafted in when a rider didn't turn up.

"I also started to go up to Stoke for second-halves, and they gave me a few second division outings in 1973.

"I went to Eastbourne the following year and things really started to click into place. But they had around nine or 10 riders competing for seven team places. It seemed to be that whoever complained the most got into the team the following week!"

Yeates took a whole second off the Arlington track record on May 19, 1974, while riding in the No.7 reserve berth.

He exclaims: "I was pretty chuffed about that. I thought it would guarantee me a regular team place but it wasn't as simple as that. From what I recall, I don't think they were going to use me the following week.

"I remember there were fans outside with banners, who refused to come in, until I was put back in the team!"

Salisbury-based Yeates began his association with Weymouth in 1975. He ended the season as the club's No.1 with an 8.31 average from 40 official matches. He says: "It was nice signing for Weymouth. Not only did I have a regular team place, it was local. Harry Davis (John's father) was the Weymouth promoter at the time. John became a good friend of mine, which he still is today."

Weymouth Wizards of 1976. Left to right: Garry May, Chris Robins, Tim Bungay, Derek Cook, Martin Yeates, Trevor Charley, Ricky Owen and Roger Stratton, with Vic Harding on the bike and Lew Coffin (coach) kneeling.

Martin (left) with Neil Middleditch and Christer Sjosten while doubling-up with BL Poole in 1976.

In 1977, Yeates moved to Oxford, where he enjoyed a terrific season, establishing himself as one of the best three riders in the National League, alongside Tom Owen and Colin Richardson.

He recalls: "That was a cracking year for me. Everything dropped into place and was just right. I was full of confidence. From memory, I scored 16 maximums that year. I also did very well in some individual meetings and ended the season as Silver Helmet holder. I enjoyed my year at Oxford."

As well as averaging 10.54 for Cheetahs, he won the Warners Grand National at Hackney and finished runner-up in the National League Riders' Championship. He would finish on the NLRC rostrum a record four times between 1977 and 1984, with two second places and a couple of thirds.

He moved up to the British League with Poole in 1978 and '79. Despite posting an average of exactly 6.00 in '78, he admits: "Those two years were pretty tough going at times.

"I had that great year in the National League in 1977, finishing third in the averages, but suddenly I was brought down to earth.

"I was back at the bottom of the ladder. It was like that for a lot of riders – it was so hard to break through in the British League. There were so many good British riders about in those days.

"When the offer came to rejoin Weymouth in the National League in 1980, I took it.

"There was sometimes a bit of friendly banter from one or two members of the press, who said I should be riding in the British League. But I could never quite see why, because I could ride in National League and also have BL rides as a No. 8 for Poole or Swindon, or whoever.

"I remember one season I did 115 meetings – all in the UK. Not like today, with riders gallivanting all over the continent. Most clubs had at least one open meeting and if you were going well, you were invited to those.

"I once did 15 meetings in 16 days and in the middle of that, my first child was born. I finished one meeting, went to the hospital to see the birth . . . and then went home to wash the bike for my next meeting!"

144

He continues: "When I returned to Weymouth in 1980, they had a new promoter in the shape of Mervyn Stewkesbury – a local businessman who had saved the club. Mervyn would be the first to admit that he knew absolutely nothing about speedway when he came in but he soon learnt. He ran a very professional ship and it wasn't long before we ended up with a highly competitive team."

One rider who started to make rapid strides through the Weymouth ranks was Simon Wigg, who was already making a name for himself in grass-track circles but was a speedway novice when he came into the 1980 Wildcats team.

Martin says: "You always suspected that Simon would make it. He was so enthusiastic and determined. If he went out and ran a third or fourth, he'd come back to the pits and ask me: 'What did I do wrong, because I was trying so hard?'

"And he would listen and digest and probably end up winning his next race.

"He eventually took the No.1 jacket off me but there was a friendly rivalry between us. His enthusiasm was infectious. We were good mates."

When the dual spearhead of Yeates and Wigg were joined by mid-season acquisition Les Rumsey in 1981, Wildcats stormed to second place in the National League.

Says Martin: "It's an old cliché but we had a great team spirit and it rubbed off and produced success."

In flying form for Oxford Cheetahs in 1977.

In his second spell with Weymouth, leading in a 4TT at Arena-Essex.

Martin riding for Swindon at British League level.

Silverware wasn't far away – and it came at the 1982 National League Pairs at Swindon. It was the only NL trophy not won by the powerhouse Newcastle side that season.

"Simon and I had been away racing somewhere and only made the meeting in the nick of time," Martin reveals. "We went through the whole meeting unbeaten, finishing first and second in each of our races – it was the first time the meeting had ever been won in that fashion."

A year later, this time accompanied by a young Simon Cross, Yeates retained the trophy almost single-handed. In the event of a shared race, the tie would be settled on which pair provided the heat winner. Cross finished last in the semi-final and final but that proved immaterial because Yeates won both races.

"That was at Belle Vue," he recalls. "It was a fantastic track. although I always seemed to struggle around there. But on that evening, it all clicked into place.

"I nearly won the Pairs for a third time, in 1985. By then, they had adopted the 4-3-2-0 scoring system and myself and Stan Bear were sat in second and third in the final. But there was an incident on the final bend and Stan was excluded."

Weymouth lost out in the final of the 1983 National League KO Cup by a single point to Exeter, with Yeates again boasting an average in excess of 10 points for the Wildcats.

It tempted him to move up to the British League for a second time, in 1984, with Swindon.

Martin admits: "It just didn't work out. I actually signed for the Robins on a full contract. But to be honest, it was a mistake.

"Mervyn was quite keen to have me back at Weymouth he had a clause in the contract to reclaim me if the balance of the transfer wasn't paid. I ended up rejoining Weymouth a couple of months into the season."

No sooner had Yeates returned to Radipole Lane than he was creating history – by becoming the first National League rider to progress beyond the British Final and into the international stages of the World Championship.

He used his major asset to his advantage – his ability to be quick from the tapes.

"Much earlier in my career, I'd come to the conclusion that being able to get out of the starts was a huge advantage. It's hard work coming from behind. Not everyone can do what Peter Collins was doing while I was riding, or what Darcy Ward does at Poole now. Nobody actually told me how to gate – I just worked on it myself and sussed out a technique. It earned me the nickname 'Trapper' at Poole. Even these days, when I go to watch meetings at Poole, people there still call me Trapper.

"The 1984 British Final at Coventry was very wet. I can't say that I really enjoyed a wet track but some of the riders were getting really upset about it. There was a right old hoo-hah going on down in the pits.

"Eventually the meeting went ahead and I was popping out of the starts, as usual, and that did it for me. I finished joint fourth and qualified for the Overseas Final.

"Kenny Carter won the meeting with a broken leg – they were lifting him onto the bike for each race. I actually beat him. He only dropped two points and one of them was to me.

"I didn't really get involved in the discussions between the riders. Most of them were England team-mates, so I didn't think they'd take much notice of me, so I just concentrated on myself."

It was a single-minded attitude that paid off. Yeates progressed while the likes of World Pairs champions Peter Collins and Chris Morton failed to make the cut.

Yeates continues: "I then rode in the Overseas Final at Belle Vue. I think I made the gate in just about every race but then we'd hit the back straight and two riders would fly past me.

"Don Godden lent me an engine for that meeting but I still didn't have the top end speed required for Hyde Road. I was sat on the back mudguard, riding flat out, but it still wasn't enough.

"I never spent an awful lot on machinery. You could get away with it in those days. We added things to the engine, such as piston rings, to make it last another four meetings."

Weymouth Speedway came to a sudden halt at the end of the 1984 season, with the Radipole Lane venue sold for redevelopment.

Martin says: "That was a big shock, I'd spent a lot of years riding for Weymouth. By that time, I had a great working relationship with Mervyn Stewkesbury and his business partner, Pete Ansell.

"It was ironic that exactly the same winter, Poole Speedway went into liquidation, so Mervyn moved in there, pretty much lock, stock and barrel. We were even called Poole Wildcats to begin with.

"I don't think the Poole fans minded dropping down a league, although I was the wrong side of the fence to really know if that was the case. I think the fans were quite grateful to end up with any speedway at all.

"When I go to Poole now, the National League era of the 80s still seems to be talked about quite a lot.

"A few statistics come out of the woodwork. I had a record I didn't even know about (regarding successive heat wins at Poole in 1985) until Jay Herne beat it in 2009 while riding for Bournemouth Buccaneers."

Poole Wildcats finished runners-up in the National League in both 1985 and 1986. During the 1987 season, Martin decided he would retire at the conclusion of that campaign.

"I was still enjoying my racing," he says, "but I was aware how astute a promoter that Mervyn had become. Quite often, he'd speak to me about team selection in the winter. He realised that you needed riders who would improve their average.

Skipper in his final season with Poole in the National League in 1987.

"I was probably no longer in that bracket! I wanted to make the decision myself to come out of the sport, before the decision was made for me. So there was a little bit of personal pride in there.

"But that wasn't the only reason. I also wanted to go off and start a business. And I'd had a long injury-free career and I think I'd started to back off a little more in some situations, so the time was right to retire.

"Mervyn kindly gave me a farewell meeting as a reward for the years I had ridden for him. We used to spend all winter haggling over terms. When I retired, he said: 'I shall miss doing that with you, Martin!'"

Other side of the fence

YEATES retired from racing while still holding down a heat leader spot at Poole. And he quickly threw himself into a new venture.

"I launched Martin Yeates Caravans, which then turned into the Salisbury Caravan Centre. It grew quite quickly and we moved into purpose-built premises."

After a five-year absence from the sport, Martin Yeates became team manager for Swindon Robins in 1993, before progressing to co-promoter at Blunsdon in 1995.

He recalls: "Mervyn Stewkesbury and Pete Ansell had taken over at Swindon and they asked me to be team manager.

"It got me involved again. The team managing side was quite interesting and we had a bit of success when Tony Olsson and Tony Langdon won the Pairs in 1994.

"I found it quite difficult, though, pulling riders out of races. I'd experienced that myself when I rode in the British League. You ended up taking riders out of Heat 8 to be replaced by a heat leader, when that was probably their best chances of scoring points. But it's something you had to do.

"The Swindon press always used to crucify me if I made a mistake. They could be very critical on that score.

"There's a lot of stuff happening in the pits that people don't see. A rider can be struggling with his bikes or carrying an injury. So there was often a reason why a rider didn't go out in a certain race. I explained it to the press afterwards but they would still say that I'd made a mistake."

A young Jason Crump, in only his second season, was Swindon's No. 1 in 1993, stringing together maximums in the second tier, just as Yeates had done years earlier.

"In some ways, Jason reminded me of Simon Wigg, in that he was fast and very determined to make it. I remember one night at Newcastle. We were losing and got to Heat 8. Jason started to put on his crash helmet, assuming he'd be out in the race.

"But, instead, I used him a race or two later, against their No.1. He couldn't see why at first but I told him: 'When you travel back down the motorway tonight and you've beaten their No. 1 three times, that'll be more satisfying than beating a second string and a reserve'. I think he then saw where I was coming from.

"But I never had any problems with Jason. He was as good as gold."

It wasn't long before Yeates wanted to move up the Blunsdon hierarchy. He explains: "After two years, I'd had enough of being team manager and wanted to move onto being a promoter. I kept on pestering Mervyn, asking him to sell it to me and he told me: 'Martin, I like you too much to get you involved as a promoter!'

"But eventually he said: 'OK, I'll sell you the club, but don't say I didn't warn you!'

"I brought in Peter Toogood as a partner – I couldn't really afford to do it by myself. We bought 50 per cent of the club each. Peter was the same as Mervyn – he came in not really knowing about speedway but was a sharp-eyed businessman.

"I looked after the team, while Pete looked after the sponsorship and the general administration of the club. Malcolm Holloway was our team manager. It worked well.

"We had reasonable success and topped the league for a while in 1996. We were rookies as promoters, so I feel we did a good job. We didn't lose vast sums of money, which I'm quite proud of, because most people do.

"We weren't obsessed about winning the league – we just wanted to be as successful as we could within what we could afford. We ran a relatively tight ship. I often think fans should be more pleased if the club isn't losing money, because it means the future is assured. There are horrifying stories these days of promoters losing an absolute fortune."

Robins finished fourth in the 19-team combined Premier League of 1996 but Martin admits he under-estimated the workload of being a promoter.

"It was hugely demanding," he admits. "It took so much time. Pete had a successful business in property and I was in the caravan trade, and we had the idea that speedway was going to be our little hobby, like a classic car in the garage that you get out and polish on the Saturday ready to drive on a Sunday.

"But it was completely the opposite – it turned out to be a full-time job. The phone was ringing day and night and it was normally aggravation. It was hard work.

"At the end of the second season, I realised that if I didn't get out quickly, then I'd lose my business. I was warned by some of the old, seasoned promoters not to take my eye off the business but I had started to do that. I was lucky to save it.

"Pete bought my half – we did a deal in 20 minutes. He carried on by himself, it was a new challenge for him. I think he did very well after I left. And, of course, he went on to become BSPA chairman.

"We're still good friends. In his latter years in the sport, he would say with a grin: 'I'll never forgive you for introducing me to speedway!'."

Martin adds: "It was such an interesting experience being a promoter. I'm so lucky to have been a rider, a team manager and a promoter. I'd say the best part was riding but I did also enjoy promoting. I didn't dislike the team managing but it was just tough going due to constant criticism from one or two press people."

These days his involvement is restricted to that of a spectator, although he hints that maybe he wouldn't mind more than that.

Yeates, now 57, says: "I've sold my business and taken early retirement, so I wouldn't mind being involved in speedway again, because I've got the knowledge of how it all works and now I've got the time. But maybe age is not on my side.

"I get down to Poole when I can. It's only 30 miles away. It's good to go and see people like Neil Middleditch. We rode together as junior riders at Poole and at Eastbourne in 1974. Around that time, he was best man at my wedding.

"My wife Jane and I spend quite a lot of time out in Spain these days, we've got a place out there. We love the MotoGP and Superbikes, so we go off to a lot of those in a motorhome. We've done Le Mans, Valencia and so on.

"I feel I've been a very lucky fellow. I got the chance to ride in Australia and Poland and places I'd never dreamt of going to.

"I consider myself to be quite fortunate to have ridden when I did. Financially, I did OK. And with the money from my speedway career and farewell meeting, I launched my business, so I think speedway has been good to me."

Where did you get your first bike and how much did it cost?

To be honest, I can't remember. I just recall that I was doing scrambles at the time and although I was doing quite well, I was getting frustrated that I didn't have the equipment to do any better. When I looked at the price of speedway bikes,

I couldn't believe it – they were half the cost of scrambles bikes. And you got paid for doing it!

The first speedway bike I rode was a hire bike at the Hackney training school (in 1975). A group of 10 or 12 of us used to go to watch Oxford on a Thursday night and you know what it's like when you're young and shout and scream at your team. One night I must have got a bit carried away and someone shouted back: 'You should try doing it – it's not as easy as it seems'. So being young and cocky, myself and Paul Tapp, who also went on to ride for Peterborough, decided we would.

A friend put me touch with Mick Bell, who lent me some leathers and we hired bikes at Hackney. We bent and wrecked a few too. They used to have four or five hire bikes and there would be 14 or 15 of us in the queue for them. I remember on one occasion one rider saying to another: 'Quick, get in before those two or there'll be no bikes left!' When our mates we used to go to Oxford with watched us race, they didn't bet on who would win – they bet on who would fall off first!

After a while Paul and I decided we needed new bikes, so we went down to see Briggo in his railway arches in Southampton and bought a Jawa each.

Who helped you most in your early days?

Pete Seaton, who rode for Peterborough and Oxford, was good. After Paul and I had ridden we used to race round to his and see who could rob bits for our bike first!

Dickie Greer too. He used to have a training track at Peterborough – it was nothing official, just an old gravel pit – and we had some rides there. Mick Bell helped me with those leathers at the very start and I ended up riding in the same team as him at Coventry.

Best promoter you've ridden for?

I'm really lucky in that all the promoters I rode for were good and that I never had a non-payment.

I rode for Danny Dunton for three years and he was a shrewd businessman. He sold me to Coventry for more than he'd paid me in wages all the time I'd been there!

I only ever had one cross word with Charles Ochiltree and that was because I doubted his word. He called me into his office and he was offended that I should do that. He said: 'I gave you my word, didn't I?'

After seven years at Coventry he told me they wouldn't be able to fit me in for the following year, so he asked if I wanted to go on loan or on a full transfer and where I wanted to go. I didn't want to do much travelling, so I went back to Peterborough – which surprised me because Martin Rogers and Charles Ochiltree were sworn enemies after Coventry closed Leicester down the previous year. There was a lot of bad feeling but Charles was true to his word.

I only ever had one cross word with Martin Rogers, and once we understood each other, everything was 100 per cent.

In fact, I wouldn't have retired when I did (at the end of 1988) if he'd still been there. He sold out to my namesake David Hawkins, who had been co-promoter for half of 1988. You didn't need to be clever to see what was coming – it wasn't going to be professional.

Career highlight/proudest moment?

Winning the British League in my first year at Coventry (1979) was an achievement. They had won it the year before as well and they say it's harder to defend it than win it in the first place.

Then, later on at Peterborough, we won the Fours (in 1988) and I was second to Neil Middleditch in the 1985 National League Riders' Championship at Brandon. It was my first year since leaving Coventry, so I got a good welcome. It didn't quite happen by accident, but I never set out to make it as a speedway rider, so to make a living from it for 13 years was something I was quite happy to do.

151

ALLAN
EMMETT

IF ever bare statistics failed to tell the full story, then this was very much the case at Hackney in 1973. All the record books still show Allan Emmett top of the Hawks' averages with a perfect 12.00 match average. One meeting, two rides, two wins. Six points out of six.

But what those basic stats fail to explain is that the promising youngster from Edmonton in North London was well on the way to his third straight victory (or at least a paid win) in his team's first British League match of that '73 campaign when his career – not just his season – literally came crashing down.

He was riding the outside line, slightly ahead of team-mate Dave Kennett, with Leicester's England captain Ray Wilson sandwiched between the home pair, when disaster struck as they roared into the third bend at high speed in Heat 11.

Some 40 years on, Allan recalled the incident that wrecked his career when *Backtrack* finally caught up with him at his home in New South Wales, Australia: "The race started OK and then Dave Kennett came flying through on the inside, hit me and took me into the fence."

It was an alarming incident and the large Waterden Road crowd held its breath as St. John's and track staff rushed to the aid of the stricken Hackney duo.

Rocket on the up . . . at Rayleigh in 1972.

Kennett escaped with nothing more than heavy bruising and a badly mangled machine.

Emmett was not nearly so fortunate. He suffered a badly broken right ankle and femur.

"I think my ankle broke when it hit the kickboards at the bottom of the fence," explained Allan, "and I busted my thigh when my back wheel spun around and whacked me on the leg.

"It was a very crushing moment – I knew I was very seriously hurt. It was heart-breaking, because I knew this could well be the finish of my speedway career."

Although he made a brief comeback attempt at Rye House the following year, the crash had taken its toll, physically and mentally, and Emmett retired after just a handful of meetings for the Rockets, who had just relocated to the Herts venue after Rayleigh Stadium was sold for redevelopment.

Since reopening in 1968, Rayleigh had produced a string of fine prospects who graduated from second division racing to their

152

Allan (inside) team-riding at The Weir with Bob Young – they are now 'neighbours' in Australia.

parent track at senior league Hackney but none possessed more potential than the stylish Emmett, who had his first second-half rides at his local track in 1970.

He explained: "I bought a second-hand JAP from Tyburn Gallows and used it to practice at Johnny Guilfoyle's training track at Chelmsford – and that's where Len Silver first saw me ride. He signed me up for second-halves at Hackney and then loaned me out to his other club, Rayleigh. I made my debut for the Rockets at Plymouth."

Allan made good early progress, although Romford's infamous concrete wall set him back a little when he broke both wrists in a crash against their Essex rivals at Brooklands.

"That one was hard to forget. I got in a tangle with Brian Foote, who was lying on my bike and I just couldn't seem to get free."

In his first full season (1971) he improved his average to 6.44 per match and struck up a good understanding on track with Australian star Bob Young. "He was a really good team partner, we gelled and always seemed to know instinctively where each other was on the track," says Allan.

"Tiger Beech was another I got on with particularly well. I remember how he nearly caused a crash when he led a race and stopped because he'd only turned on one of his fuel taps – I just managed to avoid running into the back of him."

Emmett combined speedway with part-time work renovating houses with his father but further progress on the track in 1972 brought him many more earning opportunities. Apart from 10 matches doubling-up with Hackney, his pushed his Rayleigh average up by almost another two points a match and impressed in individual meetings, too.

He won the Championship of Sussex at Eastbourne, ahead of Malcolm Ballard and Arthur Browning, and a best pairs meeting there with Eagles' Paul Gachet. By scoring a maximum for Rockets in their BL2 match at Arlington, it's clear that Allan relished the tight turns of Eastbourne, while he also names Ipswich as a particular favourite. But he was equally at home on the bigger, faster circuits. In Crewe's big Chester Vase meeting, he finished runner-up to Dave Parry and ahead of another Kings star, John Jackson.

The undoubted highlight of his '72 season, and therefore his career, was winning the British Under-21 Championship at Canterbury, where he took the coveted trophy with 13 points, a point ahead of Eastbourne's Gordon Kennett and Ipswich's Tony Davey.

Rayleigh Rockets before facing Essex rivals Romford away in 1971. Standing, left to right: Allan, Hughie Saunders, Charlie Mugford (team manager), Bob Young, Terry Stone, Dingle Brown, Alan Jackson, Len Silver (promoter). On bike: Geoff Maloney. Below: Unfortunately, Allan needed treatment after a spill during the same meeting at Brooklands.

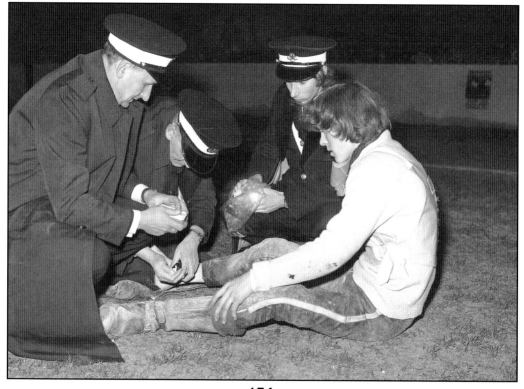

Sweet and sour . . . British Under-21 champ leaves Gordon Kennett and Tony Davey to take a beat seat.

He triumphed despite suffering a puncture while leading Dave Kennett in his first ride, which cost him two points.

It should have been a night to savour but the occasion turned a bit sour for Emmett when the Eastbourne management protested about the size of his Jawa (two-valve) engine. Instead of sipping champagne in the bar, the Rayleigh hero was detained in the pits while Speedway Control Board officials scrutinised and measured his motor amid accusations that he had cheated.

"They took my bike from me and had the motor stripped down to check the engine size, because the Eastbourne people thought it was over 500cc. But they were wrong and it was soon proven that my engine was legal."

Afterwards, Emmett described the incident as "embarrassing and humiliating". Talking about it more than four decades later, he says: "I was a bit disappointed that they thought me dishonest. I was an honest, hard-working young rider. I guess it was sour grapes on their part because I'd beaten their man (Gordon Kennett)."

He had the last laugh, though. "After what went on at Canterbury that night, my mechanic Les Westwood – who was a world champion in cycle speedway – wrote the word 'Nitro' on my fuel can, just to wind up the others!"

After collecting the 'Mr Rocket' award from his adoring Rayleigh fans at the end of 1972, most of us predicted more big things for Allan the following year – and it certainly began very brightly. Still doubling-up between Rayleigh and Hackney, he dropped just one point in his first BL2 match of the season and the plan was that after another season of advancement in the blue and yellow, he would go full-time with the Hawks from 1974. Geoff Maloney and Hugh Saunders had both moved up from Rockets to Hawks in previous seasons, so he was very much the next in line to follow in their tyre tracks.

With the Evening Argus promo girls after individual success at Eastbourne.

Looking stylish in pre-season practice at Rayleigh in 1972.

But those hopes and ambitions came crashing down in the third home meeting of Hackney's '73 season.

"Yep, I knew I was finished, I could tell by the extent of the pain and the injuries," Allan recalls. "I was in Hackney Hospital for six weeks. The rehab lasted about eight months and it was a long and difficult process."

At the age of 21, he attempted a comeback at Rye House but admits he was drained of confidence. After three official matches yielded just one point from six rides, he decided to quit racing.

"On the advice of Dr. Carlo Biagi, I had the pin taken out of my thigh before I started to ride again. But the crash was still in the back of my mind and I wasn't going to get back to where I'd been before the accident."

Given the fact that two riders were killed at Hackney after hitting lamp standards in subsequent years (Vic Harding, in 1979, and Denny Pyeatt, in 1982, who both died following incidents at the same end of the track where Emmett crashed badly), does Allan consider himself fortunate? At least he lived to tell the tale.

"Yes, I suppose when you look at it that way, I was very lucky."

And neither does he lay any of the blame at Dave Kennett, who was excluded from the rerun of that fateful race as the main cause of the stoppage.

"No, not at all, you have to expect these things can happen in a dangerous sport. I had no ill feelings at all towards speedway," says Allan, with the philosophical air of a man who has been accustomed to the relaxing Australian climate for the past 25 years.

"After I stopped racing in '74, I was spraying cars for a living and then I bought a house at Brightlingsea in Essex, got married and we had a son called Wayne."

Very few people know what happened to Allan Emmett in the years after he quit speedway but

Allan with his friend and team-mate Tiger Beech at Hackney's 1973 pre-season practice (above) and, just weeks later (below), together again in the Rayleigh pits with Allan on crutches following his terrible crash at The Wick.

Allan in 2013, at home in Toukley, NSW.

now he can reveal the personal heartache and physical pain that he suffered since leaving England for Australia in 1987.

"We made the decision to emigrate because my wife at the time had relatives there and she wanted us to join them. I thought it may be a great change for me. But when I reached Australia, she decided to leave me and take everything I had worked for over my speedway years. I haven't seen my first son since he was 18-years-old and I'm not even sure where he is at this stage.

"Looking back, though, things have turned out perfectly – my divorce led to me meeting and marrying my beautiful wife Julianne. She gave me a perfect son, Ashley, and now we have a four-month-old grandson, Harry. We have been married for 22 years now and I'm very happy."

Julianne, an Aussie girl with Irish blood in her, has clearly been a devoted rock in Allan's life since they first met at his work colleague's party when she was 26 and he was 37. She says: "When he left the UK it was only to please his wife. He was very happy and settled in England, with a good job. He owned his own home, which he paid for from what he made from speedway.

"On arrival in Australia, his wife seemed to have another man here for her, so she left Allan and took 80 per cent of his money from the sale of their UK home – that's the law here if you have one child, which they did.

"On top of all this hurt, his family (in England) turned their backs on him for leaving them behind, so it left him feeling very alone."

Apart from personal turmoil, Allan has also had to cope with a serious back injury sustained at work in March 1993 that resulted in a compressed fracture of the L4 vertebra.

He explains: "I worked for a company called CCMP that did abrasive spraying and shot blasting. Then one day a steel girder that was on a trolley being lowered by an overhead crane toppled over and landed on top of me. I was in hospital for six weeks and still can't bend down properly.

"I've not been able to do any heavy work since then, although I've done odd part-time jobs. When I lived in Sydney for four years I drove a bus for disabled school kids and for a while I was a salesman for a sports injuries spray called Painaway. I once earned 17,000 bucks in two weeks but then my friend who owned the company sold it."

Based in the town of Toukley for the past two years, Allan had lost contact with all his old friends and team-mates from his racing days but that is all set to change after Julianne's sister in Ireland recently found Retro Speedway on the Internet and put him in touch with us.

With amazing irony, Allan has just learned that Bob Young, his Rayleigh race partner, is living just 230 or so kilometres up the coast from where he and Julianne live, at Cundletown.

"I have seen speedway at a couple of tracks over here. I used to go to Gosford on a Saturday night but it's closed down now. I also went to one or two car meetings at Sydney Showground.

"Julianne found a man who was selling speedway DVDs filmed in the UK and Europe, so I bought lots of them and watch them often."

A proud Mrs Emmett says: "My Allan is the kindest, most selfless man I have ever known. He would do anything for anyone at any time. He would give his life for me and his sons and grandson at a second's notice.

"He is shy and reserved, always smiling no matter what. Even in pain or sickness, you would never know it, because he always puts others first.

"Due to the back injury that prevented him from working, we then lost our family home – the second time it had happened to him – because we were unable to meet the mortgage payments. Even then, he was a bit sad only for me and our son, because he felt he had let us down."

The Rayleigh DVD we produced at the end of 2011 has also now been added to Allan's growing collection. And the former Rockets No.1 didn't have to wait long for a visual reminder of just how much talent he possessed before cruel fate intervened 40 years ago.

Former Rayleigh promoter and team manager Peter Thorogood said of Allan: "He looked like a future international, for sure, and also a possible World Championship contender."

Tiger Beech added: "Allan was a fantastic rider. He was a quiet lad – you usually find the best speedway riders are the quiet ones."

BRIEF ENCOUNTERS WITH… Glenn McDonald

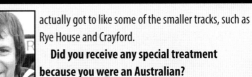

How did your move to the UK come about?

After riding for about three seasons at the Sydney Showground and Liverpool Speedways, I thought I'd try to get a start in the UK. Peter White, who was the co-promoter at the Showground, made some enquiries with Joe Thurley from Birmingham and further contact was made with Dan McCormick at Cradley Heath. Negotiations were finalised with McCormick and I arrived in the UK in March 1979 to go on loan to Nottingham Outlaws.

What were your first impressions of the UK?

Quite cold and damp and the size of London itself, what with me coming from a city of around 30,000 people. I must say that I found everyone very helpful. Dan McCormick and Bob Wasley (Cradley team manager) were the first people I met in the Midlands and they made us feel very welcome.

How different were the tracks and the racing in the UK and how did you adapt to them?

The tracks were quite different, smaller, although I had ridden throughout Northern Australia and a lot of the tracks are comparable to UK tracks in size. The tracks were very deep after wet winters. Overall, I adapted quite well and actually got to like some of the smaller tracks, such as Rye House and Crayford.

Did you receive any special treatment because you were an Australian?

I'm sure we did. I can remember going to a market in Wolverhampton, not long after we settled in, looking for some coat hangers. We asked someone where to buy some and they gave us about 50 wire hangers from their clothing stall for nothing. We shared a house with Oxford's Aussie Carl Askew and he really helped me along the way for the first season. We still keep in touch.

What was the highlight of your British speedway career?

It was an honour to ride in an England v Australia (National League) Test match at Boston in 1978. Also, riding in the Cradley team on occasions in the first division with some of the greatest riders in the world. They all made me feel welcome. This led to me looking after Bruce (Penhall) and Bobby's (Schwartz) bikes for them when they came to Australia. All the friends we made at Long Eaton, too.

And the low point?

When Nigel Wasley lost his life after an accident at Long Eaton in 1979.

By Doug Nicolson ● Issue 49 (2012)

HAMPDEN HORRORS

No-one knew it at the time, but 1972 would turn out to be Glasgow Tigers' last season at Hampden Park. Tigers fan Doug Nicolson recalls how a truly dismal season in Scotland unfolded . . .

UNLIKE the previous winter, there was no training track at Coatbridge during the close season of 1971-72. However, there was plenty of alternative action for the fans. On January 2 a long-track meeting was held at Motherwell and it may well have been instrumental in persuading the BSPA that the Motherwell promoters would be fit and able to stage speedway racing at the venue – wrongly as it turned out.

The long-track event featured Barry Briggs, Ivan Mauger and Don Godden, all proven and experienced experts on the bigger circuits who pitted their skills against various locals, some being little known second-halfers. Unsurprisingly, given the wide disparity in skill levels, many races were very strung out. Still, it was a pleasant way to have the last traces of a New Year hangover blown away.

A week later the first of a series of ice racing meetings was held at Murrayfield Ice Rink in Edinburgh. It attracted a capacity crowd and the meeting had to be held up for over half an hour while they filed in. The racing itself was a cross between cycle speedway and roller derby, but on

Glasgow Tigers soon after the start of their troubled 1972 season, before their match at Sheffield. Left to right: Jimmy Beaton, George Hunter, Charlie Monk, Jim McMillan (on bike), Paul O'Neill, Robin Adlington, Bobby Beaton.

ice. It had a certain novelty value but crowds fell with each successive meeting and the experiment wasn't repeated the following year.

However, it was probably the only bright spot in a singularly dark time. The miners' strike had so reduced the supplies of coal held at power stations that electricity had to be rationed. By rotation your local area had scheduled power cuts that meant you were in the dark and in the cold shortly after nine o'clock at night.

To add to the gloom, Harry Nilsson's turgid and depressing *Without You* topped the charts for five consecutive weeks.

End of two dynasties

TWO famous speedway families ended their association with the Tigers before the season started. It has to be said that most fans were pretty indifferent to these departures. Johnnie Hoskins and his son Ian sold their shares in the Tigers promotion to team manager Neil Macfarlane. Fans were delighted that Neil, a Tigers man through and through, was now a director.

Only a few were concerned that men as steeped in speedway as the Hoskins duo had seen the writing on the Hampden wall and decided it was a good time to get out.

The Templeton brothers, Doug and Willie, announced their retirement, although they would sign for second division Berwick shortly afterwards. Supporters had been critical of the Templetons' performances, particularly away from home, during the 1971 season and, again, were unfazed by their departure. However, the fans were to change their tune after the season was just a month old.

Lions escape Tigers

TIGERS' promotion obviously had plenty of notice of the Templetons' departure and had planned to bring in Wayne Briggs and Brian Collins, who had both spent 1971 with Wembley Lions, as replacements. Briggs was allocated to Glasgow by the Rider Control Committee but could not be persuaded out of retirement, while Collins ended up at Poole.

Tigers were allocated Paul O'Neill and given a foreign rider permit to cover the other vacancy. The season was a couple of weeks old before they signed Kjell Gimre, an unknown Norwegian rider who had had trials at Exeter but had not been offered a team place. Maybe there was a clue there.

By mid-May, O'Neill and Gimre were struggling badly and both had averages well under three, roughly half of what the much criticised Templetons had achieved the previous year. Yes, you don't know what you've got till it's gone.

Opening night blues

HAMPDEN'S opening night was a real disappointment on just about every front. First, the programme looked pretty austere. The cover no longer featured a photo but, instead, a red thistle superimposed on a Saltire – hardly the most inspiring design.

The printing throughout was in black, whereas it had previously been blue, which only added to the growing sense of gloom. The fans' main gripe was that the price had been increased fairly steeply from seven pence to 10p, although to be fair to the promotion, this increase was to avoid raising admission charges. Even so, it was now twice the price that it had been just 18 months earlier.

On entering the stadium fans were aware something was missing. No music. A local resident had complained to the council during the winter, so music was now banned. Les Whaley was planning to appeal this decision but that would be a few weeks off. So far, so bad.

Once racing started things went from bad to worse. After six heats of the 'grand opening challenge'

The less than impressive 1972 programme cover.

Glasgow trailed visitors Sheffield 26-10. Surely no-one loses their opening challenge match . . .

It is not known what was said in the pits but Glasgow made a comeback that would have impressed even Lazarus. But only the most gullible fans could have believed it was for real.

Tigers on telly

SCOTTISH Television were again looking for a sport to show on the Saturday afternoon of the (English) FA Cup Final, which the rest of the ITV region would be receiving, and chose the Tigers v Poole match.

With Dick Barrie sharing commentating duties with STV's Alex Cameron, time keeper Stan Gardner took over the announcing role, while I was co-opted to mark up a programme for Cameron and generally keep him informed of what was going on. He seemed well impressed by my description of John Langfield as "colourful and controversial" and used it on more than one occasion. My fee for being his assistant was two guineas (£2.10) – not enough to persuade me to give up my day job.

The meeting itself was fairly drab, although thankfully blessed with a dry, bright night. Glasgow won by one of the biggest margins of the season but it didn't provide a good advert for the sport and there was no improvement in crowd numbers in the weeks that followed.

Talking of speedway on telly . . . on Saturday, July 22, Tigers' fans travelled down to the West Midlands see their team at Cradley Heath during Glasgow Fair fortnight. The supporters' bus arrived in early afternoon and most fans spent a few hours wandering about Brierley Hill town centre.

Just after 3.00pm ITV's *World of Sport* programme featured the England v New Zealand internations speedway fixture and, as luck would have it, a local TV showroom had a set showing highlights of the previous Thursday's international from Wimbledon. A few fans gathered to watch and within a few minutes their number was swelled to quite a crowd. Undaunted, the showroom manager invited us in and turned on a few more sets – and even turned up the volume too. What a gentleman!

Triple wash-out

THE Hampden track had an enviable reputation of draining really well and few meetings had been rained-off there in the preceding three years. This was to change, though, with an incredible three meetings out of five being cancelled in May.

In the first of the wash-outs, visitors Sheffield were leading by 10 points at the time of the abandonment, so obviously home fans weren't too disappointed when a halt was called.

Two weeks later and the match against Oxford had to be scrapped without a wheel being turned. Les Whaley was incensed, writing in the following week's programme: "The rain ceased at 6.45 and by 7.00 the track was cleared of puddles. The referee declared the track fit, not only for RIDING but for RACING. However, certain riders had made up their minds that they were not going to ride, and that was that. It is situations like these which make me think I must be mad to promote speedway. You, the supporters, are the ones who have to suffer."

George Hunter seemed to take the view that on a wet night the best course of action was to cancel the meeting and restage it later when the weather might be better. With Jim McMillan and Charlie

Monk readily backing him up, the promotion were up against it.

Hunter certainly was a pragmatist. At a Motherwell long-track meeting there was considerable rain but, when it became apparent that the event would not be restaged at a later date, he, and indeed all the other riders, got on with riding without any complaint.

A couple of weeks later, the World Championship qualifying round became the next Hampden meeting to fall victim to the elements, although this time all parties seemed to accept the referee's decision.

Flaming June

SUPPLIES of new Jawa bikes, via UK distributor Barry Briggs, were delayed at the start of the 1972 season and it took until mid-May for Jim McMillan to take delivery of his new Czech machine.

However, just over a fortnight later, his lock-up caught fire and he lost all his equipment and riding gear – and none of it was insured. In all, about three thousand pounds worth went up in smoke.

Tigers' supporters had a collection for him and a number of English fans kindly sent donations, too, but it was still a huge financial blow and it would take Scotland's No.1 rider until mid-summer to get all his equipment and gear just the way he wanted it.

Jim Beaton's crash

LES Whaley's second division interest, Bradford, travelled to Berwick for a BL2 match that left a nasty taste. A Heat 3 crash saw Jim Beaton sustain such severe injuries to his right arm that the surgeon initially recommended amputation.

It is a tribute to the surgeon's skill and Jim's determination and perseverance that, after many operations, he would make a track comeback some years later, despite limited movement in his arm.

Feelings were running high after this incident and it would lead to a major rift between Glasgow promoters Les Whaley and James Beaton (Jimmy's father) in the coming weeks. This would greatly impact on the Tigers' promotion.

Motherwell fiasco

A COUPLE of days later, Motherwell staged its first, and as it turned out only, challenge match, when the local Golden Eagles lost to Teesside. The meeting, promoted by the stadium owners, was a complete fiasco.

The speedway track was separated from the low-rise terracing by no fewer than three circuits: a trotting track; an unkempt circuit (said to be intended for a moto-cross course); and a tarmac stock car oval. The speedway track had a board fence, which hid large parts of the track from the spectators' view.

By the second heat, most of the sparse crowd had clambered onto the stock car track to view the racing from there. The surface was soft and deep and precluded any meaningful racing. Unsurprisingly, no further meetings were ever staged there.

By George, he's out

BOBBY Beaton and George Hunter travelled to Leicester for a British semi-final of the World Championship, although (first reserve) Hunter may not have expected to take any real part in proceedings.

Beaton and King's Lynn's Howard Cole were involved in a nasty Heat 1 crash and neither took any further part in the meeting, so Hunter replaced Cole in all five of his programmed rides and

George Hunter and brothers Jimmy and Bobby Beaton trying to keep warm.

gained sufficient points to qualify for the British Final. Or so it seemed.

The following day it was announced that Hunter was ineligible. His appeal against this decision was supported by Tigers' management.

Golden moments

JIM McMillan beat Terry Betts at King's Lynn to annex the Golden Helmet. Unfortunately, the next three fixtures were all away from home but Jim did a sterling job in making successful defences against Edgar Stangeland at Newport and Geoff Curtis at Reading.

Hopes of a defence at Hampden were dashed when Christer Lofqvist narrowly beat him at Poole – a pity, because some match-races in Glasgow would have given supporters a lift.

More bad news

CITY magistrates upheld the earlier decision to ban the playing of music during meetings, dismissing Tigers' appeal. This was a real blow, because meetings really seemed to drag on without any sound backdrop and further diluted the atmosphere in what was already proving to be a downbeat season.

There was more bad news, this time from the *Evening Citizen,* Glasgow's evening newspaper, which had produced a 'Speedway Special' edition every week since the sport returned to Glasgow in 1964. It had a special front page devoted to speedway and despite carrying little editorial inside and many often quite dated photographs, it was still very much part of speedway night.

Sadly, sales were dwindling and the *Citizen* reluctantly decided to cease production of their special edition – yet another indicator of speedway's downward spiral at Hampden.

Whaley's woe continue

HACKNEY'S visit brought yet another wet night and, again, the usual suspects weren't prepared to race despite the referee ruling the track rideable. The promotion were reportedly prepared to track four juniors in their place. Fortunately, it never came to that, because Hawks also declined to get their bikes dirty.

A disgusted Les Whaley wrote in the programme: "Well, once again a rained-off meeting and this makes four out of 11. Riders blandly decide they are not going to ride despite the referee's decision that the track is rideable, so how long do they think a promotion can keep a track open under these circumstances? Last Saturday I attended Halifax Speedway, where conditions were exactly the same as for our Hackney date. This meeting started at 7.30pm and continued to the end, completing a total of 24 heats."

Hunter loses appeal

ON July 11, Whaley travelled down to London to present George Hunter's case against the SCB ruling that he was ineligible for the British Final. He argued for over an hour but the Control Board maintained that the referee had been wrong to allow Hunter to replace the injured Howard Cole in the rerun of Heat 1 and were adamant in rejecting Hunter's appeal.

Whaley wrote in his programme column: "I was amazed to find them (the SCB) admitting that a referee could be wrong."

Like the previous year, Whaley seemed to opt out of running the Tigers after the Glasgow Fair break, the last fortnight in July. Neil Macfarlane wrote the programme editorial from the beginning of August but made no mention of Les's absence. A couple of weeks later, observant fans would have noticed that Whaley's name was no longer included among the directors listed in the programme.

Again, no reference was made to this and it was not until mid-September that fans were told that Jim Wallace had bought Whaley's shares.

The main grandstand at Hampden towers above the riders roaring from the starting gate.

It is believed that the rift with James Beaton, following incidents at the aforementioned Berwick v Bradford match, together with his disillusionment over rained-off meetings and the weekly travelling from his Yorkshire base, were the major factors in his decision to sell up.

Although, like Hoskins earlier in the year, Whaley may well have concluded that Tigers' days at Hampden were numbered.

Hunter leaves

UNLIKE in 1971, George Hunter was not a settled Tiger. Some would argue he was both unsettled and unsettling. He had personal reasons for wanting to be based in the Midlands and was always the first to push for a rain-off decision when track conditions were less than ideal. His controversial elimination from the World Championship couldn't have helped either.

Things came to a head when he was excluded for tape-breaking in Heat 12 of Tigers' home match against Coventry in mid-August. Tape exclusions were hardly an unusual occurrence for Hunter and, from memory, this one didn't look unjustified. It is a bit hard to understand why he got so worked up about it. Certainly, had he won Heat 12, as the form book suggested, he would have been joint-top scorer along with Bobby Beaton and eligible to challenge Wolverhampton's Ole Olsen for the Golden Helmet.

Harsh words were spoken in the pits over the referee turning down Tigers' claims for his reinstatement and, ultimately, it led to him demanding a move. The promotion immediately agreed to let him go, claiming that George's actions of late have been undermining team spirit.

Somewhat controversially, he was sold to Wolverhampton. The intention was to buy a replacement, although from where was never made clear. It seems unlikely that any second division starlets could

One of Scotland's finest, George Hunter was unsettled before his move to Wolverhampton.

Jim McMillan gave Tigers a rare boost when he reached the World Final.

have been persuaded to come north of the border. Berwick's Andy Meldrum made several appearances in second-half races and even rode a few meetings for Tigers, but never actually signed for Glasgow.

Norwegian new boy

AT the end of July, Tigers released Kjell Gimre in order to sign Denmark's Preben Rosenkilde. Gimre's departure was certainly no surprise. His average was just over two and many felt the promotion had been more than patient in giving him an extended run.

'Benny' made his debut at Hackney, a track for whom he had previously ridden in 1971 before joining West Ham. If his failure to score in four starts was disappointing, then worse was to follow, when the Danish Motor Union banned him from riding in Britain following an incident during a meeting in Denmark.

Tigers then turned to Svein Kaasa, a young Norwegian signed from Oxford who won his debut race at Hampden against Ipswich.

World Final high

THE only bright spot in an otherwise dreadful season was Jim McMillan's qualification for the Wembley World Final, albeit as first reserve. This truly caught the Glasgow supporters' imagination and more than a dozen buses were booked to travel to London.

Most supporters had bought tickets for the terracing high up on the third bend and they raised the roof when Jim took two rides in place of Barry Briggs, who was taken to hospital with severe hand injuries following a second race crash.

Definitely the highlight of the season and possibly the most iconic moment in Tigers' history. Certainly one that will never be repeated.

Kaasa killed

WHILE Jimmy Mac's Wembley appearance gave Glasgow a boost, the events of the final weeks of the season were to leave both the supporters and the promotion completely shattered.

Svein Kaasa crashed in Heat 11 of the home match against Swindon on Friday, September 29. As crashes go, it didn't look particularly bad. Mid-race, Svein was attempting to pass Martin Ashby as they raced into the first bend. As Ashby began to slide, the gap Svein was going for disappeared and he clipped Martin's back wheel and was thrown head-first into the fence. He was taken off, face down, on the stretcher trolley.

The meeting continued and it was only at the end that a distraught Neil Macfarlane announced that Svein's injuries "had proved fatal".

A horrible feeling descended on the crowd. Everyone wanted to get out of the stadium quickly but quietly and without jostling. Once outside, no-one wanted to leave. People were milling about aimlessly. Guys that I thought were pretty hard were sobbing their hearts out. It was a truly desperate night.

Svein's desperate last moments

NORMAN Hunter was nearing the end of his first season with Swindon in 1972 when he witnessed the dying moments of a fellow rider up close.

The former England star and 1968 World Cup winner was in the Glasgow dressing rooms when Tigers' popular Norwegian youngster Svein Kaasa was brought in by medical staff fighting to save his life. The memory of this "terrible" experience is still fresh in Norman's mind almost 40 years later.

He told *Backtrack:* "I'd gone out for my first race, in Heat 3, against Charlie Monk and we were battling for first position down the back straight, with neither of us prepared to give way to the other. In the end, Charlie – who was a hard rider – came across me and took out all the spokes on my front wheel.

"I crashed, bent my bike and because I only had the one machine with me on that occasion, I couldn't take any further part in the meeting.

"I loaded up my bike and having driven 300 miles to Glasgow for less than one lap, I felt very cheesed off.

"I made my way to the changing rooms – they were huge at Hampden Park – and got myself settled into the big bath. I was feeling sorry for myself when, all of a sudden, there was a commotion and a sense of urgency around me.

"A policeman appeared at the door and told me there was a bit of an emergency going on. Then in came the St. Andrew's ambulance staff and I recognised the youngster on the stretcher as being the Norwegian lad who I'd seen signing autographs and happily chatting to fans before the meeting. Svein was dressed all in black and seemed a nice lad, just a young kid really."

In his quest to become a speedway star, Kaasa had left behind a well-paid career as a draughtsman in his home town of Gvarv. He drove several sports cars, including a Lotus Cortina in his national colours, and owned a holiday apartment in Benidorm, on Spain's Costa Blanca, and another in Norway's capital city of Oslo.

Hunter was immediately aware that the 25-year-old's life was in serious danger. He says: "I could tell they hadn't just brought in somebody with a broken leg. The doctor immediately started chest compressions and as soon as I saw him do that, I feared Svein was dead. It did something to me to see how very concerned these people were in trying to save the young lad's life.

"A few years earlier (in 1968) I'd ridden for Great Britain against Sweden at Coatbridge. I'd come off and was taken to the changing rooms, where the track doctor treated me for mild concussion. I was told afterwards that this particular doctor liked a drop of whiskey, which might have been cause for concern for some people."

The track doctor listed in the Glasgow programme on the night of the 1972 tragedy was Dr E. Collier M.B. Ch.B D.P.H. He served the club from (at least) 1964 until their move to Blantyre 1 in around 1980. The club ran a second half benefit for him when he retired, so he was obviously well thought of.

He had a small piece in the programme thanking supporters and saying that in his medicine bag he always carried some "amber liquid" to dispense to shaken-up riders!

Hunter continues: "It happened to be the same doctor who I saw desperately trying to revive Svein Kaasa in the Hampden dressing rooms. And I must say that man could not have done any more to save the boy's life. He kept on and on and made sure everyone around him did their bit, too, while Svein was laid out on the physio's treatment table.

"They were still working on Svein as I got myself dressed and went back to the pits, where I stayed until the end of the meeting. I drove back to Leicester and remember stopping at the M1 services at Watford Gap, where I met my team-mate Mike Broadbank and one or two others who'd been riding elsewhere that night."

Broadbank had featured in the fateful Heat 11, along with his Swindon team-mate Martin Ashby and Tigers' Jimmy McMillan, that had claimed Kaasa's life. But Norman had already left the stadium just moments before the crowd were told the tragic news that the Norwegian had died from his injuries.

"It was Broady who confirmed it for me when we met up again at the services," Hunter added.

"To have actually been there and seen that young lad signing autographs for girls, smartly dressed and a fine example of the modern young speedway rider, to then see him again an hour or so later fighting for his life . . . it upset me for a few days and it's stayed in the back of my mind. It was a horrible experience."

Tony McDonald

Svein Kaasa had finished third in the Norwegian Championship, behind Reidar Eide and Dag Lovaas, at the end of 1971, so his inclusion in the Norway-Denmark team for the Inter-Nations Championship series in England in the summer of 1972 was no shock. This is how the combined team lined up against Australia at King's Lynn on July 15, 1972. Left to right: Odd Fossengen, Dag Lovaas, Ole Olsen, Tore Kittilsen (team manager), Kurt Bogh, Svein, Reidar Eide and Oyvind Berg, the former Tiger who recommended Kaasa to the Glasgow management.

How *Speedway Star* reported the 25-year-old's death.

The Svein Harald Kaasa memorial stone housed at Hampden's football museum.

Norman Hunter will never forget his "horrible experience" at Hampden.

Double tragedy

TWO weeks after the death of Kaasa came another blow. George Beaton, eldest of the brothers, was killed in a car crash. Only days before, he had turned out for short-handed Oxford at Hampden.

Both Svein Kaasa and George Beaton are remembered at Glasgow Speedway to this day with memorial trophies presented towards the end of the season. The Svein Kaasa Trophy is usually awarded to the winner of Heat 15 of the Scottish Cup match with Edinburgh, while the George Beaton Trophy goes to the winner of a junior event.

Neil Macfarlane – now living in Murcia, Spain – summed up the year: "Our 1972 season will go down as one of misfortune and tragedy. We have been unsettled by team changes and management changes and fate just hasn't been on our side."

Tigers meet Tigers again

VISITS from Sheffield Tigers were certainly never boring. They opened our season with a highly unusual defeat in a challenge match. A couple of months later, they seemed well on course for the league points, leading by 10 before the rain came. A restaging date in August was duly arranged and, again, it wasn't without its talking points.

This time Sheffield's Bert Harkins arrived mid-meeting and referee Cuthbert refused to let the Scot take his remaining programmed rides. Sheffield's appeal against this decision was subsequently upheld but, in turn, Glasgow decided to appeal against the appeal! Almost predictably, Glasgow's appeal was dismissed, which meant they had lost three appeals in a row: the music ban; Hunter being ruled ineligible for the British Final; and now the club's counter-appeal over Harkins.

Sheffield returned as the second part of a double-header with Oxford, which turned out to be our last-ever British League fixture at Hampden – and not one to remember. It dragged on badly and, reportedly, some fans who stayed to the bitter end had to walk home after local transport services had ceased operating.

Those who left in time to catch last buses certainly didn't miss much. Sheffield won by a staggering 50-28 – Tigers' biggest ever home defeat in BL Division One. Apart from Jim McMillan, who scored 12 from five rides, there was little Glasgow resistance.

What a way to end league racing at Scotland's biggest sporting venue.

Bleak winter ahead

THE '72 season closed with rumours again suggesting that Charlie Monk would be looking for a move. This rumour had circulated before but now it had a lot more credence.

Monk had not been in good form or the best of health, while the long drive from his Wakefield, West Yorkshire base to home meetings had also taken its toll. He would soon be transferred to his local track, Halifax.

So within 18 months Tigers lost virtually a complete team in Oyvind Berg, George Hunter, Monk, the Templeton brothers and Bill McMillan, as well as promoters Hoskins and Whaley.

With only four riders that they could be certain would return the following season, Jim McMillan, Bobby Beaton, Jimmy Gallagher and Robin Adlington, the club's prospects looked bleak.

There were troubled times ahead – and Glasgow Speedway would never return to Hampden.

In 1973, they moved their first division operation to Coatbridge.

TONY
DAVEY

IT's the age old question most sportspeople contemplate when they take stock and reflect on their careers in retirement: 'What if?' In moments of introspection, it's what we have all asked ourselves at one stage or another.

In the case of Tony Davey, it's a question he is fully entitled to ask himself even though I sense he rarely, if ever, has.

You will never find this popular son of Suffolk wallowing in self-pity. And yet, as he faces the camera to record his thoughts for our *Memories of Ipswich Speedway* DVD, you can't help but feel that the Witches legend and one-club man deserved so much more from a career of such great early promise.

For starters, ask yourself how good would he have been but for three serious injuries that seriously hampered his career and ultimately ended it a few days short of his 29th birthday in 1980.

THREE serious bangs for a rider renowned for his steady, measured approach to racing, who lightly caressed the throttle rather than thrashed it? Lady Luck didn't exactly deal him a fair hand, did she?

Ipswich Witches at Romford early in 1971, Tony's sensational first full season. Standing, left to right: Pete Bailey, Ted Howgego, Clive Noy and Ted Spittles, with John Louis and Shrimp kneeling and Ron Bagley on machine. Tony went on to record a 15-point maximum and break the Brooklands track record that night.

By the time disaster struck at Leicester in 1978, he had finally emerged from the huge shadows cast by more celebrated Foxhall Heath heroes John Louis and Billy Sanders to earn a return to the England Test team, having just enjoyed by far his best ever season in the sport.

Then there was the cruelly mysterious engine failure in the British Final that robbed him of a hard-fought place in the Golden Jubilee World Final at Wembley. Ironically, the same year in which he gained some substantial sponsorship and the mechanical back-up that enabled him to have the best equipment he had ever known.

What if he'd been on good gear from the outset?

The down side to spending all of his 10 years in the saddle with his home-town club was that it denied him wider acclaim and, in pure financial terms, many extra open bookings for a rider of his stature. Back in the days when every track staged at least one prestige individual meeting a year, promoters were keen to book the number ones, much less so the numbers two or three. Louis was a shoe-in everywhere, at both second and first division level in the early 70s, while Sanders got more opportunities in accordance with his status as arguably the top Australian.

Malcolm Simmons left King's Lynn because he was fed up riding in the shadow of Terry Betts, then blossomed into an international star and World No.2 at Poole.

What if Tony had taken himself out of his comfort zone at Ipswich. Would he too have become a superstar in his own right elsewhere?

King's Lynn wanted him, as did Hackney when he was still at the novice stage, but his heart and soul belonged to Ipswich and nothing was ever going to change that, or his immensely likeable homespun personality.

"I was always overshadowed by JL and Billy but that never fazed me. I was happy being at Ipswich, getting paid for what I loved doing," says a typically humble 'Shrimp', the nickname that has stuck since his teenage scrambling days as one of the Eastern Centre's greatest discoveries.

A diminutive man with a huge heart, that's the Framsden Flier.

Local heroes

ALONG with many other young motorbike-mad lads growing up in the Suffolk backwoods, Davey was inspired by the legendary exploits of local scrambles hero Dave Bickers. "JL used to work in Dave's motorcycle shop in the town and when you saw Bickles racing on the telly, on the Saturday *Grandstand* programme through the winter, we all wanted to be like him and do what he was doing for a living," explained Tony, whose introduction to speedway late in the 1970 season came more by chance than expectation.

"I went down to Alf Hagon's shop to collect a new set of leathers and while I was there I spoke to Bill Mathieson, who was running the Rye House training school. He suggested that I gave speedway a go, so I hired a bike at Rye House and it went from there.

"I was offered second-halves at Hackney and won my first junior race there. That's when Len Silver tried to get me to sign for him but I decided that if I was going to take up speedway, Ipswich was the only place for me. I still don't think Len has forgiven me."

It seems crazy when reflecting on Davey's rapid emergence as an overnight sensation to think that he actually had to phone Ipswich consultant Howdy Byford – who was advising John Berry and Joe Thurley in their formative period as the new kids on the block – to ask for second-half rides at Foxhall. He must have shown enough promise because before he knew it, he was thrown in at the deep end for his Witches debut . . . in the KO Cup final!

"I failed to score a point in the first leg of the cup final at Berwick and didn't get anything in the return match either, so I picked up a cup winner's medal without even scoring a point," he laughs.

171

This Good Friday crash with Hackney's Roger Wright cost Shrimp (6) a finger.

Perfectly balanced, Shrimp powers round Foxhall during a practice session.

By then, Louis was nearing the end of his brilliant first full year on shale and had established himself as the hottest property in British League Division Two. His meteoric rise, from local scrambles star to the new king of Ipswich Speedway, inspired Tony, who took himself off to the Olle Nygren training school at Boston in the winter of 1970-71 to hone his technique and gear himself up for his first full season in the blue and black racejacket.

"Olle gave me a few good pointers but it was really a case of me learning how to ride the bike and improving my technique over the four days of the training school."

Although Louis began 1971 in the same blistering form he'd shown throughout the previous season, he suddenly had the relatively unknown Davey for company at the top of the score chart. Not that the red-haired discovery in green leathers would stay unknown for long. Just days, in fact.

His first five matches produced three full and one paid maximum. The only point he dropped in the other meeting was to Ted Hubbard at Canterbury.

In Witches' match at Romford, both Louis and Davey scored maximums but 19-year-old Tony claimed the Brooklands track record, as well as 15 points from the reserve berth. Not bad considering it was his first visit to the Essex track whose unforgiving concrete 'safety' wall put the fear of death into many an experienced campaigner.

Track conditions and all the different shapes and sizes never did trouble Tony, whose scrambling background taught him to take the rough with the smooth. "I never disliked any track," he says. "I used to love fast, banked places like Halifax and Exeter. The only track I could never master was Belle Vue – it was a good track but, for some strange reason, I just never did well there."

As we know, John Berry was a demanding man never known to lavish praise lightly but he famously described Shrimp as the most naturally talented speedway rider he ever saw – at a time when his own No.1 Louis totally dominated the second tier and Peter Collins was pulling up trees with Rochdale in BL2 while also benefiting from regular rides with Belle Vue in the top flight.

"I was surprised when I read what JB said in his first book. It was flattering, I didn't realise that he thought as much of me as he did."

Davey was renowned as one of the fastest starters, although he has no idea why. "I never practiced starts or anything like that. I just seemed to get grip out of the gate."

Unusually, he always preferred the outside grid positions and was happy to give up what were generally the more popular inside gates to grateful team-mates. "I mostly rode at No.3 and the reserves I was paired with liked to be on the inside, as did JL and Billy when we rode together in Heat 13, but that suited me fine. Mind you, you had to make the start off three or four, otherwise you were nowhere."

After leaving his job at the garage where he worked as a mechanic to become a full-time speedway rider, Tony admits his stunningly brilliant 1971 season brought him a standard of living he could only have dreamed of before taking to the shale, as well as another KO Cup winner's medal and a 10-point average.

Not bad for a 'country boy' from the sticks.

Although he would no doubt have cleaned up had he remained in the lower division for a second season, the decision to move up into the top flight in 1972 was virtually made for him when the ambitious, fiercely driven Ipswich management bought West Ham's first division licence.

The dawning of an exciting new era couldn't have started better as tens of thousands descended upon Foxhall Heath on that eagerly awaited Good Friday afternoon of March 31. The record-breaking crowd was officially declared as 13,000 but another 5,000 probably swarmed in without paying once the decision was taken to open the gates to avoid further prolonging an already delayed start.

Hackney were the visitors and the need to crack on with the opening day show was further influenced by the fact that Witches and Hawks were due to lock horns again a few hours later down the A12 at Waterden Road – the first of what became traditional Good Friday home and away fixtures between the rivals.

Except Good Friday very quickly became Black Friday for Tony Davey.

Black Friday
QUITE unexpectedly, Tony found himself thrust into Heat 1 after both of the programmed home riders, Sandor Levai and Alan Sage, were excluded for tape offences. Shrimp, Witches' No.6, picked up a point but barely had time to catch breath before he was out again in the second race, his first scheduled ride.

What happened next would define his career, if not ruin it completely, and he still bears the

Billy Sanders, John Louis and Tony Davey in 1974 – one of the strongest heat leader trios in British League history.

physical scars of that first bend tangle with Hackney reserve Roger Wright.

"I think he came down and I hit him," says Tony, trying to recall the gory details of an incident that didn't look as bad as it undoubtedly proved to be for Shrimp. "My left hand got caught in his back sprocket."

After wincing at the mere thought of the pain he experienced, I can see Tony through the camera's viewfinder, clasping his hands together while attempting to explain the full extent of the permanent damage. "They amputated the little finger on my left hand and there was a lot of nerve damage too," he went on.

"I was racing again in three months, although we had to adapt my handlebars so that I could work the clutch. Basically, we cut the handlebar, inserted a thinner piece of metal into the hole and then bent the bars forward so that it fitted comfortably into my left hand. It didn't have any adverse effect on my ability to gate."

The Ipswich team that won the British League championship for the first time in 1975 and then completed the league and KO Cup double the following year was built on an all-for-one-and-one-for-all philosophy, where team spirit and collective input was prized way above the pursuit of individual glory.

"I think the biggest factor behind what we achieved was the fact that we were all local boys, living within a 10-mile radius of Ipswich Speedway. As well as winning the league and cup in '76, I think we also won the Spring Gold Cup, while John and Billy added the British League Pairs title.

"The team spirit in general was excellent. For his good company and to share the cost of travel, I'd drive to a lot of away matches with Ted Howgego."

While Tony is full of admiration and respect for the late John Berry, he also has words of praise for the role Ron Bagley played in helping to establish Witches as one of the greatest teams in British League history.

"As a team manager, Ron had a nicer way than JB of getting you going and he was a big help and

174

inspiration to me," says Shrimp.

After five seasons in which he consistently averaged somewhere between 7.47 and 8.37 from official fixtures, 1978 saw him burst through the nine-point barrier for the first time at first division level. "It was a brilliant season for me," he recalls.

Recalled by England manager Berry to the international arena for the Test series against Australasia, top-scoring on his home track in the third Test, Tony received further recognition when chosen by the promoters for a rare crack at the Golden Helmet match-race title. He challenged England No.1 Peter Collins and it was some feat to take the season-long holder to a third leg of what was then a monthly event.

"I didn't always believe in my own ability," says Tony, "and I think that showed again when Peter beat me by 2-0 at Belle Vue."

Davey reversed that result with a 2-0 victory at Foxhall before the Aces' No.1 won the decider at Hackney by the same emphatic margin. PC retained the coveted headgear throughout the season, successfully defending the title seven times. The only leg he dropped was to Davey.

In 1978, the British qualifying rounds of the World Championship were combined with the Grand Prix competition, with points counting towards both. Each rider contested three rounds and for added spice the best Australians and New Zealanders, including Ivan Mauger and Billy Sanders, were included, although their points only counted towards the GP series.

Tony was attacking forcefully on two fronts, his form as bubbly as his then fashionable permed hair. The night after winning the Poole round, he finished third behind Louis and Michael Lee in a run-off for top spot at Ipswich and then boosted his aggregate points tally with 11 at Halifax to cap a satisfying qualifying campaign.

The British semi-final draw (without the Anzacs) took him back down to Poole, where another outstanding display saw him win the meeting after a run-off with White City's Gordon Kennett. Before the next step on the world title trail at Coventry, Tony was among the top five qualifiers for

Local heroes: After winning their first British League title in 1975, the Witches (minus Billy Sanders, who had returned to Australia) were guests of the town's Mayoress. John Louis signs the visitors' book surrounded (left to right) by Ted Howgcgo, Mick Hincs, Tony, Trevor Jones, Mike Lanham, Dave Gooderham and team manager Ron Bagley.

the VW-Daily Mirror Grand Prix Final at White City, where fourth place on the day earned him fourth in the overall series scorers, behind Chris Morton, Louis and Malcolm Simmons.

Starr treatment

TONY never received the big money sponsorship deals many riders much less talented than him did but he could lay claim to one of the most unexpected and famous backers.

For shortly before the GP Final at White City, he was bought a brand new engine by TV comedian Freddie Starr.

Daily Mirror columnist Graham Baker, whose interview with Shrimp sparked Starr's interest, explained the backdrop to this bizarre tie-up when he wrote in the 1979 edition of Peter Oakes' *Speedway Yearbook:* "Nothing gave me greater pleasure than to witness the tremendous improvement shown by Ipswich rider Tony Davey.

"Shrimp surprised the whole of speedway by taking the fourth highest qualifying place for the final with 25 premium points.

"But when I interviewed him just four days before the Final, Davey revealed that he would have to sell his car to survive in speedway.

"He said: 'It's sickening to hear what other riders are making. I see them buying big houses and £10,000 cars while I am literally living from day to day.

"Some of them get £500 a meeting appearance money but I have to think myself lucky with £25. I must buy a new engine soon if I'm going to make it really big but I'll have to sell my car to do that'.

"Neither Davey nor I could have anticipated the reaction literally hours after the story appeared in the *Daily Mirror.*

"Comedian Freddie Starr, that great speedway fan, read the story – and immediately phoned Davey (who he had never met) to offer him £1,000 for a new engine.

"I phoned Starr, who was appearing in his summer show at Paignton, Devon, and he told me: 'The cheque is in the post. As soon as I read your story I realised something had to be done to help Tony'.

"Starr was as good as his word. Within 48 hours Davey had collected a brand new Weslake to use at White City.

"And although Starr had recently been suffering from flu, he promised to get to London to watch Davey – and his old mate Reg Wilson of Sheffield.

Leading Peter Collins in the Golden Helmet, 1978.

"Sure enough, he arrived to give a real showbiz flavour to the third Final. He finished the meeting by ripping off his shirt as he ran round the stadium to the cheers of a 15,000 crowd and the Penthouse Pets."

Recalling the story for *Backtrack*, Tony explained: "I received a phone call here at home a few days before the Grand Prix final from a bloke who said he was Freddie Starr's manager. I couldn't believe it and thought someone was messing around but he said Freddie wanted to have a word with me.

"He came on and asked what I needed. I told him I needed an engine that would cost about 700 quid, so he said: 'If I gave you a thousand pounds, would that do you?' I said: 'That would

On the Wessie engine bought for him by Freddie Starr, Tony roars clear of eventual GP winner Chris Morton and Ivan Mauger in the 1978 final at White City.

do me more than well, thank you!'.

"Next morning, just as promised, Freddie's cheque arrived along with a signed photo of himself.

"Freddie was my most unusual sponsor but I was also grateful to others . . . Dave Bickers and Fred Cotton, who was the manager at Dave's shop, and then there was Bob Steward, who bought me engines, clutches and other things in the last couple of years of my career. Bob looked after me and my family really well. He always said to me: 'If I'd known you earlier in your career, you'd have been World Champion'."

Two points away from Wembley
WITH the GP done and dusted, in August '78 all attention turned to the British Final at Coventry, where a perennially tough qualifier became even more cut-throat because the top four went straight to the Golden Jubilee World Final at Wembley. In most previous years, eight points would have been sufficient to ease Tony through but this time it left him an agonising two below the cut.

After winning his first heat from John Davis, Malcolm Simmons and Alan Grahame, Shrimp's dream of making it to a World Final was effectively shattered in a second ride machine failure. It was a double blow, because two of the riders he gifted precious points to – Dave Jessup and Kennett – both ended up among the quartet bound for the Twin Towers.

"I was leading when my bike just stopped and I never did find out the cause of it," he says, reflecting on the disappointment of scoring eight points from three of his five rides and nothing from the other two. A second place in his third outing and then a win over the Sheffield stars Reg Wilson and Doug Wyer, plus his old mate Louis, in his fourth appearance had kept his hopes alive going into the all-important Heat 19.

"But I was up against Peter Collins and the Morton brothers, Chris and Dave, and I suppose nerves

Tony at the start of 1979, a year that began full of promise but ended abruptly on a disastrous night at Leicester.

got the better of me again and I finished last. I just blew the race."

Typically deflecting praise from himself, Tony attributes his upsurge in 1978 to a new tie-up he enjoyed with a local firm, Scholar Engineering, who tuned his Weslake engines. "Had I known then what I know now, I could have been a better rider. Yes, I was earning reasonable money but there wasn't much spare cash to throw at my bikes. Besides, I was winning races and feeling happy.

"I just wish I'd believed in myself more. When I put my mind to it, I could beat anyone on my day."

But then Shrimp was always happiest being Shrimp and we love him all the more for being true to himself. He couldn't force himself to become, say, an Ivan Mauger.

Leicester agony

ABOARD well-prepared, top class machinery and imbued with a new sense of self-confidence, 1979 should have been the year in which Tony pushed on to even bigger things. Instead, just nine meetings and one league match into the new campaign, he landed back in hospital nursing his second career-threatening injury.

"I was on a high after '78, when I also got my first continental booking. Me and John (Louis) finished third in a best pairs meeting in Germany and because I scored a few more points than he did, I was invited back there the following year. In fact, we had just come back from Germany when I rode at Leicester early in '79 and my good run came to an end."

Describing what little he can recall from the back straight crash with team-mate Mike Lanham at Blackbird Road on April 24, he continues: "All I can remember is leaving the starting gate and then waking up in Leicester Royal Infirmary.

"I was told afterwards that the kick-boards at the bottom of the safety fence had been sticking out a bit and I must have clipped them. The bike stopped dead but I kept going. They reckon I went as high as the lamp standard and came down flat on my back. I broke six vertebrae and my left femur.

"I think I broke my leg when I slammed against the handlebars. The other (right) thigh was black and blue too, so it's a wonder I didn't break both legs."

To compound his misery and prolong the recovery process, the operation was botched so badly that John Berry said later that Tony could have successfully sued the hospital.

"The break was too low down to pin it, so they had to plate it on the outside of the bone," explained Shrimp. "When the swelling around the knee wouldn't go down, they wanted to re-admit me but by that time I'd been up to Scotland to see Dr Carlo Biagi, who told me the swelling wouldn't ease unless the plate was removed."

But rather than face the ordeal of a second operation, Shrimp decided to endure the pain and make a comeback in September. "It really did hamper me on a bike, though. Even just laying in bed, the leg hurt like hell.

"Looking back, the most sensible thing would have been to have gone through the whole surgery procedure again but I never did like hospitals. Who do!" he asks rhetorically in his deepest Suffolk accent that he is prone to unleash in quick-fire bursts that are not always easy to decipher.

Carr crash

WITH his testimonial year set for 1980, Tony had every incentive to fight his way back to a reasonable level of fitness but after struggling tentatively through to early August, careful not to take any unnecessary risks that might lead him back to a hospital ward, he re-broke the same thigh in the home match against Belle Vue.

To compound the pain, the simple-looking first bend spill, which observers say happened almost in slow-motion, came just three days before his testimonial meeting, set for Sunday, August 10.

"This time I broke the thigh higher up, just above where the plate finished. Ironically, I'd got out of the gate in front for the first time in a long while . . . and then Louis Carr came straight into the side of me.

"I knew as I lay on the track that the leg was broken again. JB kept telling me it wasn't – the first thing he did was give me a cigarette! – but I knew it was.

"I was sick with pain when I got to Ipswich Hospital and begged them to plate it again, which thankfully they did. I made up my mind there and then that I was finished in speedway. That was it.

"It was very unfortunate that it happened a few days before my testimonial meeting but they very kindly still went ahead with it. Later, I was presented with a photo album containing pictures of the riding line-up, some race action and shots of other things that went on, which I've kept to this day. After the meeting, a few of the boys – including JL, Bettsy and Michael Lee – came to see me in hospital, which was very nice of them."

Berry always had the greatest respect and reserved a special place in his heart for Shrimp. It's probably not stretching the truth too far to say that Witches' boss felt those painful moments that blighted Tony's career almost as acutely as the unlucky victim himself.

"JB was a shrewd businessman and although a lot of people outside of Ipswich didn't like him, he was friendly and generous to me. He didn't pay big money up front but he was always there if you

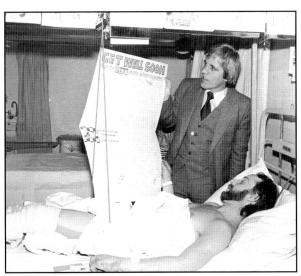 

In hospital at Leicester after his bad crash in 1979. Right: Memories and mementoes . . . Tony in 2014 with the metal plate that caused him so much pain in his left thigh.

Proud parents Audrey and Tony with new-born Claire. Right: Tony and Audrey in 2014, at home in Framsden.

needed help. He helped me through some bad times," said Tony.

"After my hand injury in 1972, he paid for my wife Audrey and I to go to Jersey for a week's all-expenses paid holiday. And after I broke my leg at Leicester, he offered to pay for Audrey to stay nearby. She didn't go because she had our daughter Claire to look after and was expecting Simon at the time, but it was another typically kind offer from JB.

"The second time I broke my leg he gave me a bit of money to help me out, because he knew I hadn't earned as much as expected that year.

"He was a brilliant man, a brilliant promoter and a good friend."

More breaks on the grass

AT 29, Tony's chequered speedway career came to an end after 10 years in the saddle. But he still had plenty of laps left in him, some extra gas in the tank. He just needed a new outlet for his adrenalin – and found it not far from home.

" I was told that if I broke my leg again, I could possibly lose it, which is why I packed up speedway. But like an idiot, I then took up grass-track racing and kept riding for probably another 20 years. I suppose I missed speedway and just liked racing for a bit of fun.

"I broke my wrist and two bones at the top of my back riding on the grass but I still enjoyed it," he laughs.

"When I packed up on the grass about seven years ago, I spent another couple of years riding in pre-65 moto-cross events.

"I got our son Simon involved in grass-track from the age of six. He won the British Best Pairs in his first year and went on to win the Eastern Centre Championship three or four times, on both 250 and 500cc. He carried on until he was about 22, got married to a nice girl and settled down without risking any more injuries. We used to race in the same group, although he was much quicker than me – I was an old man.

"Simon had a go at speedway, at Ipswich and King's Lynn. Even though we never encouraged him to race – we'd lost one child and didn't want to lose another – Audrey and I still supported him and I drove him around."

Family guy

ONLY parents who have been through the sad and horrifying anguish of losing a child can fully comprehend what Tony and Audrey must have suffered when their beloved 14-year-old daughter Claire was taken from them.

Courageous Claire had been fighting leukaemia for a couple of years before she passed away in 1990. Pictures of the pretty schoolgirl continue to adorn the Davey's home in the tranquil village of Framsden, some 10 miles north of Ipswich.

Their son Simon, who was 10 when his sister died, gave the Daveys the strength and purpose to carry on. "There would have been no point in us going on if it hadn't been for Simon," said Tony.

"It was obviously a terrible time for both Audrey and myself but having Simon helped us to get through it."

Simon and his wife Hayley have three children - Emilie (aged eight), Cadence (six) and Logan (four).

Claire would have been pleased and proud to know that more recent Ipswich idols, Jeremy Doncaster and Mark Loram, rode in a grass-track meeting near Norwich in her memory and raised £2,200 in charity for Addenbrookes Hospital, Cambridge.

Now 63, Shrimp and his brother Jim, who used to help him to prepare his speedway bikes, continue to run the Evergreen Garage at nearby Crowfield, where they carry out servicing, repairs, MOTs, etc. But when he's not at work, the family come first.

"Audrey spent 40-odd years running around after me and my time is now with her and the rest of our family," Tony added.

If Shrimp does have any lingering regrets about his decade on the shale, he is very good at disguising them.

"I got paid money like I'd never seen before I did speedway," he admits. "I knew second division boys who were earning more than I was in the first division but I was happy being paid for doing what I enjoyed. I've had a wonderful life and done everything I wanted to.

"The years I had with Ipswich in the 70s were far and away the best in speedway. The success we achieved as a team full of local blokes will never be done again – not at Ipswich or any other track."

By John Berry ● Issue 47 (2011)

MEN OF HONOUR

Testimonial and benefit meetings have been routinely added to the annual fixture list since the mid-70s. JOHN BERRY looks back at some of the most deserving recipients . . .

I WELL remember when Reg Fearman and Eric Boothroyd, on behalf of Halifax Speedway, announced at a BSPA general council meeting that they wanted to apply for Eric Boocock to be granted a testimonial meeting in celebration of his long-term loyalty to the Dukes, specifically after having served 10 years with the same team.

The room was full of old-school promoters, many, if not most, of whom had been riders themselves before joining the ranks of track bosses. They found the very notion of granting such a request to be utterly against the long-held belief that riders rode, promoters promoted and they each sat on opposite sides of a huge divide.

Eric waxed lyrical about how it was the right thing to reward loyalty, like the cricketing fraternity, with a one-off bonanza payout that didn't actually have to come out of the promoter's back pocket.

OK, in theory a rider was locked into a particular promotion by the retain and transfer system but even then, in 1974, those riders who wanted to move tracks were finding ways of doing so and this was seen as providing an incentive for a rider to remain loyal to a particular team.

Of course, the more cynical among us would have understood this carrot would also be something of a negotiating ploy when sitting down with a rider to thrash out his pay deal for the upcoming season – especially those riders who were entering into their seventh, eighth or ninth season with the same club and who might feel they could pick up a better deal if they touted themselves around. It should be pointed out that this was at a time when the old system of centrally negotiated pay rates had finally broken down.

Not that every rider needed such an incentive to remain loyal to a club and especially those who rode at Belle Vue. I cannot imagine for one moment why any rider would want to leave Belle Vue (Hyde Road). Having the 'Zoo' as a home track was such a clear advantage to all riders and over the years there were very few, if any, who left the place of their own volition. Most had to be winkled out with a crowbar. Even Ivan Mauger found himself squeezed out against his wishes when he departed for Exeter in 1973.

For the years Peter Collins and Chris Morton graced the fast flowing circuit, how they loved the wide open spaces with its multitude of lines, where making good starts was nowhere near as essential as at most tracks. It could be argued that the grand old place was fair to everyone and, indeed, most riders enjoyed their visits. However, like playing lawn bowls, anyone could ride it but it required lots and lots of practice to understand its full potential. Another bonus was that the home riders were able to take the confidence it gave them and put it to good use away from home.

Not surprisingly then, Belle Vue can claim the highest number of testimonial recipients – five – during the period 1974 to 1990, although not all can be said to have met all of the requirements. Of course, Peter Collins and Chris Morton ticked all the boxes with plenty to spare (Mort getting very close to a double) but Belle Vue relied on Soren Sjosten have ridden for the Aces pre-British League (with a break in between) to justify his event in 1975 during his ninth unbroken year. Alan

The programme cover for the first ever speedway testimonial meeting to honour Eric Boocock's 10 years with Halifax. Right: Booey riding flat out at The Shay.

Wilkinson's eight years with the Aces (and one at Rochdale under the same management) really means his day in 1979, the year after the crash that saw him wheelchair-bound, was more of a benefit than testimonial, while Peter Ravn was somehow granted a day in the sun during 1990. Shawn Moran also had his testimonial at Belle Vue's next home, Kirkmanshulme Lane, in 1989, although that was his reward for nine consecutive seasons with his former club Sheffield, and it wasn't his fault that Tigers closed down at the end of the '88 season.

Many other riders, in fact the vast majority, qualified for testimonials because they simply enjoyed riding for their local track and were being loyal and true to their local roots. There's no doubt riding for your local team adds pressure. Have a bad meeting and you can't just go home and forget it until next week. Everyone wants a piece of you, good or bad. Ipswich staged four such events in the same number of years from 1979 to 1982.

John Louis set the ball rolling in 1979 with eight years in Division One following two in the second division. Next came Tony Davey (nine and one) and then Billy Sanders in 1981 (actually a 'benefit meeting' because by then he had been moved to Hull against his wishes). It was Mike Lanham's turn in 1982 after having been at Ipswich for 11 years.

Interesting also is the number of pairs of stars who stayed together at clubs over a long period. Once again, Peter Collins and Chris Morton head the list with 14 shared years, with Reg Wilson and Doug Wyer at Sheffield not far behind. Martin Ashby and Bob Kilby might well have topped the list for Swindon had both of them not been forced by Rider Control to do stints at Exeter at different times. John Louis and Tony Davey shared 11 seasons together at Ipswich and eight of Billy Sanders' 11 years there were shared with Louis.

They were good friends, as were Terry Betts and Malcolm Simmons at King's Lynn, but that didn't prevent a certain amount of competitive tension between them! No such tension between Tom and Joe Owen up at Newcastle where they dominated the National League instead of racing with the big boys where they patently belonged. Tom had his testimonial in 1982 during only his eighth year

183

Nigel Boocock and his wife Cynthia salute a packed Coventry crowd before his testimonial meeting in 1975.

at the club and then Joe, after he had five highly successful years at Hull, returned to Newcastle to be granted his testimonial meeting one year later, and two years into his second spell. Mind you, Ian Thomas was no stranger to stretching situations. Hull had given Bobby Beaton a testimonial in 1978, just four years after the Vikings had begun racing in the top league!

Gordon Kennett was another curly one. Eastbourne to Oxford, Oxford to White City and then White City back to Eastbourne. Three different venues in the 10 years but because Bob Dugard was on the promoting team of all tracks he claimed that meant Gordon had done 10 years with the *same promotion*.

Trevor Hedge, on the other hand, did nine solid years for Wimbledon and then found himself moved out in the very year he should have had, and fully deserved, his big event.

Malcolm Simmons never qualified for a testimonial by way of 10 years at one club but was granted not one, but two, special benefit meetings (at Hackney and Kings Lynn) in his silver jubilee season of 1987. George Hunter had a similar meeting at Edinburgh celebrating his 25 years of service to the sport. Others, too, have had a 25-year benefit.

Barry Thomas receives a presentation from Ronnie Russell on the occasion of his second testimonial at Hackney, in 1989.

Doctor Carlo Biagi was granted a testimonial in 1981. As far as I know he is the only non-rider to be afforded such an honour but I defy anybody to suggest he did not fully deserve it for his selfless service to the sport. Barry Thomas is the only rider who actually had two testimonials at 10 and 20 years' service for Hackney.

I'm not sure when the original testimonial was granted to Eric Boocock that anyone thought different to the 10 years having to be consecutive and at the same track. I'm not sure appearances as a number eight filling in for injured riders should have constituted a qualifying year but as per usual it was easier to shrug one's shoulders rather than be seen to be a killjoy. Also, with only a couple of exceptions, at that time even star men were hardly topping the rich lists and middle order riders were doing it tough, so why not give them a chance to gain a bonus?

Testimonial or benefit? Are those words interchangeable? Probably to you and I but my understanding is the tax man accepts the rewards from a testimonial, if it meets many and various conditions, are tax-free, but rewards from a benefit meeting are not. These conditions meant that, in theory anyway, all testimonial activities should have been organised through a testimonial committee with specifically the rider and his promoter excluded from being involved. This actually raised a question as to who was the promoter of the meeting and given that only licensed promoters were allowed to stage speedway events . . . of course, this was carefully overlooked, with the rider and his family working alongside the promotion to stage the meeting.

Benefit meetings, as apart from testimonials, were not supposed to happen. Or rather, if they did happen, the regulations stipulated that the profits had to go to the Speedway Riders' Benevolent Fund (SRBF). Somewhere along the line this regulation went by the board. Who would doubt that it was reasonable to hold a benefit event for a rider who, for instance, was wheelchair-bound? The trick is to know where to draw the line.

These days it seems as if there is a benefit meeting for somebody every other week. Not just a reward for long service to a club any more, but farewell meetings for riders who may or may not be retiring. Each of these meetings for star men who have already done well out of the sport all seem to want to outdo the one before, leaving the poor old regular promoter having to make do with just staging the bread and butter meetings and seeing these riders taking both the jam and the cream.

Somehow, though, in my romantic and naïve little brain, I can't help thinking about riders like Mike Keen, Pete Reading, Bernie Leigh, Mike Lanham, Ian Turner, etc. Never superstars but always there and ready to claim the odd few points that were more often than not the difference between their team winning and losing. They rode speedway for the love of it, not to become millionaires, and surely these and others like them deserved the testimonials they earned. In fact, to my mind these were the kind of riders the idea of a testimonial was designed for.

Alan Wilkinson and his wife Jean with the Belle Vue management and the riders who supported Wilkie's benefit meeting at Hyde Road in 1979.

SID
SHELDRICK

THESE days Sid Sheldrick gets his kicks fixing and flying Piper airplanes around Blackpool Tower and beyond, taking part in Civil War Re-enactments with his film star pal Sean Bean and enjoying the occasional tear-up on his grass-track bike.

Three years ago, at the age of 60, he won the Northern Grass-Track Championship after finding a bike in a barn in Newcastle which had been lying there for 15 years.

"The owner told me to take it because his son was frightened to death of it and after rebuilding it, I had a go and won six races on the trot. Not bad at 60. I'm proud of that."

But back in the late 60s and 70s, Sid was a handsome young speedway star who had the girls at his feet and certainly has some stories to tell of a track career that took him from Sheffield to Nelson, Bradford, Wolverhampton, Newcastle, Hull, Barrow, Paisley, Scunthorpe and the German Bundesliga.

Two of the best concern how he became 'The Lion King' after an unwelcome brush with a fiery Scotsman who was to become the most iconic football manager in the British game.

In fact, Sid desperately wanted to become a professional footballer in his home city of Sheffield.

"I was on Sheffield United's books as a 16-year-old goalkeeper and got as far as playing for the reserve team against Manchester City. But we got beat 3-0 and on the Monday morning I was called into the office and told I was too small to make it as a goalkeeper and was being released.

"The bloke who told me was the club's England international goalkeeper Alan Hodgkinson and he wasn't exactly the biggest.

"At that age, it destroys you. I went home and threw my boots in the corner and decided I would become a speedway rider instead.

"My parents had always been interested in speedway and followed Sheffield Tigers. I got involved with 'Uncle Frank' Varey at Owlerton and had a few rides there when I started out. But I ended up joining Mike Parker's empire because I thought there were more opportunities.

"I rode for Parker at Nelson, Newcastle, Wolverhampton and Bradford, where Les Whaley became the promoter."

Sid was a blossoming second string with Nelson Admirals and moved with them to Bradford's cavernous Odsal Stadium in the middle of the summer of 1970.

Sid's first full season with Nelson in 1969.

186

"Nelson was a bit of a trick track but once you found out how to ride it, it gave you a massive advantage in home meetings. My best pal was Gary Peterson, the New Zealander who would have become World Champion if he had not been killed in a track crash at Wolverhampton.

"The night he was killed I was racing somewhere else and was called into the speedway office and told the devastating news. I went to Gary's funeral and it took me a long time to get over his death, because I was so close to him and we rode together for Nelson and Bradford."

Sid admits that the mid-season move from Nelson, where the promoters struggled to make ends meet, to Odsal was a massive culture shock.

"We had a 10,000 crowd at the opening meeting against Eastbourne and the atmosphere was unbelievable. Odsal was vast and just walking out in front of such a big crowd was a daunting experience.

"I fell off in my first race and was knocked unconscious when the handlebar went through my 'pudding basin' helmet. Later, in the bar at Odsal, I met the Halifax rider Bob Jameson and he sold me a Bell helmet. I was one of the first riders in British speedway to have a full-face helmet. Then our captain Alan Knapkin got one and we were known as the 'Northern Spacemen'.

"Odsal Stadium had such a history as a speedway venue and the sheer adrenalin made you give your best. OK, I didn't score maximum after maximum but I loved racing there in front of those fans and always gave it everything. I wanted to entertain them.

"At that time speedway was the second best-supported professional sport to football and even second division racing was very spectacular. It was a hard division but you had more control on the old two-valve Jawas than today's bikes and you could come from the back."

Sid wore a white football shirt over his leathers just to be different.

Sid in full flow at Odsal in 1971 wearing his familiar white full-face helmet, shirt and boots, so that his mum couldn't miss him.

Barrow Bombers in 1974. Left to right: Sid Sheldrick, George Graham (promoter), Mick Sheldrick, Chris Roynon, Alan Middleton (team manager) and Joe Owen, with Graham Tattersall and Terry Kelly kneeling and Tom Owen on machine.

"It was so my mum could pick me out from her seat in the stand, because nearly every rider in those days just wore black leathers. The only exceptions were Mike Broadbank at Swindon, in his all-red leathers, and 'Little Boy Blue' Nigel Boocock at Coventry.

"Another reason I liked wearing white was because I had heard a lot of stories about Ken Le Breton, 'The White Ghost'. But the person who really inspired me to wear white was Cradley Heath's Ivor Brown.

"Later, in 1972, Bradford became the first team to have 'team leathers' made for us by Lewis Leathers of Sheffield.

"We had a lot of success at Bradford and nearly won the Division Two title. I had such a good relationship with the fans that I never wanted to leave. I loved the crowd and it was where I made my mark.

"But after a couple of injuries and a couple of mediocre seasons, I was getting a bit despondent and my pal Eric Boocock suggested a change of track might do me a world of good.

"Before that, my father said to the Bradford promoter Les Whaley: 'You need to drop Sid from the team. It might give him a shock and get him going again'. But Les told him: 'I can't afford to drop him because he puts bums on seats. He is worth a few hundred on the gate'.

"I don't think you get loyalty like that in speedway any more but Les was always a perfect gentleman.

"Anyway, I moved to Barrow in 1973 and, career-wise, it was the right thing to do. Les Whaley had left and Alan Knapkin took over as promoter. I never had a problem with him because I used to partner him and I know he would have had me back.

"Alan loved his speedway and he loved Bradford but he was trying to do everything on a shoe-string. He wanted to bring back the good times but when you plough your life savings into a business it doesn't always work.

"Anyone who puts their money into speedway these days must be very brave. If the crowds are not there, you can't pay the riders' wages and they all want fortunes because the sport is so expensive.

"I used to ride for 10 shillings a point in old money and 10 shillings a start. But I would have paid to ride.

"And I loved going back to Bradford at every opportunity – even if the fans started booing me!"

England hero

THEY didn't boo him when he rode for England at Odsal and he particularly recalls an international there when he wasn't in any fit state to take part.

"I crashed at Barrow on the Tuesday night and the next morning, the day of the international at Odsal, my left knee came up the size of a football. My parents had a small hotel in Blackpool and knew the physio of the local football club. He gave me some treatment and I went to Bradford.

"Joe Thurley, the England team manager, said he would put me at No.8 so I might not have to ride, because I couldn't put my foot on the floor. Anyway, it got to the point where Joe said: 'I need you in this race' and I got a 5-1 with Carl Glover.

"My knee was killing me but I got two more 5-1s and I'd done my job. I remember the headline in the *Bradford Telegraph and Argus* the next day: 'Sheldrick the hero of England's win'. When you get to my age you look back at things like that. But I can't remember whether it was against Poland or Czechoslovakia!"

Thumbs-up for Lions

ANOTHER injury pre-empted Sid's next team move, from Barrow to Paisley in 1975, and two of his favourite stories.

"I crashed at Barrow and lost the end of my left thumb when I got it caught in the chain. I thought that was my racing career finished but Eric Boocock took me up to Galashiels to see Dr Carlo Biagi and he said: 'Don't worry, I'll grow you a new thumb!' And he did.

"It meant having my thumb fastened inside my stomach for six months but while I was in hospital, supporters came from all over Scotland to visit me and so did Neil Mcfarlane, who I knew from Coatbridge.

"Meanwhile Barrow had closed and I had fallen out with the promoter Ian Thomas, so there was no chance of me moving to his Newcastle track.

"But Neil said: 'Sid, I am opening a track at Paisley next year and I want you to be my No.1 and captain'. I couldn't believe it but what an incentive to get better. Here was a promoter who had faith in me.

"So when I was fit again and had a new thumb, my dad drove me up to Paisley from Sheffield and parked up at Love Street Stadium, the home of St Mirren Football Club, alongside some offices.

"The next thing, this red-faced guy comes storming out of one of the offices screaming four-letter words about how we had parked in his parking space. My father took exception to the guy's tone of voice and they finished up in a nose-to-nose confrontation.

"The guy turned out to be Alex Ferguson, the St Mirren manager. Dad was ex-Royal Navy and had boxed for the Navy, so he was ready to give as good as he got and more. If other people hadn't intervened I am sure the two of them would have finished up rolling in the dust.

"My father's claim to fame is that he nearly knocked 'Fergie' on his backside although, funnily enough, they did become good pals."

Only after the Sheldricks had a blast from the infamous 'Fergie hair drier' long before he joined Manchester United.

Sid with Leo the line on opening night at Paisley in 1975.

National pride: Sid before an England v Australasia Test at Workington in June 1975. The Paisley star scored 10 in a 58-50 victory.

"We all know what Sir Alex can be like and nobody can dispute his outstanding achievements in football but, effectively, it was down to him that the Paisley Lions only lasted two seasons. The football club was begging for extra revenue when speedway opened at Love Street but didn't want us any more once Fergie got them promoted to the Scottish Premier League. I suppose he did what he had to do."

Nevertheless, speedway got off to a great start at Love Street in April 1975, when 6,000 turned up for the opening meeting against New National League big guns Birmingham.

And promoter Neil Mcfarlane demonstrated his skill as a showman by producing a real live lion cub for his new captain to lead out on the opening night.

"Without warning, Neil just handed me the lead and said: 'You have got to take Leo out on parade'. It was only a few months old but it was certainly playful and had big teeth," recalls Sid.

"Arthur Browning, the Birmingham captain, was a big guy who used to do the stunts for the Milk Tray adverts but he wasn't happy when Leo started mauling his leg. Fortunately, Leo took a shine to me and was trying to lick me to death when we were posing for photographs.

"It was one of the biggest nights of my life. I had ridden in plenty of big meetings but the opening night at Love Street was something else and I'll never forget Leo the Lion. He became a full-grown lion and lived to a good age in Edinburgh Zoo.

"My brother Mick and I were No.1 and 2 at Paisley and although speedway only lasted two seasons at Love Street and the team wasn't very successful, the fans were brilliant and we had a terrific re-union up there two years ago. It would be great if someone would organise one at Bradford."

Sid was the first English rider to captain a Scottish team and claims the reason he left in the middle of the Lions' second campaign was "to save the club".

"Scunthorpe came in with a ridiculous offer for me and it gave Neil Mcfarlane the money to finish the season. The Lions had run into financial difficulties, so I left to save them from closing. I have a lot of time for Neil and owe him a lot. I really enjoyed my time at Paisley.

"I liked Scunthorpe, too, but it wasn't a good career move, although I had two

Mick Sheldrick in action for Paisley in 1976. The brothers had previously ridden together two years earlier at Barrow.

seasons there before I went off to ride in the German Bundesliga for a couple of seasons.

"I came back in 1979 and Jim Beaton, who was the promoter at Blantyre, asked me if would ride for England against Scotland there to try to pull in a few fans from my Paisley days. It was a one-off and my last-ever speedway meeting. Not a bad way to go out—riding for England against Scotland.

"I had started my own garage business in Blackpool and it took off. So it was time to call it a day as far as speedway racing was concerned.

"Now I am a Civil Aviation Chief Engineer with a fleet of planes based at Blackpool Airport. Fancy a flip round Blackpool Tower, upside-down?

"I still follow Sheffield United and I'm quite pally with Sean Bean, another big Blades fan who is also into Civil War Re-enactments. Cromwell and the Roundheads and all that stuff.

"We hit it off straight away when he found out

Sid in 2013, on his bike and surrounded by speedway memorabilia where he works at Blackpool Airport.

I supported the Blades and, of course, he was in the TV series *Sharpe*. We go around the UK re-enacting battles from the Civil War. It's great fun but a lot different from speedway."

Sid and I had a great time chewing the fat in the club bar of his company Fly Blackpool Ltd, where I met his chief executive Robert Murgatroyd and Sid's brother Mick.

Speedway? Would you do it all again, I asked him. "I miss it every day," was his response. "I loved every minute. There is nothing better than throwing your motor bike sideways and sitting on somebody's back wheel at 65mph. The adrenalin is out of this world. And you feel 10 feet tall when you pull on that Union Jack body colour to represent your country."

One final memory. His most satisfying race. "Riding for Wolverhampton at Hull in the first division. I was a second division rider and Wolverhampton needed a 5-1 in the last heat to win the match.

"Jim McMillan and Bobby Beaton were the Hull pairing and Ole Olsen and Tom Leadbitter for Wolves. Leadbitter went through the tapes and because our other reserve had used up his rides, that just left me to ride with Ole.

"He said: 'We can win this but you must make the gate and ride on the outside'. I did make the gate and Olsen, who was on a 15-point maximum, pushed me out to the dirt and shut the door on McMillan and Beaton on every turn. On the last corner I thought I had better ease off to let him through for his maximum. I didn't have to. He left me for dead.

"But we got the 5-1 and it was probably the best four laps of speedway in my entire career."

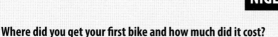

Where did you get your first bike and how much did it cost?

When I was a kid we lived two doors away from the Grahame brothers' parents, so when I was about 14 I got into speedway and I used to go round there and clean their leathers. I soon knew I wanted a career in speedway and Andy Grahame lent me the money to buy a two-valve Jawa. It cost £175 and he said I could pay him back £10 a week. I was on a YTS scheme at the time earning £25 a week. I paid £10 a week housekeeping and gave Andy a tenner, so I was a 17-year-old lad with a fiver a week to live on.

Who helped you most in your early days?

The Grahame brothers – they taught me all I know about speedway. I first got involved in the sport in 1982, when I helped John Grahame by mechanicing for him. After that I mechaniced for Alan Grahame when he was at Cradley (Birmingham had closed by then). I did it for two years and the promoter Colin Pratt used to arrange it so I could have a go after the meeting on some of the away tracks. I started off in the juniors with Cradley but Mick Evans, who was team manager at the time, didn't seem to want me in the team – I think he thought I was only there because of Alan Grahame. But John Jones, the junior No.1, broke his leg and I was thrown in at the deep end.

In 1985, after I'd broken into the Cradley team, Erik Gundersen asked me if I'd go to his house and help him with his machinery. I thought, 'this is my chance to learn how to be a World Champion' – it didn't quite work out like that, though. One night before a meeting me and Phil Collins were at Erik's house – we had a few beers and a take-away. It was a lads' night in. Erik got a bit drunk and he slept in until about four o'clock the next afternoon while I was working on his bikes. That night, though, he scored 14, while I got my usual four or five.

Best promoter you've ridden for?

Chris van Straaten – he was so professional. When I was struggling at Exeter I phoned him to ask for some help. He told me to take my bike to Carl Blomfeldt, the expert tuner, and to send him the bill. OK, Wolves owned my contract but I wasn't even riding for them at that time.

Track(s) you never looked forward to visiting?

Peterborough. I had some good races and decent scores there – but the amount of times I've ridden the line and still been passed on the inside by a home rider with both wheels inside the white line. Mick Poole was one who used to do it.

Which team-mate did you most enjoy partnering on-track?

Andrew Silver at Arena-Essex. He really looked out for you.

Worst crash/injuries?

It was at Mildenhall when I was riding for Arena. I had a coming together with Eric Monaghan and fractured my kneecap.

The ambulance was from the nearby American air base and the driver got lost going to the hospital. We were in the back for ages and it was a really bumpy ride. Eventually we stopped and we thought we must be there. Then we heard this American voice say, 'Hey buddy, do you know where the hospital is?'

The most frightening crash I had, although somehow I came out of it unscathed, was when I was riding for Cradley at Coventry. Alun Rossiter went into the corner and pulled a big locker, I spun round and was laying face up on the track with my legs apart. Paul Fry went right over my nuts and over my head. I could see the engine going over the top of me.

At the time we had a spate of wearing different coloured goggles and mine were tinted red, so when everyone came over to me, they thought it was blood in my eyes!

Career highlight/proudest moment?

I won the first ever Midland Junior Championship in 1985.

I scored a maximum for Arena against Coventry and beat Dave Mullett to win the Silver Helmet. I went home and slept in it all night – it was really uncomfortable with those wings on the side!

MARTIN
DUGARD

MARTIN Dugard succinctly sums up his one and only World Final appearance when asked what, with the benefit of hindsight, he would have done differently.

"Turned up wanting to win it!" he laughs.

The 44-year-old from Worthing, a two-club man who retired from racing after the 2001 season, reached the last 16 for the only time in his career at Bradford's Odsal Stadium in 1990.

It was the year Sweden's Per Jonsson defeated American Shawn Moran in a run-off to take the title. Dugard's evening wasn't anywhere near as momentous as Jonsson's, his big night debut proving rather inauspicious as he finished down among the also-rans with just six points.

He did have a race win to look back on, although 24 years down the line, he admits his recollection of arguably the biggest night of his career is not exactly crystal clear.

"I don't really remember that much about it," he says. "I've watched it on video when I can remember little bits and pieces of it but, no, I don't remember it to be fair."

In the build-up to the meeting, Dugard, like every rider, was interviewed by *Speedway Star*. He was astonishingly frank when he told the magazine: "There's no way I'm going to win it, that's for sure. I'm not up to it yet and I'll be happy if I can come away with just one race win. At least I'll be able to say I've won a heat in a World Final."

Perhaps a little more self-belief wouldn't have gone amiss and nearly a quarter of a century on, he admits: "I was a bit naive. I didn't really understand how you get to a World Final and what you had to do when you got there. With me, if it was going to happen, it was going to happen. If it wasn't, it wasn't.

"The thing was, I wasn't really trying to get to a World Final and I think it would have been better for me if it had been held in another country. It would have meant more to me. But unfortunately, or fortunately as it was, the World Final was at Bradford.

"There was a full house there, however many thousand people that was, but I don't think I was too laidback about it. I just believed Bradford wasn't particularly my sort of place. It was a fast track, I hadn't had good meetings there before and I hadn't really mastered it.

Martin looking typically laid-back before the 1990 World Final at Bradford.

194

SPEEDWAY FAMILY: Martin's grandad Charlie Dugard was part and parcel of Eastbourne Speedway from Day One. Father Bob, seen here in the colours of Wimbledon in 1968, has long been the driving force at Arlington. Uncle Eric lining up for the Eagles in 1978. Martin with younger brother Paul – 'like chalk and cheese' – while riding together for Oxford in 1989.

"When you only go somewhere maybe twice a year, it's the last place you think about. I was just pleased to get that far but as much as I wanted to go and get to another World Final, I didn't, apart from when I was reserve at Wroclaw in 1992.

"I won my last race and I was pleased with that (Dugard defeated Roman Matousek, fellow Brit Richard Knight and Toni Kasper in Heat 20). To win a race in a World Final was something to be proud of but it's so surreal when you get 15 or 20 years down the line and you think, 'I wish I'd done that instead'."

So what do you wish you'd done? "Turned up wanting to win it! If you speak to any of the speedway boys, you generally know when you're going to have a good night and you know when you're going to have a bad night.

"A World Final is a little bit different because there are so many people out there who can trip you up, as it were. Like when your bike goes into scrutineering, they can say, 'that's not right', or they'll say, 'you've got to do this', and then someone else will say, 'you can't put that on there'.

"Because my bikes were so light, we were putting chains under the seat, duct-taping them and fixing them to the seat with cable ties and they're saying, 'no, it's got to be fixed properly'. It just seemed that everybody was there trying to make it hard work for you, even before the meeting started, and that's when you realise the World Final is on a completely different level for someone like me. It was my first World Final but for Hans (Nielsen), maybe it was his seventh or eighth, I don't know.

"I did enjoy the experience but it was a bit different to what I expected, as in it was just a glorified British Final in a way, but I still found it very strange that if you went to Poland (for a World Final), everyone there would want the Poles to win. Go to Sweden, they all want the Swedes to win. But go to a British World Final, and they want the Swedes, the Poles, the Germans, whoever, to win. That's the only thing I found very hard in the UK.

"I would have loved to have ridden at Wembley in a World Final but I never even saw one there. I went to the '88 Final in Vojens, though, the one with the run-off between Hans and Erik (Gundersen) – that was the only other one I saw."

Apart from 1992 in Wroclaw, where Dugard was a non-riding reserve – through choice. "Rick Miller was excluded and I should have been out as a reserve to replace him," he explained. "But I wasn't going to get all my stuff dirty just for one ride when it was right at the very end of the meeting. I couldn't be bothered.

"I helped Havvy but when it came to having a ride myself, I didn't want to get covered in it just for four laps."

Dugard, in fact, holds a unique place within the annals of speedway history. He is the only Brit to have appeared in both a British World Final and a British Grand Prix.

Martin, whose family name is synonymous with the Eastbourne

His first big individual win, ahead of Kevin Smith (left) and Steve Schofield in the 1986 Southern Riders' Championship at Poole.

Eagles, made that one and only World Final appearance at Odsal in 1990. He also made three GP wild card appearances – at Coventry in 1998 and 2000, when he recorded a famous win, and at Cardiff in 2001, the first-ever Grand Prix at the Millennium Stadium.

He didn't ever qualify for the GP series outright and says: "If I had, I would like to think I could have finished about halfway but I wouldn't have been consistent enough. For me to be consistent all the time, I would have had to give something else up, so I could really concentrate on it.

"When you get a little bit older, it's like the old saying: 'the older you get, the better you were'. I do regret some of the things I've done and not doing some of the things I should have done. For instance, I should have listened to other people when they told me to go and ride in Germany on a Sunday, instead of staying with my club.

"You should go and do these meetings when you're offered them but the problem is it's no good going there if you don't understand what's going on around you.

"When you go to the big individual meetings, they are like a World Final. You have a pit area and that's it. It's not like in England where you have a pit area and a bench, you have a number on the wall and what you stick in that pit area is up to you. You have to stand on your own two feet and that's where it is very different compared to what you get in the UK. We do pamper everybody when really we should be saying, 'no, you go and fight a little harder for your place'.

But we don't, we're not that sort of nation."

Family dynasty

IT all started for Dugard back in the early 80s and given his family's connections with the sport, dating back to speedway's very earliest days, it was inevitable that Martin would follow his grandfather and father on to the racetrack.

Grandad Charlie Dugard was one of the founders of the club and was later followed at the Eagles' helm by his son Bob, Martin's father. Brothers Bob, John and Eric all rode on the shale.

"I don't think there was ever an opportunity for me to choose another path," says Martin. "Obviously the family connection to speedway was pretty tight. My grandfather owned the machine tools business as well as the speedway, and the speedway was very profitable compared to the machine tool company during the years around the war. It's only in the last 30 years really that the speedway has started to lose itself, while the machine tool business is still good because everybody still needs engineering in the world, so that holds its own.

"I didn't know anything else apart from speedway. I basically grew up at Arlington and, as far as I was concerned, there was only Eastbourne. I didn't realise there was a big league out there. We just concentrated purely on Eastbourne. We went to the track, it was run as a business, we came home and that was it.

"There's such a big connection when you speak to people now and they know a member of the family or they know someone who did speedway. But you go somewhere where they've bought a machine from us and they don't connect the speedway with the machine tools. As much as you push the speedway, some people are totally oblivious to the fact it even exists. Sometimes, it's quite disheartening.

"But there are people who followed Tai Woffinden in the Grand Prix last year and that lifted speedway up a little tier of the ladder. How long it will last, who knows?

"My own opinion is that I don't think speedway would have survived without Sky Sports. Speedway has always survived but for how much longer, no-one really knows.

"When I first started to ride in the mid-80s, the crowds that I saw then were nothing compared to what Gordon Kennett and people like that saw in the late 70s, and through to the early part of the

80s when the crowds started to die off.

"The biggest crowd I ever rode in front of was the World Final in 1990 and when I was at Oxford, there were pretty good crowds there all the time but that was only because of the World Champion Hans Nielsen and the fact it was a pretty good side. But then to now is chalk and cheese.

"Eastbourne always had a good following in the 70s when it was on a Sunday afternoon but I don't think it matters what division you are in now, you are not going to get the same amount of people. How they can call it the Elite League now, I don't know. But it's one of those things – it's easy to sit back and criticise but when people are losing thousands and thousands of pounds, *you* come and put your money where your mouth is. You lose that amount of money every week but you think you're going to make it better by advertising, so do you pump that money in as well? And then, if that doesn't work, you've lost double the amount."

Kids on the right track
DUGARD cut his racing teeth on the mini-track at Arlington in the early 80s, which was built behind the terraces on the first and second bends.

Martin recalls: "There was a big group of about 10, people like me, Gary Tagg, Scott Swain, Kevin Pitts, David Norris and the Standings, Dean and Darren. Bob would be doing the main speedway track, so we were told to go and play elsewhere.

"We had a couple of tyres on the floor and then it was, 'hey, we can cut a track out in there' and that's what we did. They realised we were having fun and then Alan Johns became involved. He made the first junior bikes for everyone and we had a couple of fence panels go up to make a corner and that was it really, it was all built from there.

"We all started on a standard bike, it was one Alan made, no-one else made them, and we did what we could with the equipment that was available at the time. It was the upright Honda engines, the Honda step-through that now they deliver pizzas on, but that was all that was available at the time.

"In 1983, we had a Schoolboy Championship and I won it but really anybody could have won it out of all of us there. None of us was particularly any good but that was where the fun came from. I can't remember a lot about the meeting but I think there was quite a good attendance for a kids' event.

"It was real grass roots. It didn't matter if you fell off, or someone else fell off. Whoever couldn't ride, someone would lend a bike. That's what it was like in those days and I think that has gone out of speedway at the moment."

Despite the development of the mini-track, Dugard didn't spend every waking hour on the circuit. "No, not really because we live half-an-hour or 40 minutes away from the stadium, so we could only go over there when Dad was going. He was very protective of the main track. It was, 'no, you can't ride on it, go and do something else' and 40 years down the line, he's exactly the same, nothing's changed!

"As kids, we would go out and do a race at the interval and then we'd do a couple of races during the second-half. As we progressed, we got 350cc engines and then we went up to 500s."

Whirlwind start
BY 1985, the winner of that 1983 Schoolboy Championship had graduated to the Eagles team, making his league debut on Sunday, July 7 in a 52-26 home win over Exeter. The 16-year-old scored five paid seven from three rides.

"I had half a season that year and it was like a whirlwind," he recalls. "I went to lots of places I'd never seen before. I had Exeter at home in my first match and I was really happy with my score, but what I didn't realise was that Exeter was huge and they didn't go round Eastbourne very well.

"The next day, I cleaned my bike and it was off to Exeter. Oh, my God! I looked down the straight there and it was like a whole lap round Eastbourne. I thought we were at the wrong place! I think I scored one point and I didn't click with the place because I didn't really know much about set-ups.

"I have to be fair and say that for most of my early years of riding, most of the set-ups I had came from Keith Pritchard. Gordon Kennett was good but Keith was the sort of person who would talk to you about it and explain why you had to do stuff.

"I didn't realise what I was doing. I knew people changed gear but how they changed it and what they changed it to was all new to me. It was good of Keith because he was No.2 in the team, so he was in between reserve and second string, so it wasn't going to be long before we changed positions. But he was one of those very down to earth, professional sort of guys and he would take the time to help me. That was what I needed.

"We would go on a northern tour to places like Newcastle, Glasgow and Edinburgh, then stop at, say, Stoke on the way back down. We probably did four meetings in four days, which was quite hard on the equipment but good fun. You don't see that now. Once you've been to places before, you know what's going on because you write it down and you don't forget it."

The teenage Dugard posted a more than respectable 5.69 first season average and was part of an Eastbourne team that defeated Ellesmere Port in the Knockout Cup final. There was more silverware to come in 1986 and 1987, much more in fact, as Eagles pulled off back-to-back league and cup doubles.

Dugard's average shot up to 9.75 in 1986 and then 10.40 in '87 but he says: "I was part of a team, it wasn't just what I did. It has always been quite friendly at Eastbourne, team-wise, and we had a good young side. But it was a team in which everybody wanted to win, in a nice way. There was a

Happy days: Eastbourne Eagles of 1987, when speedway was still fun. Left to right: Steve Chambers, Kevin Pitts, Martin, Keith Pritchard, Gordon Kennett, Russell Lanning (team manager), Andy Buck, Dean Standing, Darren Standing, Dean Barker.

competitive spirit between us because no-one wanted to think, 'I've let the side down' or 'I haven't scored enough'.

"Winning the league and the cup like we did, I thought that was just normal."

Oxford blues

IN 1988, the British League beckoned and Dugard moved out of his Eastbourne comfort zone to join Oxford in the 'big boys' league. Cheetahs were one of the powerhouse teams of the top flight at the time, boasting a couple of the sport's biggest names in Hans Nielsen and Simon Wigg.

There was competition for the up-and-coming Dugard's signature and Martin admits now, with the benefit of hindsight, that moving to Cowley was perhaps the wrong decision. "Cradley wanted to sign me, as well as Oxford, but Oxford was a lot closer and my dad had ridden there, so he knew a lot of people. Looking back now, was it a mistake to go to Oxford? Possibly.

"I think I should have gone to Cradley. It was a bigger track and would have given me a broader sort of outlook on life. You had Cradley, Coventry and Wolverhampton and when Cradley went to somewhere like Wolves, it was, 'open the doors, we're coming' with Billy (Hamill) and Greg (Hancock) in their side.

"Yes, you had people like Hans at Oxford but he was an individual. He said what was needed to be said in terms of the team but, really, he was purely on his own mission. Unfortunately, I'd come from a place where it was all about team spirit.

"You get so used to riding in a team and thinking as a team and that was my biggest problem – I was always team-orientated and not an individual. I wasn't selfish enough to be an individual.

Silver Helmet holder in 1987.

"At Oxford, they were all very much individuals. You had Simon (Wigg) who was a class above everybody else with his World Long-track titles. He was very much the man to beat on the grass and long-track scene.

"Hans was the speedway person, so you had to try and bang those two together and get the best out of them. Then you had Marvyn (Cox) who wasn't quite in Hans' league in speedway and not quite in Simon's league in long-track, but he could mix it with both of them. It was best to learn from Marvyn really.

"Hans was great until you started beating him, then he just clamped up. Simon was great, I rode with him in Sweden as well and he was very good but as soon as you start beating people who aren't used to being beaten . . .

"I was still quite green around the gills, as it were, but I have got to say respect to John Davis. When I went to Sweden, he always looked after me. He was a great ambassador for the youngsters and that's where Lee (Richardson) learnt a lot. John was a great influence on me

Beating Bradford's Marvyn Cox, a former team-mate at Oxford, at Odsal in 1990.

because he would look after me – from when I met him at the airport to when I came home.

"He wasn't shy about helping you and being on your side, rather than not wanting to be beaten by you. John was good but throughout those years when I was at Oxford, you had Hans who would help you if he had to, Wiggy would help if he had to but Marvyn was very open.

"All of a sudden, you go from being a top National League rider to going straight in at No.2 with Hans Nielsen and against all the top number ones. You think you've shot yourself in the foot, from having, say, an 11-point average in the National League to going down to reserve in the British League. That's what I did and then it was, 'oh my God, how hard is this league going to be?'

"I would say it was a harder league then than it is now. It would be like someone from the current National League (third tier) going straight into the Elite – at No.2. It was unbelievable. The professionalism of everybody was quite frightening.

"I think I got a six-and-a-half to seven-point average in my first season and that wasn't bad but I was in my own sort of world really, in that I was on a small home track that suited me. I hadn't been anywhere else, only Eastbourne.

"For me, it probably would have been better to go to Cradley because, as a track, Oxford was the easy option. I should have looked at it and thought, 'nothing in life is easy' and I wish I'd stuck with Colin Pratt because he looked after people well. But I didn't and going to Oxford is what happened."

Whether Dugard's career would have turned out differently had he signed for Cradley rather than Oxford is a moot point, but Martin says: "I'm almost certain it would. But having said that, I'd never been abroad either and raced there. I think it would have been better for me if I could have done what the boys do now, but there just wasn't that opportunity back then. You're talking 24 years ago.

"It was only when they had the FIM World Championship rounds that all of a sudden I was going abroad with Marvyn Cox.

"In 1990, I did my first meetings in Poland. You thought you would just walk in and start picking up points straight away. Big mistake! Those boys, even in those days on inferior equipment, were still fast. You thought, 'here we go, I'll go pick up 10 or 12 points in Poland', as you'd done here the night before, but little did I know.

"Looking back, I would say my early years were my best years because I enjoyed them more. It started off as a sport, friendly, something I enjoyed but when I went to Oxford, it suddenly became a lot more intense. It became a business. My job.

"When I left Oxford and came back to Eastbourne, there was 100 times more pressure because: a) I was the local lad; and b) everybody thought it was going to happen for the club. Yes, we had a good run but it was quite hard work, everything was 'pressure on' and that wasn't enjoyable at all.

"That's when you get to the stage when you hate your job and I thought, 'this isn't for me anymore'. Maybe I would have been better off shutting my mouth and sitting it out for a year.

"I was only 31 when I retired, so that wasn't old. Look at Greg (Hancock) or Peter Karlsson today. If I'd taken a year out and come back refreshed, who knows where I could have got to? But hindsight is a fantastic thing.

"I still enjoy going out and having a ride now and again. I went out to America a couple of years ago and had a skid there and that was enjoyable. But then again, it's a completely different set-up and scenario over there, it's far more laid-back.

"I've had a couple of laps at Arlington too. I'm still fit enough – or fat enough! – but I obviously have an oxygen tank now like a diver! I don't think it would take long to regain fitness but the problem with being a speedway rider is that you have to be 100 per cent fit or it's not going to do it for you. You can't just be a little bit fit. I don't know how Screeny (Joe Screen) got away with it all the years he rode, the size he was!"

Best of British

THE individual highlight of Dugard's career came in 2000, when he pulled off a shock win in the British Grand Prix at Coventry as a wild card. A title that always eluded him, however, was the national championship, something he claims was "far more difficult to win then than it is now".

Martin says: "The British Final would always be about the third week in May, beautiful and hot for that one day, and you probably had 5,000 or 6,000 people there, maybe more. It was very hard to tell in those days but there was certainly a lot more people than go to it now.

"All the riders who would be at the British Final were pretty much all No.1 for their clubs. There would be Screen, Wigg, Havelock, Loram, Louis, me, they were all there, then there would be the likes of Dean Barker, Neil Evitts, Paul Thorp and Dave Mullett. At one meeting, out of the 16 riders, I think nine of them were the top riders in their teams.

"Andy Smith won it three times in a row and yet you probably wouldn't have classed him as a No.1, would you? He could do things like that, he would go and pull his finger out and win it, and that just shows you how hard it was."

The best Dugard could manage in a British Final was three podium places, firstly as runner-up to Gary Havelock in 1992 followed by two bronze medals in 2000 and 2001.

But that all paled into insignificance alongside the best night of his career at Coventry on July 29, 2000, when he won the British GP. Ten years after his World Final debut at Bradford, Dugard's laid-back approach at Brandon worked wonders.

"The rules were that you had to sign in the day before, so I did . . . and then I came home. I just

In his second spell with Eastbourne, leading at Belle Vue from Aces' Bobby Ott and Paul Smith, with Stefan Danno at the back.

went up there and signed in," he recalled.

"Brent Collyer was with me and we came back via Oxford because he was riding for Young Australia in a match against Young England and I was mechanic for him there.

"Afterwards, we took all of his stuff out of my van and put mine back in and by the time I got home, it would have been half-past 12 or one o'clock. We had to be back up at Coventry the next day and shot up there no problem at all. I fell asleep in the van and I spent the rest of the time trying to fix a little telly in my van. More than anything else, that was my biggest priority.

"I probably woke up about 45 minutes or an hour before the start of the meeting, the bikes had gone through all the scrutineering and I really didn't have a care in the world. We were all so laid-back.

"I'd ridden there a week before for Eastbourne and I think I got 11 out of 12 and that was the bike I was using for the GP. I just turned up as if it was a normal meeting.

"I remember after the meeting, I had to go and meet all the press but when I came back after that, no-one would believe that the bike that was filthy, dirty was the bike I had ridden. They asked to see my spare bike.

"I said, 'it's over there, but it's all clean'. They said, 'but this one's got all standard parts'. I said, 'well, that's because it's a standard motor'. Everyone was horrified because in those days, all the top boys, like Tony Rickardsson, would build an engine just to do a practice and a meeting. But mine was just my standard Eastbourne bike. For me, it is what it is and it was just another meeting.

"I'd never done so many rides as I did that night and we didn't even have enough tyres to do the whole meeting because we'd thought, 'well, we might make the semis but that will be it'. It was only because Todd Wiltshire had got knocked out that he ended up lending us a tyre.

Bob Dugard offers a fatherly word of advice before Martin's senior England debut against Denmark at Oxford in May 1987.

Martin gets the better of Andy Smith at the 1992 British Final.

"It all just fell into place that night. Whatever happened, it was one of those nights when it was going to be a good night.

"As an individual, Coventry was the highlight of my career but there was also the Southern Riders' Final in 1986. I remember that one because I wasn't expected to win it. Andrew Silver was the top dog then."

On the back of his Coventry triumph, Dugard was offered a wild card role at Cardiff the following season for what was the first GP staged at the Millennium Stadium.

"I wouldn't say I was having a particularly great time at Eastbourne that year but they did offer it to me and I thought I might as well go and have a go because of the fact that I might never get the chance to ride there again," he said.

"I turned up with the same sort of attitude as the year before . . . 'my normal bikes will be OK, it's a very small track and we'll be all right', but that was a big mistake.

"Cardiff is a funny place. You needed the ultimate bike with power. When we first went there, the surface they put down just zapped every ounce of power out of your engine.

After fixing his telly, Martin looks relaxed before what turned out to be his biggest individual success – the 2000 British GP.

"The problem was that I couldn't get enough power to the track. Dropping the clutch out of the start wasn't a problem, everybody can do that, but I was just putting big holes into the track rather than going forward. And when I was trying to chase everybody down, it was just taking all the power out of the engine. It was like the sort of track you'd find on the continent.

"We had a very limited practice because of the way the track cut up when they laid it and we were chasing our tails right the way through the meeting. It wasn't particularly enjoyable but at least I can say I was there. I did Cardiff."

Danish pastings

RIDING for his country was also a source of great pride: "I remember riding for England when I was one of the youngest in the team, before Screeny came along. It was against Denmark at Oxford. I beat Wiggy, even though he was on my side, and then realised that, actually, he was very upset with me for beating him.

"It was his home track and he was England captain but, as far as I was concerned, I just wanted to race and beat whoever was out there. I was a little bit outclassed but it was another big step up from the National League for me and people like Andrew Silver to join the big boys, as it were.

"What an experience, though. It was enjoyable but that was when the Danes were in their heyday, so it was another hiding from hell.

"I hadn't experienced anything like it before. Colin (Pratt) and Eric (Boocock) did as much as they could but, unfortunately, the England side was not as strong as it needed to be, especially against teams like the Danes. It was probably all right against the Young Australians but it was no match

Martin in 2014, as part of the promotion team at Eastbourne.

for the Danes.

"These days, you couldn't fill an England side, could you? Not properly anyway. People like Scott Nicholls and Chris Harris, they don't want to ride for England anymore but in our day it wasn't about the money factor. You wanted to ride for England because that was something you wanted to do.

"Nowadays it's all about what they can line their pocket with. But when you ride in Poland and someone is your team-mate, then you go to Sweden and swap sides and then come back to England, and you've met that same person maybe four days in a row, in four different teams, it does make riders all seem and feel a bit individual."

Home comforts

DESPITE all the team success, and the British GP win at Coventry, when asked if he thinks he under or over-achieved, Martin replies: "Under . . . just like my school reports! Really, I should have listened and taken a bit more from people away from the Eastbourne side of it.

"My biggest problem was my parents being Eastbourne through and through. Running Eastbourne, they had no ambition for me to go and ride anywhere else and I didn't know there was even anywhere else for me to ride.

"I could have ridden at Eastbourne forever and would have been none the wiser. Dad was a big influence to a degree but you've got to say he was running a business, he was running the speedway, so really I did most of it myself. Eastbourne always came first because it was made to come first.

"There were no international meetings for me, because we always ran at half-past three on a Sunday.

"My brother Paul rode as well. He was at Oxford, then went to Swindon for a bit with Andrew

Silver, because he was very friendly with Andrew. He was a little bit too lazy and laid-back and was pushed into doing speedway rather than actually wanting to do it.

"I suppose they had me on the one hand where everything was speedway, I wanted to do speedway and I would get up at five o'clock in the morning to do it. But Paul would get up at five o'clock in the afternoon and get someone else to do his bike. We were chalk and cheese when it came to drive and ambition.

"Sometimes, my father being the promoter was definitely a negative but it was always the sort of place where you'd be paid straight away, you never worried about not being paid. I was always paid at Oxford on the dot and paid at Eastbourne on the dot and never, ever had a problem regarding payment.

"But when I finished with speedway, I realised they'd been conning me all those years because I wasn't getting paid enough!

"Nowadays you hear of these top riders not getting paid at all for half a season." Dugard says his earliest times in the sport were his happiest as he sought to make a name for himself with Eastbourne.

"I enjoyed the friendly days early on at Eastbourne before it all started getting too busy and too commercial, from 1985 up to about 88-89," he says.

"Overall, I was very lucky and when you look back, I had a great career. I sustained injuries, just like everyone else, but it was generally only collar-bones, fingers, bits and pieces like that. The biggest one, and the one that hurt the most, was a crash with Stefan Andersson when I dislocated my thumb, cracked my pelvis and had a bang to the head – from which I've probably never recovered!

"No-one ever gets away completely injury-free. Maybe Leigh Adams was the only one but then he ends up in a wheelchair through a moto-cross accident.

"It can be a glamorous lifestyle but it's a very hard life too. You can say to someone that you went out to Italy to ride and they'll say, 'very nice, bet it's lovely out there' but they don't know it was an early hours of the morning flight, a smelly old minibus to the track where it's sweltering hot, do the meeting, then straight in the minibus again to the hotel and finally back home. Yeah, that's right, it's lovely!

"People don't realise how hard it is sometimes but then you wouldn't want to swap it for anything else."

By John Berry ● Issue 39 (2010)

BEST OF BRITISH: THE SEVENTIES

THE 1970s was generally an outstanding period of unprecedented success for British speedway, featuring as it did six World Team Cup victories for GB or England teams, four World Pairs wins and, of course, Peter Collins' individual World Championship in 1976.

But it wasn't just in the international arena where the Brits flourished like never before. In the domestic British League there was no shortage of very talented riders challenging, and at times toppling, the overseas giants led by Barry Briggs, Ivan Mauger, Ole Olsen and Anders Michanek.

So who were the top Brits from this glorious decade and how would you rank them now? It's a tough task but *Backtrack's* JOHN BERRY has never ducked a challenge.

We asked JB to list, in order, his best 20 UK riders from the 70s, disregarding all performances before and after the cut-off dates. The term 'best' takes into account club and personal achievements from 1970 until 1979 inclusive.

See how many of his choices you agree with . . .

1 Peter Collins

Not as automatic a choice as you might think. Fair or not, I consider the fabulous Hyde Road track and the chance to double up with Rochdale and Belle Vue throughout 1971 gave Peter a real advantage at the start of his career. On the other side, his not wishing to ride at No.1 throughout most of his time meant he met the opposition top gun twice in every match, making his BL average all the more of an achievement.

Much as the World Championship race seems to have become the holy grail in speedway, I have always felt its importance is overstated and it should not be the sole arbiter of success. Certainly that was the case in the 60s, where all the world's best riders were to be found in the British League. Having said that, Peter was able to pull out that little extra for special events in a variety of conditions and, as such, he litters the individual record books for the entire period.

If points could be awarded for style and flair, then PC would also be right at the very top. No doubt his never-say-die effort and number of passing moves assured him of being the People's Favourite. Style, flair and runs on the board.

On second thoughts, maybe the decision was easy!

2 John Louis

I hear cries of bias here, maybe justified, but the stats are there for all to see, although what the figures do not show is the way John carried the Ipswich team almost from day one. Not only was he a brilliant team rider, he was prepared to put the art into practice time after time in the interests of the club.

John's individual record is excellent. He can claim medals at every level except the Big One, where third was his highest, but his high ranking from me comes because of his team orientation, both at club and country level. No trick bike hidden away for special events for JL. Every event was equally important to him.

He, and maybe Ray Wilson before him, stand out as true leaders who were always worth more than their points alone showed.

JB's TOP 20

1 Peter Collins
2 John Louis
3 Malcolm Simmons
4 Dave Jessup
5 Michael Lee
6 Ray Wilson
7 Terry Betts
8 Martin Ashby
9 Jim McMillan
10 Chris Morton
11 Nigel Boocock
12 Eric Boocock
13 Gordon Kennett
=14 Doug Wyer
=14 Reg Wilson
16 Trevor Hedge
17 John Davis
18 Bob Kilby
19 Dave Morton
20 Steve Bastable

3 Malcolm Simmons

4 Dave Jessup

5 Michael Lee

Malcolm at King's Lynn was all set to become another of those very good speedway riders who never fully arrived. I put this down every bit as much to the sad loss of Maurice Littlechild and Malcolm having to live in Bettsy's shadow. The move to Poole, with the influence of Charles Foot and the Knotts, was a major turning point in his life and helped him mature and achieve greatness.

Some riders simply thrive on responsibility being thrust upon them. 'Simmo' was one who needed people to believe in him to make up for a lack of belief in himself and the Poole influence helped him become not just an excellent England captain, but an ambassador for the sport. One step off the world crown but handfuls of other gold medals.

Describing Dave as a 'gun for hire' might sound derogatory but isn't meant that way. His reserved manner and unspectacular riding style were never going to make him a folk hero but what he lacked in pizzazz he made up for with professionalism, reliability and integrity.

Dave was an administrator's dream. No histrionics, no need for mollycoddling or nursemaiding, no need to explain what was needed at any given moment, he did his talking on the scoreboard.

There was never, ever, any questioning of his pride and loyalty towards the England cause and he always gave full service and commitment to whichever team he rode for in the League. Some riders remain aloof. DJ was never that, nor would you ever suggest he was anything like big-headed. He just preferred to do things his own way and regarded his family as perhaps the biggest part of his life.

Bearing in mind Michael was only 11-years-old when the decade began, it seems incredible that he should figure so high up in the table. With only five years of racing under consideration, it simply demonstrates just how huge his talent was, and just how much went into the father/son pairing.

The world crown came a year after our 1979 cut-off date but I still offer no apology for putting him in front of so many other brilliant star names. Quite simply, Michael was a phenomenon and could easily have gone on to have been the greatest rider ever.

Still, we are only talking 70s here, so we can glory in Michael's on-track discipline and professionalism while noting he was a lovely fun-loving kid to be around and managed to push aside so many of the established riders of the time without there being one bit of jealousy or resentment towards him, such was his delightful manner.

6 Ray Wilson

Averages in the high tens in his first three seasons in the decade tell us just how good Ray was but it was as World Cup Willie he was to capture the imagination in 1971, '72 and '73 with stirring performances in the World Team Cup. He was the one who fired the English imagination after the home of speedway had lived with years of domination from the Swedes and New Zealanders, as he led Britannia's charge to the top of the tree.

The avalanche of talent thundering through from the second division and a perhaps ill-advised move away from Leicester in 1977 saw the 'Bostik Kid' come unstuck quite rapidly during the second half of the decade when he should have still been in his prime.

But we can all remember the sight of him bustling through from the back time after time in his heyday.

7 Terry Betts

The promoter's dream. Looks, ability, charisma, charm and not a little talent on a speedway bike. In Simmo and Michael Lee he had two exceptional talents attempting to steal his glory but 'Bettsy' was always Mr King's Lynn.

In all respects Terry was the David Gower of speedway. He was a natural talent and although he took the sport seriously, there was always time to see the lighter side of life. He had a wicked sense of humour and there was always a merry quip for every occasion. He was through and through an 'Essex Boy' even before the term was invented.

In Bettsy's days the England riders quite reasonably saw the World Championship as just another event, perhaps even looking somewhat askance at the time and effort the foreign 'mercenaries' put into what represented such a small part of the season, and therefore, like so many Englishmen of his generation, should not be judged on the one competition alone.

8 Martin Ashby

Another of speedway's gentlemen but maybe lacking some of Bettsy's massive outgoing character, 'Crash' served a three-year exile at Exeter with stoic panache before returning to his home track of Swindon in 1971, going on to represent Robins with style and grace for a long period.

Perhaps at a more glamorous or ambitious club he might have received greater national recognition but anyone who could follow in Briggo's footsteps and come out with flying colours must have had a great deal of internal fortitude to go with the talent and class.

Because of his quiet, unassuming manner many people regarded him as a bit of a pushover, and maybe he wasn't stirred up enough in individual meetings to reach his full potential, but when fully charged up there were few riders who could get the better of him.

9 Jim McMillan

North of the border sportsmen, so the saying goes, are British when they win and Scottish when they lose. Speedway officialdom's casual interchange between 'English' and 'British' has always left Jimmy Mac as something of an outsider in terms of 'national' selection. Therefore he cannot look back on a long history of international performances but nobody would doubt his long and distinguished service to the British League.

Enforced moves from Glasgow to Hull and then on to Wolverhampton were accepted without demur, propping up weak and unfashionable teams and all the time as the No.1 man just about throughout the decade.

One wonders what he might have achieved had he been born south of the border. He was a durable, class act fully deserving of top 10 recognition.

10 Chris Morton

It is easy to forget Chris didn't join Division One full-time until 1974 and never finished at No.1 in the Belle Vue averages at all during the 70s. Every other rider in this list headed his club's averages at least twice in the decade. Then again, not every other rider had Peter Collins as a team-mate.

At first glance it is difficult to reconcile putting Mort behind, for instance, Jimmy Mac, but we are comparing the whole of the 70s and only the 70s here. One was a top rider for the whole decade, the other a superstar but a large portion of that was in the 80s.

Mort's popularity can be best judged by his Queen's honour, no doubt due to the sheer delight he brought speedway supporters of all persuasions with his wholehearted and brave dashes from behind time after time, and for his great character.

11 Nigel Boocock

The 'Blue Boy' had already established himself as a huge star at Coventry before the 70s arrived. He still remained the top man over the next five years but the many injuries early in his career had begun to take their toll.

That Nigel continued to ride for so long after his best years were behind him tends to deflect from his many years as a huge star. If his 10-year reign as Coventry's No.1 man had all been in the 70s, he would have been in the top three.

Even so, his riding did extend throughout the 70s and let's be fair, anyone who was prepared to have Eastville for a home track deserves a high score, if only for guts. Nigel was actually the highest English rider at Bristol in both 1977 and '78. In fact, he was just about the only English rider in the Bulldogs team.

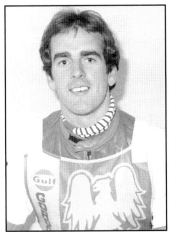

12 Eric Boocock

Like Nigel, Eric also spent 10 years as his club's No.1 rider but, again, at least half of his achievements fell before 1970. Otherwise, like his older brother, he would have been top three material in this list.

The sudden retirement at the end of 1974 at only 29 years of age was in stark contrast to Nigel and cut young Booey's 70s performances off after just five seasons. If for no other reason, this puts him behind his brother on my list, although it should be mentioned that he spent the rest of his working life helping others in British speedway.

13 Gordon Kennett

In contrast to the Boococks, Gordon spent the first half of the 70s learning and then honing his speedway skills. It was not until the move to White City and its tie-up with Weslake in 1976 that Gordon sprung to prominence. The 1977 season turned out to be a special year for both Gordon and the Rebels, as he skippered the west London team to the league title.

If 1977, with a 10-point-plus average, was a stellar club year, '78, as second in the World Final and a partner to Malcolm Simmons in winning the World Pairs, was the pinnacle internationally.

Those years were the stand-outs in a five-year period as the White City/Eastbourne No.1 and sees him onto this list, even if he still had a large part of his career still ahead of him.

= 14 Doug Wyer

Doug Wyer and Reg Wilson both rode for Sheffield in every year of the decade. They always finished next to each other in the averages, Doug on top five times, Reg on top five times. Both riders were fiercely loyal, hard as nails and extremely talented.

Reg might have been marginally better on the smaller tracks, Doug on the bigger, but really there was little to separate the two in performance. Sheffield tended to give something of a home advantage to riders but like the Exeter circuit, this possibly worked against Tigers' riders away from Owlerton, so in the end the results probably even out.

Both riders were very much a part of the BL Division Two Boomers and as such found themselves facing plenty of competition for international

= 14 Reg Wilson

recognition, although both performed admirably when called up to represent their country.

Reg was a little more flamboyant than the gritty Doug and was perhaps my own personal favourite between the two, but that is a subjective thing. Although Doug had a World Final appearance in 1976 that others might set great store by, I cannot split them on performance.

16 Trevor Hedge

'Hedgey' had just four seasons at Wimbledon to be considered for this table. In that time he headed Dons' charts once with a 10-point average in front of Ronnie Moore before his performances began to fade.

He was quiet and considerate off the track and graceful, rather than forceful, on it but was very much a special part of Wimbledon, where he maintained a strong cult following.

He was another who continued to grace the speedway scene for many years, becoming a hugely liked and respected engine tuner. A really genuine nice guy.

17 John Davis

John was intelligent enough to have left quite a substantial imprint on the speedway scene in the 70s through clever self-promotion, flamboyant mannerisms and good nature, so it seems strange to find his name so far down the list.

His best claims to fame for the period, however, was a 10-point-plus average to lead the Reading scorers in 1979 and a one-off appearance in the 1977 World Team Cup Final in Poland, where he scored six points from the reserve spot to help England regain the trophy.

Like many of the other younger riders on the list, he was still learning his trade during the first half of the period. A full decade in the top league would obviously have seen him higher up the list.

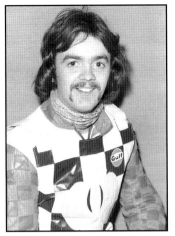

18 Bob Kilby

The late Bob Kilby was Swindon through and through. Rider Control saw him pushed out to Exeter and Oxford for a couple of years each (where he headed the score charts for one of the two years at both places) before returning to Swindon, where in the main he played second fiddle to Martin Ashby.

'Kilb' will be remembered most for his fast gating and his volatile character when in leathers but away from the track he was a genuine good bloke. Ten solid years, three as a No.1 man, sees him included in the list in front of some very good riders.

19 Dave Morton

From the wide open spaces of Crewe up in Cheshire to the relatively small Hackney circuit in east London was quite a big trip for Dave when he made the permanent jump in 1975 after doubling-up the previous year. The move looked to have worked brilliantly when he topped the Hackney list in 1975 and '76, the latter year with a 10-point-plus average. He looked set to be every bit as much of a star as his younger brother.

But a broken leg made him miss nearly all of 1977 and a move to Wolverhampton the next year never really saw him return to the same heights of success. Dave was a very good and level headed rider who looked set for a great career before the thigh injury.

20 Steve Bastable

Plenty of competition for the last place on the list but I finally plumped for Steve, probably second youngest on the list behind Lee. Steve worked hard to climb the ranks at Cradley and had the one stellar year in 1978 before being pushed back into the shade by the emergence of Bruce Penhall, Alan Grahame and Phil Collins the following year.

Injury and a fall out with the management saw him move from Dudley Wood and he continued to have a very successful career into the 80s.

Special mentions: Ian Cartwright, Tony Davey, Arnold Haley, Chris Pusey, Barry Thomas and Alan Wilkinson.

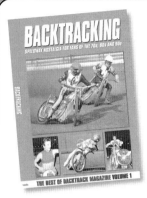

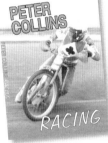